Comparative Health Policy

Robert H. Blank
Brunel University

and

Viola Burau
University of Aarhus

First published 2004 by
PALGRAVE MACMILLAN
Houndmills, Basingstoke, Hampshire RG21 6XS and
175 Fifth Avenue, New York, N.Y. 10010
Companies and representatives throughout the world

PALGRAVE MACMILLAN is the global academic imprint of the Palgrave Macmillan division of St. Martin's Press, LLC and of Palgrave Macmillan Ltd. Macmillan® is a registered trademark in the United States, United Kingdom and other countries. Palgrave is a registered trademark in the European Union and other countries.

ISBN 0–333–98598–2 hardback
ISBN 0–333–98599–0 paperback

This book is printed on paper suitable for recycling and made from fully managed and sustained forest sources.

A catalogue record for this book is available from the British Library.

A catalog record for this book is available from the Library of Congress.

10   9   8   7   6   5   4   3   2   1
13   12   11   10   09   08   07   06   05   04

Typeset by Cambrian Typesetters, Frimley, Camberley, Surrey

Printed in China

Contents

List of Boxes, Figures and Tables

Boxes

Figures

Tables

Preface

We wrote this book to fill a gap in comparative health policy. Although there have been many books published about the health policy of particular countries and fewer books that compare several nations, our past research across a variety of countries convinced us that a more inclusive coverage was needed in order to explain the issues and problems surrounding health care in the twenty-first century. Therefore, we have taken our collective knowledge of rather disparate health care systems to write this introduction to comparative health policy. Although primarily written for students, we feel that it is highly accessible to other readers, including health policy makers, who have an interest in the future of health and health care in their own country.

In order to determine the extent to which the problems facing health care systems have common causes or spring from specific national circumstances, this comparative assessment of health policy focuses on a set of key themes and issues that run throughout the book. How do the main types of health systems in the developed world address health care problems, and do different systems make a difference? Or is health policy in these countries converging, as some commentators argue? The book analyses what lessons can be learned about public/private mixes, policy and funding frameworks, professional organizations, and acute and preventive services from the varied health systems. In order to do this, the systems of Australia, Germany, Japan, New Zealand, the Netherlands, Sweden, Singapore, the UK and the USA are systematically covered. In addition, discussions of France and Italy and appropriate data from additional nations are included where we felt it would be helpful for a better understanding of the topic.

Throughout the book, we try to put health care in a broader social context and demonstrate its interdependence with factors often excluded from analysis. Health care, we argue, cannot be separated from other issues that impinge on health such as economic inequalities, the environment and social services. Thus we include in-depth discussions of home care and a range of public health measures that cumulatively have more impact on health outcomes than medical services. We also explore whether the medical model and the heavy emphasis on curative medicine is the most effective way to address people's health problems.

Chapter 1 introduces the reader to health policy and to the impact of global trends of population ageing, technology diffusion and heightened public expectations on the health systems of developed nations. It also discusses the importance of comparative health care analysis and presents the typologies used to classify health systems. Chapter 2 looks at the cultural and historical context of health care across our countries and posits a more integrated model of health that accounts for these differences. It also discusses the varying importance of alternative forms of medicine across these countries.

Chapter 3 shifts attention to the provision, funding and governance of health care and the nature and scope of health reforms across the countries. Our countries show considerable diversity, both across different health systems and across the sub-systems of each health system, and only a few countries fit existing typologies. Chapter 4 continues and expands this discussion by examining priority-setting in health care. It illustrates the difficult allocation and rationing issues facing all health systems and discusses how these countries are responding. The profession plays a key role in health policy and is at the centre of medical decision making in all countries, although its influence does vary. Chapter 5 looks at the organization and power of doctors in these health systems with special emphasis on how this has changed through recent health care reforms. Although the face of medical practice has changed significantly, in many cases doctors have retained considerable power.

Chapter 6 moves the discussion to home care to demonstrate the interdependence of health with other care services. Again, the impact of ageing populations is evident here and the response to this challenge in times of cost containment across these countries varies. Nevertheless, there are common trends across countries, most notably the more formal support for women as informal carers. Chapter 7 takes the discussion even further afield from the dominant medical focus found in individual, patient-centred acute care to public health, where the focus shifts from individuals to populations. It demonstrates that health outcomes for populations are more closely tied to health promotion and disease prevention efforts which, in turn, may have nothing to do with medicine and more to do with income distribution, public services, housing, social conditions and the environment. The concluding chapter returns to the broader themes introduced in Chapter 1 and on the basis of the evidence provided in the previous chapters assesses the appropriateness of existing typologies of health systems. The discussion points to the continued importance of country-specific differences within overall trends of convergence, as well as to the complexity of health systems. Complexity arises from differentiation of health systems into often quite distinct sub-systems and from the fact that health care encompasses so much more than health systems.

ROBERT H. BLANK
VIOLA BURAU

List of Abbreviations

ACC   Accident Compensation Commission
AMA   American Medical Association
BMA   British Medical Association
CDC   Centers for Disease Control
DRGs   diagnosis-related groups
GDP   gross domestic product
GMC   General Medical Council
GP   general practitioner
HACC   Home and Community Care
HCFA   Health Care Financing Administration
HMOs   Health Maintenance Organizations
IPA   Independent Practice Association
JMA   Japanese Medical Association
MRI   magnetic resonance imaging
NHI   National Health Insurance
NHS   National Health Service
NICE   National Institute for Clinical Excellence
NZMA   New Zealand Medical Association
OECD   Organisation for Economic Co-operation and Development
OSHA   Occupational Safety and Health Act
PACE   Program for All Inclusive Care for the Elderly
PHS   Public Health Service (USA)
PPO   Preferred Provider Organization
QALY   quality adjusted life years
QWB   Quality of Well Being
SARS   Severe Acute Respiratory Syndrome
SES   socio-economic status
TCM   traditional Chinese medicine
UVB   ultraviolet B
WHO   World Health Organization
WHPP   Workplace Health Promotion Programme

Chapter 1

Comparative Health Policy: An Introduction

Health care has always been a complicated policy issue, but in the last decade it has become a major area of concern in all developed nations. Ageing populations, the proliferation of new medical technologies, and heightened public expectations and demands, among other factors, have made health care the central issue in the public view. Pressures on political leaders to meet rising public demands for expanded service conflict directly with the need to constrain health care costs and to manage scarce societal resources. Despite major differences among countries in how health care is funded, provided and governed, therefore, no government has been able to escape the controversy and problems that accompany health care in the twenty-first century, although some seem to be coping significantly better than others. Why is that so?

Given the universality of health care as a problem, one must question whether or not what governments do about it – what policies they adopt – makes a difference. And if it does matter, what approaches and strategies offer the most hope of resolving or managing the problems of health care? Does simply spending more money improve the health of a population? If not, what does? This book addresses these questions by examining health care policy across a selection of countries that have taken divergent approaches and established a variety of mechanisms for covering the health needs of their populations. It also analyses trends within and across these countries in order to determine whether or not there is a convergence in health policy among developed nations, as argued by some observers.

• Despite variation in health policy across countries, there are several factors that are critical to all developed nations. In the wake of falling national incomes and increasingly scarce resources for social spending, all countries, no matter how much they vary, face growing problems in the financing and delivery of health care. Table 1.1 clearly demonstrates that while countries vary considerably as to the percentage of their gross domestic product (GDP) that they devote to health care, in virtually all cases it has increased significantly over the last three decades. This means that health care costs are increasing at rates exceeding that of economic growth, a pattern that most countries will not be able to sustain.

1

Table 1.1   *Health expenditure as a per cent of GDP, 1970–98*

	1970	1980	1990	1992	1998	% change
Australia	5.7	7.0	7.9	8.2	8.6	2.9
France	5.7	7.4	8.6	9.1	9.4	3.7
Germany	6.3	8.8	8.7	9.7	10.3	4.0
Italy	5.1	7.0	8.1	8.4	8.2	3.1
Japan	4.6	6.5	6.1	6.3	7.4	2.8
Netherlands	7.2	8.0	8.5	8.9	8.7	1.5
New Zealand	5.2	6.0	7.0	7.6	8.1	2.9
Singapore	n/a	n/a	2.8	3.2	2.9	0.1
Sweden	6.9	9.1	8.5	8.5	7.9	1.0
UK	4.5	5.6	6.0	6.9	6.8	2.3
USA	6.9	8.7	11.9	13.0	12.9	6.0

n/a = not available

Sources: Data from OECD (2001b) and Singapore Ministry of Health (2001).

The increase in health care costs is not by itself a problem. As Duff (2001: 138) points out, an expansion of spending on other goods is welcomed as contributing to economic well-being; why, then, should increased consumption on health care be a problem? The prime reasons are because of the critical role of the state in funding it and because it does not respond to normal market forces. Another cause for deep concern, however, is that the funding problem and the recent reform efforts in every Western nation are to some extent a reaction to three major factors: ageing populations, rapid advances in medical technology, and expanded public expectations and demands. Although there is variation by degree across these countries, these trends represent ominous signs for the funding of health care in the coming decades.

The problem of ageing populations

As indicated in Table 1.2, on the basis of demographic projections most countries will experience substantial ageing of their populations over the next 30 years. Although the ageing process will take place earlier and more rapidly in some countries, all countries are expected to experience the ageing process which began in the 1970s and which is accelerating, especially in the non-European countries where there is currently a lower proportion of elderly. This ageing of populations is a

Table 1.2   *Percentage of population aged 65 and over*

	1960	1980	1990	2000	2020	2030	2040
Australia	8.5	9.6	11.1	12.2	15.4	18.2	19.7
France	11.6	13.9	14.1	15.9	19.5	21.8	22.7
Germany	10.8	15.5	15.3	16.8	21.7	25.8	27.6
Italy	10.5	13.2	14.9	17.6	19.4	21.9	24.2
Japan	5.7	9.1	12.1	16.7	20.9	21.0	22.7
Netherlands	9.0	11.5	12.8	13.6	18.9	23.0	24.8
New Zealand	8.7	9.7	11.1	11.7	15.3	19.4	21.9
Singapore	n/a	4.9	6.0	7.0	18.5	19.0	22.0
Sweden	11.8	16.3	17.8	17.8	20.8	21.7	22.5
UK	11.7	15.0	15.7	15.7	16.3	19.2	20.4
US	9.2	11.2	12.4	12.3	16.2	19.5	19.8

Sources: Data from OECD (1988) for all but Singapore (Singapore Ministry of Health, 2001).

product of two major factors: a decline in fertility and increased life expectancies.

The primary cause of the ageing of Western societies is the precipitous decline in fertility rates that has naturally increased the proportion of elderly. Furthermore, this trend is exaggerated because the sharp upturn in birth rates after the Second World War produced a bloated age cohort in the baby boom generation, the first wave of which is now reaching retirement age. Even if life expectancy is unaltered, this wave of ageing baby boomers, along with declining fertility rates, guarantees an increasing proportion of elderly.

The second factor contributing to the ageing of populations is increased life expectancies. In the years between 1950 and 1980, life expectancy at birth increased by 8.5 years for females and 6.0 years for males. These significant gains resulted from improved social factors, health habits and the new capacities of medicine to reduce infant mortality and extend the life span. It is important to note that in the past gains in life expectancy have been underestimated, meaning that there could be even more significant increases in average life span in the coming decades. Moreover, substantial differences in average life expectancy in Organization for Economic Co-operation and Development (OECD) countries at present strongly suggest that further gains could be made in a number of countries. Many of these gains might follow the adoption of healthier lifestyles and other health promotion activities. Ironically, these health-improving steps, together

> **Box 1.1   A warning: 'profound consequences' as the EU grows older**
>
> EU-wide, the share of the elderly in the total population is expected to rise from 21% now to around 34% by 2050. Those 80+ are predicted to rise from 4% of today's population to some 10%. By 2050, 37 million people are expected to be octogenarians+. Eurostat says these big rises in the elderly will have 'profound consequences' for social protection systems – particularly pensions, which are funded mostly by workers and employers. Health spending is also likely to 'increase significantly'. (Eurostat News Release, 29 July 1999)

with low fertility rates, could add considerably to population ageing and add to funding problems (Box 1.1).

These ageing trends are accompanied by two critical changes in the population structure. First, within the overall trends towards older populations is the ageing of these elderly populations themselves. At present the most rapidly growing segment of the elderly population is the cohort aged 80 and over. As illustrated in Table 1.3, this proportion is expected to climb to over 30 per cent in 2050. The second trend within a trend relates to the sex composition of the elderly population. As a result of their longer life expectancy, women outnumber men significantly in the elderly age cohorts. Furthermore, the sex imbalance increases with age, meaning that as the very elderly cohort expands, the proportion of elderly women will grow. Even though this imbalance is projected to narrow over time, especially at the younger end of the elderly age group, women will continue to constitute a substantial majority of the elderly and this factor will remain particularly marked among the most elderly. As with the other trends this will have considerable impact on health care needs of the population.

Table 1.3   *Estimated age structure of the population over the age of 65 (%)*

	1980	1990	2000	2010	2020	2030	2040	2050
65–69	34	32	31	32	31	31	27	26
70–79	48	46	48	44	46	46	47	43
>80	18	22	22	24	22	24	26	31

Source: Data from OECD (1988: 23).

These trends towards ageing populations have clear ramifications for the distribution of societal resources and for determining social priorities. Resources now devoted to children and young families, particularly education and family benefits, will be shifted towards health care, pensions and other support services directed towards the large and politically potent elderly populations. Table 1.4 illustrates these shifts in expenditure among selected countries in terms of major programme and age group. On average, spending on education is projected to decline by almost 40 per cent between 1980 and 2040, falling from 27 to 17 per cent of the social budget, while the share of pensions is projected to increase precipitously to comprise nearly half of all social expenditures (48 per cent) by 2040. As a proportion of social expenditures, health care is expected to show modest gains in most of these countries. Similarly, the proportion of social expenditure going to those under 15 is projected to fall by one-third whereas expenditure on those 65 and over will rise on average to over half of total social spending, with a high of 62 per cent in Germany. Although the timing and extent of these expenditure changes varies significantly by country, the trends are consistent with only a few exceptions regarding health.

Although the proportion of social budgets dedicated to health care show only modest aggregate gains as compared to pensions, for many countries these growth rates represent a sizeable cumulative increase in the resources necessary to finance health care purely because of the ageing factor. Setting aside differences among countries, it appears likely that by the year 2030, OECD countries will be faced on average with total health expenditures some 30 per cent higher and per capita expenditures some 20 per cent higher solely as a result of population ageing. Any increase in utilization and intensity of care per person that leads to an increase in real benefits per capita and any increase in health care prices over the general rate of inflation would add to this financial burden.

What does it matter for health care if the populations age? It matters because at present a disproportionate share of health resources go to the elderly, particularly those over 80, the fastest growing age cohort. As illustrated in Table 1.5, in most countries those over 65 account for at least double the expenditures their size alone would indicate, and in most cases at least triple (in Australia, for example, 12.2 per cent of the population use 40.2 per cent of the resources). At the extreme, in the USA the 12.3 per cent of the population over 65 and older consumed nearly half (48.8 per cent) of total health care expenditures in 2000. How can these governments possibly continue this spending pattern as their populations of elderly increase? Ironically, because of medical improvements and technologies that prolong life, chronic disease requiring frequent medical care has become an increasing drain on scarce

Table 1.4 Estimated changes in distribution of social expenditure by major programme as implied by ageing populations

	Education		Health		Pensions		% total of 65+		% total < 15	
	1980	2040	1980	2040	1980	2040	1980	2040	1980	2040
Australia	31	19	25	29	29	40	28	49	27	16
France	21	13	22	21	42	56	40	54	24	16
Germany	20	11	25	23	47	61	46	62	17	10
Italy	23	13	24	24	47	59	35	50	15	9
Japan	31	17	29	30	28	46	29	52	32	17
Netherlands	23	13	20	23	34	46	27	49	22	13
Sweden	23	18	31	33	39	44	45	56	23	18
UK	28	22	26	29	34	40	36	48	24	19
USA	32	20	22	24	40	52	39	56	21	14

Source: Data from OECD (1988: 37).

Table 1.5   *Percentage of health expenditures and persons aged 65 or more, 2000*

	% 65+	% Total Expenditure
Australia	12.2	40.2
France	15.9	30.0
Germany	16.8	34.1
Italy	17.6	34.3
Japan	16.7	42.4
Netherlands	13.6	41.2
New Zealand	11.7	42.1
Sweden	17.8	54.2
UK	15.7	43.0
USA	12.3	48.8

Source: Data from OECD (2001b).

medical resources. Furthermore, because of the concurrence of multiple and often chronic conditions, the cost of prolonging life at older ages is higher than at younger ones, and especially since the introduction of antibiotics in the 1940s reduced the incidence of death from illnesses such as pneumonia.

Table 1.6 illustrates the estimated increases in health expenditures going to the elderly. Although there is again significant variation by

Table 1.6   *Proportions of public health expenditure going to population aged 65 and over*

	1980	*2000*	*2020*	*2040*
Australia	34.5	40.2	46.4	56.0
France	28.4	30.0	35.8	41.1
Germany	32.7	34.1	40.0	49.4
Italy	33.2	34.3	38.9	46.8
Japan	31.3	42.4	52.5	55.9
Netherlands	37.0	41.2	49.6	60.1
Sweden	51.5	54.2	59.6	63.3
UK	42.5	43.0	45.6	54.1
USA	47.0	48.8	56.9	62.9

Source: Data from OECD (1988: 41).

country, the trend towards a heightened concentration of health care resources in the elderly is universal with most countries registering over 50 per cent by 2040. The ageing population not only increases health care spending and shifts it towards the elderly, but it also has considerable potential impact on the type of health care provided. Obviously, the growing number of old people will generate a greater demand for geriatric care and thus a proportionate increase in geriatric facilities and personnel.

Several additional aspects of the ageing of populations are critical to an understanding of the full range of implications in health policy. Although attention here has focused on the increased expenditures generated by the growing proportion of elderly, the other side is that as populations age the size of the productive sector decreases, thus raising concern over the capacity of society to support the new demands. The ability of any country to finance increased costs associated with the ageing population depends upon the relative size of the productive population (usually measured by dependency ratios of some type), as well as unemployment rates and productivity. As the workforce, and the tax base, is reduced through ageing and continued low levels of fertility, the pressures on the remaining working age population will intensify.

Finally, just at the time where there is an increased need for long-term care-giving, social changes have undermined traditional, largely informal care mechanisms for the elderly. The decline in the extended family, increased mobility, and trends towards more working women and fewer children in many countries have reduced the willingness and ability of families to care for the elderly. Although women continue to provide significant levels of long-term care for family members, coverage is saturated and as a proportion will decrease (see Chapter 6 for details). As a result, the demands for formal long-term care services will intensify and such services will depend increasingly on public funds. Those countries without adequate planning and funding infrastructures for long-term care are most vulnerable to severe problems in this regard.

Medical technology and health policy

Another force impacting on all health systems is the rapid expansion of medical technology. Simply put, we have a lot more technologies today for intervention and many of these new techniques are very costly on a per case basis. Medical technologies that did not exist a decade or two ago account for a large proportion of current health care costs (Newhouse, 1993). Vast improvements in surgical procedures, tissue matching and immuno-suppressant drugs are making repair and replacement of organs increasingly routine. Likewise, improvements in diagnostic machinery are continuing to accelerate. Computerized axial tomography (CAT) scanners and magnetic resonance imaging (MRIs) have been quickly followed by position emission tomography (PET) and other specialized diagnostic machines, but at high cost. Moreover, human genetic technology, stem cell research and pharmacology dramatically promise an expanding array of costly diagnostic and therapeutic applications that will increase both the range of intervention options and the pressures on health care systems to deliver.

This continuous development of new medical technologies has contributed to a growth in health care expenditures. Callahan (1998) suggests that more than any other factor, this proliferation of medical technology explains the expansion of health spending. According to one study, new medical technologies account for up to one-third of the rise in annual health care costs (Zwillich, 2001). Medical technology affects outlays by adding to the arsenal of feasible treatments and by reducing the invasiveness of existing interventions, thus increasing the number of patients who might enjoy net gains from diagnosis and treatment. In addition to leading to significant increases in the use and intensity of care, many new treatments are expensive. Although not every technological advance necessarily leads to increased expenditures, the net effect has tended to raise costs due to extensions in the range and intensity of care. Even relatively inexpensive advances, such as antibiotics, which appear to reduce health care costs by treating common diseases at a lower cost than conventional treatments, add significantly to medical spending.

The impact of technological advances is likely to be exaggerated by increases in the number of very elderly people who are the heaviest users of many medical innovations. Advances in technology have enabled the prolongation of life of persons with illnesses that would have been untreatable in the recent past. Moreover, while much curative treatment is beneficial to patients, the marginal gain in terms of length of survival and quality of life is difficult to judge. This uncertainty is complicated by the fact that most medical procedures have not been subject to controlled assessment to determine their effectiveness in particular cases and how they compare in outcome to less expensive alternative approaches. According to Eddy (1991), in the USA alone the difference between the attitude of 'when in doubt do it' and that of 'when in doubt stop' could add up to $100 billion annually.

Despite the fact that medical technology is global and contributes to cost escalation in all health systems, many studies demonstrate that policies adopted within nations can have a significant impact on the use of new technologies. McClellan and Kessler, for example, found 'enormous differences in how quickly and widely treatments diffused into medical practice' (1999: 253), especially those high-technology treatments with high fixed costs or high variable costs per use. They also found more modest differences in the times at which new drugs, procedures or devices become available across countries. The approach of some countries reflects the view that new technologies should be made available quickly while others are likely to be more cautious in funding them and thus encouraging their widespread diffusion. The result is that medical spending growth across nations has become more divergent as some countries have implemented cost-containment policies designed to curb the diffusion of medical technology. These different approaches and their impact on technological innovation and health care funding are discussed in Chapter 4.

Rising public expectations and demands

The primary forces behind technological medicine come from the providers of health care community who instil a demand in the public. Providers are trained to do what is best for their patients and in some countries this has produced a do-everything, 'maximalist' approach (Fuller, 1994). Also, as noted earlier, health care is big business with huge financial stakes. The health care industry itself is a powerful shaper of perceived needs and it benefits significantly from an ever-expanding notion of health care. Not surprisingly, any attempt to place limits on access to the newest technologies risks condemnation from practitioners, their patients and the public. Such cases of denial of access result in dramatic news stories and difficult questioning of those officials who dare to deny such care (see Box 1.2). Unless constrained by government or other third-party actions, the health care community embraces the technological imperative with enthusiasm.

These public expectations and perceptions of medicine have resulted in an overutilization of and reliance on technology (Ubel, 2001). Patients demand access to the newest technologies because they are convinced of their value. Popular health-oriented magazines and television shows extol the virtues of medical innovations. Physicians have been trained in the technological imperative, which holds that a technology should be used despite its cost if it offers any possibility of benefit. Third-party payment provides no disincentive against this overutilization of medical technology. Any limits on the allocation of medical technologies, then, must come from outside the health care community itself. The only agent with the power to enforce such limits is the government, but it can do so only within the context of rising public expectations and demands.

The expectations and demands of the public for health care are potentially insatiable and they are fuelled by the medical industry which

---

Box 1.2   Media campaigns for treatment denied

In New Zealand a 76-year-old man is denied kidney dialysis by the public hospital. The man and his family take his case to the media accusing the health authorities of denying his rights to life-saving treatment. The media portrays him as a wronged War Veteran and includes emotional interviews with family members and his MP. Unrelenting media pressure forces political officials to overrule the hospital authorities and give him dialysis despite their argument he was a very poor medical risk for reasons they could not disclose due to patient confidentiality. He received kidney dialysis but died within 5 months due to heart failure. Were the politicians right in bowing to public pressure? Meanwhile, in the UK, multiple sclerosis sufferers are furious and go to the media when the National Institute for Clinical Excellence, the government's cost-effectiveness agency threatens to ban a new drug on the ground that at £10,000 per year per patient it is simply too expensive for its relative benefits. One mother of two children with the disease is quoted in the press as saying: 'My children are dependent on me – how can you put a price on that?' Should the government step in and fund the drug for these young children and, if so, where will the money to do so come from?

---

has much to gain by continual expansion of the scope of medicine. Health care costs have increased in part because citizens expect and often demand higher and higher levels of medical intervention, levels undreamed of several decades ago. In some countries, this aggrandized view of health care has been encouraged by politicians, governments and other third-party payers who place heavy emphasis on the rights or entitlements of individuals to health care with few apparent limits. Furthermore, in most Western countries there was in the mid-twentieth century a shift towards the notion of positive rights to health care that placed a moral duty on society to provide the resources necessary to exercise those rights. The long-term results in the light of expanding medical technology mean that setting limits became increasingly difficult politically once the population took health care rights for granted.

In some countries, the suggestion that we limit medical expenditures on an individual in order to benefit the community contradicts the traditional patient-oriented mores of medicine (Drummond, 1993). Thus there are strong pressures for intensive intervention on an individual basis even in the last days of life, often despite the enormous cost for very little return in terms of prolonging the patient's life. In other countries, with more communal or collectively-grounded cultures, this maximalist approach to health care is more malleable and the public less critical of limits (see Chapter 2 for discussion of these cultural differences: p. 41). Public opinion studies, for instance, have found that

Table 1.7   *Views of the elderly about their health care systems*
                         (%)

	Australia	Canada	NZ	UK	USA
System works well	34	38	22	39	25
Needs fundamental change	38	40	45	44	44
Needs complete rebuilding	24	18	31	15	26

Source: Data from Commonwealth Fund (2000).

public support for specific health care systems varies considerably across countries and support seems to have little correlation with the amount spent on health care (Table 1.7). One must look closely at the cultural factors and value systems of the specific countries to explain these differences in support in which systems delivering fewer services are rated more highly by the public than those with much higher provision levels.

Public expectations may be elevated unrealistically because of a tendency to oversell medical innovation and overestimate the capacities of new medical technologies for resolving health problems. At the centre are the mass media, which are predisposed to unrealistically optimistic and oversimplified coverage of medical technology. Frequently, the initial response of the media, often encouraged by medical spokesmen, is to report innovations as medical 'breakthroughs'. Because most health care is routine and not newsworthy, the media naturally focus attention on techniques that can be easily dramatized. By and large media coverage in many countries solidifies public trust in the technological fix and 'stimulates their appetite for new, expensive, high technology procedures' (Kassler, 1994: 126).

Moreover, media coverage, along with a freedom of information climate in many countries, has forced the rationing process out into the open, making it much more explicit. Users of health care are less willing to acquiesce to a gate-keeper role for their general practitioners, especially when they read in the paper of inconsistencies and problems in the health care system. Particularly in those systems such as New Zealand and the UK that have traditionally had implicit supply-side rationing, making the system more transparent under media and consumer scrutiny makes it potentially more politically explosive. As a result, politicians in many countries find it difficult not to join in the call for expanded access to new technologies while the media seems to relish uncovering and dramatizing cases of denied treatment.

Arguments in favour of containing the costs of health care, while acceptable at the aggregate, societal level, are often rejected when applied at the individual level. Thus, while a large proportion of the population might support in theory the need for cost containment, when one's own health or that of a loved one is at stake, limits on the availability of health care resources are viewed as unfair: 'I know the government needs to cut health care costs but not when my child needs an expensive new drug.' It is little wonder that many elected officials are unwilling to make decisions that conflict with these emotionally held values. Again, it is important to note that although there are global forces working to increase public demands and expectations, these are more evident in some systems than in others and variation continues.

It has been observed that no matter to what extent health care facilities are expanded, there will remain a steady pool of unmet demands (Cundiff and McCarthy, 1994). Despite the policy statements of some officials, there is evidence that additional facilities and money alone will not solve the health care crisis. Instead of resolving the problems, this approach actually increases the demand for solutions to an ever-expanding range of technical medical problems. Although wealthier countries devote substantially higher proportions of their resources to health services than poorer countries, the demand for services does not abate; instead, the public comes to expect a level of medical care that cannot be imagined by those from less affluent countries. Moreover, as more of these expectations are met, demand for expanded health services actually escalates.

Types of health care

In order to analyse the ultimate attainment of health goals for society, it is important to understand the competing categories of health care. Table 1.8 describes three categories that largely define the range of activities normally included as health care. Although the terms used to define these categories vary, *primary care, curative medicine* and *chronic care* are used here. Primary care normally encompasses visits to general practitioners (GPs), ambulatory care and health education efforts, and includes a strong health promotion/disease prevention element. In contrast, curative medicine, which represents the core of modern health care discussed in Chapters 3–5, centres on acute care in hospitals and has a reliance on specialists and technologies to restore health to those acutely ill. Finally, as illuminated in Chapter 6, chronic care constitutes the range of services provided to people in long-term facilities, hospice facilities, home care and so forth, many of which have significant social as well as medical dimensions.

Table 1.8   *Categories of health care*

Primary care	Curative medicine	Chronic care
General practitioners	Acute/hospital care	Long-term facilities
Well-patient physicals	Outpatient clinics	Nursing home
Ambulatory care	Technology based	Hospice
Health promotion	Specialists	Home care
Education/prevention	Intensive care	

Public health, discussed in Chapter 7, largely falls within the realm of primary care although it is inextricably linked as well with chronic care, especially those services outside the institutional setting. At times threats to public health requiring broad public compliance can mean taking away a person's negative right to freedom of movement if that is perceived by public health officials as a health risk to the population. More importantly, as detailed in Chapter 7, public health often takes us completely out of the realm of health care per se into areas of education, social welfare, science and employment policy.

The 'health policy' of any country will constitute a mixture of these types, but there is considerable variation in the weight given to each dimension depending on the assumptions and goals of the policies. As illustrated by the scope of coverage in this book, health care today is dominated by curative medicine. When one thinks about health care, hospitals, highly trained specialists, and the latest technologies often come to mind. As noted earlier in the discussion of the expansion of biomedical technology, health care is often equated with medicine despite evidence that such an unbalanced approach has limits. Even the term 'curative' is misleading because in many cases the patient is not cured, but is rather rescued from death and often maintained in a state of health that is lower than it was before the person became ill. Instead of 'curing' the person, these interventions support or preserve a particular level of personal health by creating a continued dependence on further medical treatment or medications.

Prior to the Second World War, health care was predominantly primary care and public health oriented, in part because its curative capacities were limited and often ineffective at best. Through the early decades of the twentieth century, health care was normally limited to performing 'public health' functions. Hospitals were primarily designed to protect the public health, often by quarantining patients rather than treating individual patients, and largely served only persons who could not afford a private physician. Those with private resources would avoid hospitals like the plague because often plagues were there. Families were the primary long-term care-givers and most people died at home rather than in the intensive care wards of high-tech hospitals.

During the 1950s and 1960s, the emphasis in health care shifted perceptibly towards curative medicine even in health care systems in countries such as the UK, Japan and New Zealand which had strong roots in primary care and prevention. Although other countries have not bought into curative medicine to the same degree as the USA, as will be evident in the chapters that follow, there are strong pressures for aggressive medical interventions in acute care settings. The increased demands of the public for higher levels of technological medicine traced earlier produced indelible alterations in the health care community, most clearly manifested in the growth of medical specialities at the expense of primary care physicians and, especially, public health workers. As a result, the modern medical profession has developed primarily around the search for finding cures to disease rather than promoting health, preventing disease and protecting the public health. The growth of high-tech medical centres, the expectation of ever more sophisticated diagnostic capacity, and expansion of dramatic life-saving procedures changed the nature of medical care.

Health care as public policy

The term 'policy' has a wide range of meanings in current English usage. Politicians and parties present their intended actions as policies to be pursued and defend past actions as policies to be extended. Political commentators often talk about a government's housing policy, crime policy or drug policy in general terms, while others debate a specific government action. Policy, then, can be used to refer to general statements of intention, past or present actions in particular areas, or a set of standing rules to guide actions. Although all organizations have policies, at least in the latter sense, the focus of this book is on the policies of government. 'Public policy' is defined here as an action taken by the government or on behalf of it. It is a goal-driven course of action designed to promote, maintain or prevent a particular state of affairs. As noted by Jones (1992: 241), it is difficult to adopt or pursue a policy without having some idea of what our goal is, why we are pursuing it, and why we are pursuing it in that particular way. Policy here refers to the actions of a government that prioritize and allocate the limited resources at its disposal to achieve given ends.

Only the government has the legitimate authority to make decisions that are binding and carried out in the name of the people as a whole. Other organizations, such as medical associations and nursing societies, often make decisions that affect many individuals as well as the health care system as a whole. While their decisions might indeed have a bearing on what the government ultimately does, they are not binding by force of law. Although this book includes a discussion of actions by private and voluntary organizations that impact on health care where appropriate, the focus of attention is on governmental action or nonaction.

᾿ Health policy is defined here as those courses of action proposed or taken by a government that impact on the financing and/or provision of health services. It is crucial to note that all health policies involve a fundamental choice by a government as to whether to take a specific action or to do nothing (see Howlett and Ramesh, 1995: 5). Non-action in the health care arena has proved to be a more common policy than action in some countries. Also critical is the fact that, although health policy conceptually can be distinguished from other areas of public policy, in reality it is highly interrelated with social and economic policy in general. It will be apparent in following chapters that health and health policy cannot be understood in isolation from social welfare, unemployment, poverty, housing and general economic policies. In fact, it can be argued that the health of a population is as dependent on these policies as it is on formal health policy.

᾿ It is useful to categorize public policy as to one of three basic types: regulatory, distributive and redistributive (see Lowi, 1966). Regulatory policies impose constraints or restrictions on the actions of groups or individuals: they provide rules of conduct with sanctions backed up by the authority of government. Distributive policies provide services or benefits to particular segments of society. Often distributive policies are based on the notion of entitlements or 'public goods', which are normally defined as those goods and services that will benefit all individuals but which are unlikely to be produced by voluntary acts of individuals in part because they lack the resources. In other words, societal-wide effort is needed to effectuate these goods for the population. Public goods are defined by each society differently depending upon how broadly government responsibility is interpreted. Much activity of all governments centres on this provision of public services and it is often accomplished without undue controversy until scarcity causes tradeoffs to be made as to what groups get what goods. Redistributive policies, in contrast, frequently are controversial in principle because they are deliberate efforts by governments to change the distribution of income, wealth or property among groups in society. The reallocation of resources through progressive taxes and other mechanisms is present in all democracies, but it is central to the functioning of the welfare state.

Health care encompasses all three types of policy. The regulation of the health care sector through fee scales, licensing requirements, approval of drugs for use and other constraints on medical practice is extensive. Health care is one of the most regulated sectors in all developed countries in spite of their divergent types of health systems. The distributive policies of health care are most obvious under national health services, but occur to some degree in all countries through medical education programmes, the funding of health care research, the provision of public health services and health promotion activities. Finally, redistributive health care policies are based on the concepts of need and entitlement and encompass a range of efforts by government to shift resources from healthy to non-healthy citizens. They are usually based on a society's conception of equality. Mechanisms for such policies include the use of general revenues to provide services to those who lack resources, means-tested social insurance schemes for the poor, and programmes that redistribute societal resources from general revenues to the elderly or indigent.

  Health policy is a complex amalgamation of these various types of policy as governments attempt to influence the provision of health care to its citizens. Of all areas of public policy, health care is one of the most controversial because it always entails conflicts, especially in the regulatory and redistributive modes. This is not surprising given the high emotional and economic stakes involved in any government policy involving life, death and huge amounts of resources.

  In addition to the potential life/death stakes inherent in any policies regarding health care, health policy is distinctive because of the critical role of the medical profession in shaping and constraining it. Because of this centrality of health professionals to the delivery of health care, if a policy is to be successful it must have at least the tacit support of the medical community. Furthermore, since medical professionals largely define health need and the means necessary to meet it, any attempts by a government that are perceived as imposing constraints on the profession risk condemnation from these key stakeholders. Another characteristic that makes health policy especially difficult is the inability of individual users to distinguish between good and poor quality services and to know the value of the services they need or use. The complexity of providing health care and the inherent uncertainty surrounding medicine further reinforces the power of the health care providers to influence the delivery of medical services and thus health care policy.

  Due to the highly concentrated use of health care resources, the skewed patterns of use and the widely varied needs for health care across age, ethnic, sexual and cultural lines, the goal of equality requires a heavy redistribution of resources from a largely healthy population to the high users of health care. Table 1.9 illustrates that the use of health care resources is concentrated in a very small proportion

Table 1.9   *Distribution of health expenditures by user groups in the USA (%)*

Ranked by expenditure	1963	1970	1977	1980	1987
Top 1%	17	26	27	29	30
Top 5%	41	50	55	55	58
Top 30%	n/a	88	90	90	91
Bottom 50%	5	4	3	4	3

n/a = not available

Source: Data from Berk and Monheit (1992).

of the population in the USA. The top 1 per cent of health care users (usually heavy hospital care users) in 1987 consumed over 30 per cent of the total resources, and the top 5 per cent well over half. This means that the remaining 95 per cent of the population is largely healthy and in total constitute a minority of health care cost. These figures also show a clear trend towards greater concentration of health care resources going to a very small proportion of the population.

Although some observers point out that these only reflect high users in a given year and that specific individuals in this category will vary from year to year, a long-term comparative nation study found that even over a period as long as 16 years a small minority of the population uses most medical care and the majority uses very little (Roos, Shapiro and Tate, 1989). Data from France and other countries are comparable to those of the USA. More importantly, from an equity and need stand-point, the heaviest users of health care come predominantly from two groups: the elderly and people of all ages who engage in high risk behav-iour, thus causing or contributing to their own ill health. This concen-tration of need for health care, therefore, requires the redistribution of significant resources from young to old and from those who live healthy lives to those who do not.

Many of the most challenging dilemmas in democracies emerge as governments struggle with finding the proper mixture of these policy types in the light of often conflicting interests. Because of the heavy emphasis in many countries on rights to health care, the distinction between negative and positive rights is an important one to make here (see Heywood, 1997: 281). Negative rights are those rights which impose obligations on governments and other citizens to refrain from interfering with the rights bearer. They relate to the freedom to be left alone to use one's resources as one sees fit. Under negative rights, each person has a sphere of autonomy that others cannot violate, but no one is further obliged to take positive action to provide that person with the resources necessary to exercise the right. The only claim on others is a freedom from intrusion. Health care as a negative right would allow patients with adequate personal resources to maximize their use of health care. Negative rights are always in conflict with redistributive social welfare policies which deprive individuals of the free use of their resources.

In contrast, positive rights impose obligations on others (society?) to provide those goods and services necessary for each individual to exercise her/his rights. Although the level of positive rights is generally ill defined, this additional dimension requires the presence of institutions that guarantee a certain level of material well-being, through governmental redistribution of resources where necessary. Positive rights imply a freedom from deprivation, the entitlement to at least a decent level of human existence. The welfare state is based to a large extent on this more expansive notion of positive rights. One question of health policy is whether all citizens have a positive right to health care and, if so, what it should entail. How far does a right to the freedom from ill health go in requiring societal provision of health care resources to all citizens? What limits can justifiably be set on these entitlements to health care? For instance, could treatment be denied to an individual who causes his own ill health and who refuses to change his self-destructive behaviour despite repeated warnings?

Comparative health policy

This book attempts to place health policy in a comparative context in order to demonstrate the similarities and differences in approach among various countries' efforts to resolve health care problems. Although it is dangerous to transfer uncritically policies that work in one country to another, comparative public policy is useful in expanding policy options and demonstrating the experiences of a wide range of applications. Ovretveit, for instance, argues that travel and information systems are making it both easier and more necessary to understand cultural and national differences. For Ovretveit, 'health managers can improve their services by sensitively adapting ideas that have worked elsewhere' (1998: 15). Moreover, he argues that comparative health research has a role in building relations between nations and different communities, 'by creating knowledge that helps people understand their differences and similarities' (1998: 15). Harrop agrees that 'by examining policies comparatively, we can discover how countries vary in the policies they adopt, gain insight into why these differences exist, and identify some of the conditions under which policies succeed or fail' (1992: 3).

Comparative public policy is, therefore, a source of generalizations about public policy, which in turn are valuable for understanding policy in any particular country.

On the other hand, comparative policy analysis can demonstrate that factors which might be viewed as overpowering in one nation, such as the attitudes of the medical profession or the uniqueness of its liberal tradition, have resulted in different outcomes in other nations. According to Immergut, the 'comparative perspective shows that some factors are neither as unique nor as critical as they appear, whereas others stand out as truly significant' (1992b: 9). Ham (1997: 50) adds that an examination of international experience is illuminating in demonstrating both the difficulties faced by and the wide range of approaches available to policy makers. Comparative studies then give us cross-cultural insights as to what works or does not work in a wide variety of institutional and value contexts. Given the complexity of health care and the plethora of potential health care systems, only comparative studies can generate the evidence necessary to consider the full array of options.

Comparative policy analyses can also illustrate the commonalities of problems and variables across countries. Although to some extent health policy is unique to each nation, no longer can we ignore the globalization of problems and potential solutions. Immediate transmission of knowledge about new medical technologies through the mass media raises public and professional expectations and demands for access to these innovations. Through the Internet, citizens are informed about the newest available treatments and demands rise accordingly. Likewise, international medical conferences and journals transfer technologies and knowledge quickly from one side of the globe to the other, thus working to globalize professional standards.

These global forces are seen by some as reinforcing the *convergence theory*, which argues that as countries industrialize they tend to converge towards the same policy mix (Bennett, 1991). The convergence thesis, bolstered by globalization, would suggest that health policies across disparate country environments would have a tendency to become more similar over time as the various countries develop economically. Gibson and Means (2000), for example, argue that recent restructuring has led to convergence of the health systems of Australia and the UK despite quite dissimilar goals and strategic emphases.

Based on an examination of trends across industrialized democracies, Chernichovsky (1995) agrees that despite the variety of health care systems, health system reforms have led to the emergence of a 'universal outline or paradigm' for health care financing, organization and management. This paradigm cuts across ideological (private versus public) lines and across conceptual (market versus centrally planned) frameworks, as it combines principles of public financing of health care with principles of market competition applied to the organization and management of its consumption and provision (1995: 340). Similarly, Harrison, Moran and Wood (2002) found a policy convergence in approaches regarding the management of medical care between the USA and the UK during the 1990s.

Critics of convergence theories, however, argue that they oversimplify the process of development and underestimate significant divergence across countries (Howlett and Ramesh, 1995: 107). Convergence, they argue, downplays the importance of country-specific factors other than economic development, and most studies that find evidence of convergence do not find it applicable across the board, thus allowing for divergence in other areas. Although this book is not designed to test the convergence theory directly, its current prominence in the literature dictates that where appropriate its assumptions be addressed in the following chapters and that its explanatory power across these countries be explored more fully.

Why study these countries?

In order to provide a useful cross-country analysis of health policy, we selected nine countries for primary coverage, with the inclusion of examples from France and Italy where appropriate for comparative purposes. The core countries included for analysis were selected in order to give the reader systematic exposure to the full range of health systems as discussed in the typology section below. They were also selected because they represent countries across a wide spectrum of political, cultural and economic environments for health care. The group of case countries includes some, such as Germany, the UK and the USA, that are often included in comparative studies of Western nations and others, such as Australia, the Netherlands, New Zealand and Sweden, that are less often included. Also covered in the analysis here are Japan and Singapore, which offer valuable insights to health care policy that are often overlooked in more limited and US/European-based studies. Individually, each of the countries has unique contributions to make to the study of health policy. In combination, these countries serve as a good sample upon which to analyse the dynamics of Western health care policy in the twenty-first century.

Obviously, even the relatively large number of countries covered here does not exhaust the vast array of variation in health care systems found across the world. All of these countries are developed countries with Western-type medical systems. Even Japan and Singapore, the two non-Western countries, have highly developed medical systems and have affluent populations with similar levels of expectations and demands. Excluded from this comparative analysis, then, are the many developing nations from Africa, Asia, the Middle East and Eastern Europe which together have over 5 billion people. Although inclusion of some of these countries would have been illuminating, it would have altered the level of analysis because the issues in these countries are vastly different from those discussed here that apply to sophisticated medical systems.

One of the drawbacks trying to cover even nine developed countries is that it is not possible to provide a thorough analysis of any one of their health care systems. As regards specific countries, then, the objective of this book is to be an introduction, not a comprehensive analysis, and to provide a context within which to study individual countries. To this end, readers with an interest in a particular country or countries should make use of the Guide to Further Reading on pp. 220 ff. These suggestions will provide a valuable basis for building on the foundational knowledge offered in this book. In addition, the list of websites given in the Appendix (p. 225) provides links to the most recent information and data on these countries.

Health care systems

No two health care systems are identical, although many share certain characteristics that allow us to develop typologies which are useful in analysis of any particular system. It must be noted that while typologies are useful for teaching purposes because they allow us to simplify a complex reality and focus on the most important aspects, they must always be viewed as a heuristic tool, not a full representation of reality. The specific configuration of any health care system depends on a multitude of factors including the political system, the cultural framework, the demographic context, the unique historical background and specific events, and social structures inherent to that country. Societal goals and priorities develop over time and shape all social institutions and values, which themselves are fluid and changeable.

As Moran notes, health policy is about more than health and modern health care systems are about more than delivering a personal service: 'Health care facilities in modern industrial societies are great concentrations of economic resources – and because of this they are also the subject of political struggle' (1999: 1). With huge amounts of public resources being spent on health care, it is the source of intense political battles in which all governments are forced to participate. Both because health care is so fundamental to the interests of individuals and society as a whole, and because it involves such high economic stakes, it is always a volatile issue area for any political system. Not surprisingly, health care has taken centre stage in the politics of most countries in recent years.

The most obvious dimension of the political context encompasses the formal institutions that have been created for making public policy decisions. The term *policy arena* is used to define the institutional setting in which policy making takes place. The policy arena includes not only the formal political institutions such as legislatures, executives and courts but also regulatory agencies, semi-public bodies and specialized committees and commissions. These institutions define the distribution of power and the relationships among the political players by setting the *rules of the game* regarding access and interaction within arenas. As such they give distinct advantages or disadvantages to various groups in society. Equally important to understanding public policy, then, are the informal practices and structures that have evolved within a particular formal institutional framework. These traditions and rules of the game define a different political logic in each country. They too are critical to the environment within which interest groups, political parties, bureaucrats and individual politicians vie for influence over policy. Together these formal and informal political institutions shape how politics is conducted and create a strategic context for political conflict within the arena. 'Political factors help to determine whether a problem is defined as a public policy that requires action, they shape the way in which the problem is defined, and they intervene in the resolution of that problem' (Immergut, 1992: 10). Although institutional variables are not the only ones to matter, variation in institutional conditions across countries yields different opportunities for the actors involved in policy making in each country (Timmermans, 2001: 1).

Classifications of health care systems

Despite apparent widespread variation among the health care systems of developed nations, at root they represent variants or combinations of a limited number of types. As with political systems, typologies here can be valuable in simplifying what can be a complicated set of cross-cutting dimensions, but one must be cautious in interpreting them because they represent ideal types of specific macro-institutional characteristics. As will be demonstrated in this book, the real world of health care systems is considerably more complex.

For initial comparative purposes then, several such typologies that have used to classify health care systems are introduced here. The first classification scheme centres on the dimension of the degree of government involvement in the funding and provision of health care. At one extreme is the potential of a completely free market system with no government involvement, while at the other extreme is a tax-supported government monopoly of provision and funding of all health care services. Though in reality neither of these extremes exists and public involvement in the funding and provider roles may vary, along the continuum are three models that together represent the core types of health care systems operating across these countries (see Figure 1.1).

	Private **Insurance**	**Social** **Insurance**	**National** **Health Service**	
Free Market **System**	|------------------------------------|			**Government** **Monopoly**

Figure 1.1   *Types of health care system by provision and funding*

As illustrated in Figure 1.1, the *private insurance* (or consumer sovereignty) *model* is that with the least state involvement in the direct funding or provision of health care services. This type is characterized by the purchase of private health insurance financed by employers and/or individual contributions that are risk oriented. This system is also largely based on private ownership of health care providers and the factors of production although it might include a publicly funded safety net for the most vulnerable groups such as the poor, the elderly, or the young. The basic assumption of this approach is that the funding and provision of health care is best left to market forces. This type is most clearly represented by the USA and (until recently) by Australia, but many systems contain some elements of this type.

The second basic type of health system as to state involvement is the *social insurance* (or Bismarck) *model*. Although there is significant variation as to organization, this type is based on a concept of social solidarity and characterized in effect (though not always by design) by a universal coverage health insurance generally within a framework of social security. As a rule, this compulsory health insurance is funded by a combination of employer and individual contributions through non-profit insurance funds or societies, often regulated and subsidized by the state. The provision of services tends to be private, often on a fee-for-service basis, although some public ownership of the factors of production and delivery is likely. Germany, Japan and the Netherlands are often viewed as examples of this type. Singapore, with its compulsory Medisave system, is a variation on the theme of social insurance.

The third type, and the one which might approach the government monopoly in its pure form, is the *national health service* (or Beveridge) *model*. This model is characterized by universal coverage funded out of general taxation. Although this model is most identified with the UK, New Zealand created the first national health service in its 1938 Social

Security Act which promised all citizens open-ended access to all the health care services they needed free at the point of use. The provision of health care services under this model is fully administered by the state, which either owns or controls the factors of production and delivery. Although they have all moved away from this pure model to varying degrees the UK, Sweden and New Zealand are examples of the national health service model.

Another scheme used to categorize health care systems is based on the dimension of the method and source of financing. At one extreme are those systems fully dependent on private sources of funding, and at the other are those fully funded by public sources. Based on this criterion there are four main types of funding:

- direct tax/general revenues
- social or state insurance
- private insurance
- direct payment by users.

Within each type, however, there might be many variants. For instance the direct tax might be levied by the central government, by sub-units such as states or provinces, or by a combination of governments. Similarly, the social insurance system might be based on a single national scheme or on multiple insurance schemes more or less rigidly regulated or controlled by the government. Furthermore, there is a wide array of possible combinations both of basic types and their variants that are used often within a single health care system. The most that can be said about health care finance types therefore is that 'all health-care systems are pluralistic with respect to financing (and organisation) with tendencies to one method rather than another' (Appleby, 1992: 10).

In addition to the wide variety of combinations of these funding methods in each country, different countries apply them in different ways. Some, such as the USA (and, to a lesser extent, Australia), use general taxation for particular groups such as the poor and elderly, but depend on private insurance or direct payments for the remainder of the population. Other countries distinguish between specific forms of health care. For instance, New Zealand heavily funds hospital care through general taxation but depends on direct user payment for most primary care, except for specified categories of patients such as children whose care is subsidized. When examining health care policy, then, it is critical to examine not only how health care is financed based on these types, but also under what circumstances it is targeted from particular sources.

Another way of categorizing countries is to rank them on a single variable that is considered appropriate for the comparisons being made. For instance, one measure of state involvement that is often used to

Table 1.10   *Public funding as percentage of health expenditures,*
1970–98, ranked by 1998

	1970	1980	1990	1998	% change
Sweden	86.0	92.5	89.9	83.8	–2.2
UK	87.0	89.4	84.3	83.3	–3.7
Japan	69.9	71.3	77.6	78.5	+8.6
France	74.7	78.8	78.2	77.7	+3.0
New Zealand	80.3	88.0	82.4	77.0	–3.3
Germany	72.8	78.7	76.2	75.8	+3.0
Australia	62.3	62.8	67.4	70.0	+7.7
Netherlands	61.0	69.2	67.7	68.6	+7.6
Italy	86.9	80.5	78.1	67.3	–19.6
USA	36.3	41.5	39.6	44.8	+8.5
Singapore	70.1	68.0	n/a	26.0	–44.1

Source: Data from OECD (2001b).

compare countries is the extent to which health care is publicly funded. Table 1.10 shows the ranking of our countries on that criterion, ranging from nearly 84 per cent in Sweden and the UK to only 26 per cent in Singapore (see also Box 1.3). It should be noted that this ranking can tell us nothing about whether one system is better or worse than another; it simply illustrates how the countries array themselves on this dimension. Another use of this data is to trace changes, both for particular countries and collective patterns, and to compare the country rankings over time.

Whatever categorization schemes are used, health care becomes understood in terms of specific systems of financing, provision and governance. This approach has been central to the work of the OECD and a series of comparative studies on health care funding and delivery (OECD, 1987, 1992). The OECD scheme of three types discussed above has also been widely used by other scholars (Ham, 1997a; Wall, 1996), but it is problematic. Even in those cases where the health system of a country is dominated by one of the types identified in these models, traces of many variations are identifiable countries. Most countries, however, demonstrate mixes of characteristics in finance, provision and governance across the various types and there often is variation across time and space within a single country. These typological schemes, however, raise several questions to test in following chapters: in terms of state involvement do our countries fit the categories, and are the typologies useful or misleading in explaining health policy?

Box 1.3   The unique Singapore system: low in public funding, high on individual responsibility

Of all the systems discussed here, Singapore is most unusual as reflected in its very low level of public funding. The main reason that Singapore only registers 26 per cent public funding is because in 1984 it instituted Medisave, a compulsory savings scheme that shifted responsibility to individuals. Under this scheme, every working individual (and employer) is required to contribute to Medisave. These contributions are then deposited in an individual savings account in that person's name which can then be drawn on to pay for health insurance or hospital expenses incurred by the person or his immediate family. While the scheme is compulsory in the form of a tax on income, because each account is private it is considered to be privately, not publicly, financed.

The Singapore health care system is based on a unique interpretation of individual responsibility and is designed to provide incentives to reduce consumption and offer protection against 'free-rider' abuses while guaranteeing affordable basic health care through government subsidies. Individuals can in effect choose the level of subsidy they wish to receive in public hospitals – if they opt for a fancy ward the subsidy is low or non-existent whereas if they go to a less fancy ward the subsidy is higher. The key principle is that patients are expected to pay part of the cost of medical services that they use, and pay more when they demand a higher level of service. 'The principle of co-payment applies even to the most heavily subsidised wards to avoid the pitfalls of providing "free" medical services' (Singapore Ministry of Health, 2002b).

Conclusions

Health systems of all countries face major problems as regards the issues raised here. Whether health care represents a crisis in a particular country depends on one's perspective but certainly there is much variation in severity across nations on more objective measures as well. To what extent are these differences the product of health policies of the countries and to what extent are the problems beyond the direct control of policy makers? Put another way, what steps can governments take, if any, to maximize the chances of framing sustainable health care systems that can weather the ageing population, the proliferation of technologies, the heightened public expectations, and other forces driving up the costs?

What should be already evident from the discussion so far is that there are significant differences as to how well counties are doing in constraining costs, providing universal and quality care, and protecting the public health. It has yet to be demonstrated convincingly whether universal, global forces are moving the health policies of industrialized counties towards convergence. Even if that is the case, it is imperative to examine closely the variations and similarities of the health care systems of countries and to appreciate the implications for the provision of health care to populations. Chapter 2 begins this task by examining the political, cultural and historical context of the health systems of these countries in order to get a better understanding of how and why each country's health system emerged the way it did. As such, the chapter provides a framework for studying the intricacies of the systems and comparative health policy in the chapters that follow.

Political, Historical and Cultural Contexts

·The health policy of any country at a particular point in time is the product of a multitude of factors, the most important of which are ' displayed in Figure 2.1. These factors include the intrinsic social, cultural and political fabric of a country, including social values and structures, political institutions and traditions, the legal system, and characteristics of the health care community. As a start, policy-making authority might be highly centralized or widely dispersed across multiple levels. Moreover, in some countries unions and/or corporate structures are strong factors in determining social policy and might, in effect, have a veto power over proposed policy changes made by the government. Likewise, the influence of the medical industry and medical associations varies widely, as does the power of the insurance providers in shaping health policy.

The practice of medicine also can be strongly affected by the legal system and its role in compensation claims and the definition of legal rights to health care services. Moreover, in some countries the courts can challenge and even negate government policies, while in others the government is supreme and its decisions are the law. Social values, too, are important forces, with some traditions emphasizing individual rights and entitlements and others putting heavy stress on collective or community good. The boundaries as to what is a 'public' good and what should remain in the private sphere also impacts on health policy. Countries with stronger socialist roots are likely to define public goods and services much more broadly and include universal coverage. Furthermore, in some societies, the extended family still plays an important role in health care while in others even the nuclear family has diminished importance in the delivery of health care.

In addition to the values and institutions of a country, health policy is also shaped by the composition of its population and by demographic patterns. Heterogeneous, multi-cultural populations require more complex health systems than more homogeneous ones. Likewise, older populations have different needs from younger ones. Health policy and the way in which medical resources are distributed also reflect the current state of medical technology and the public expectations and

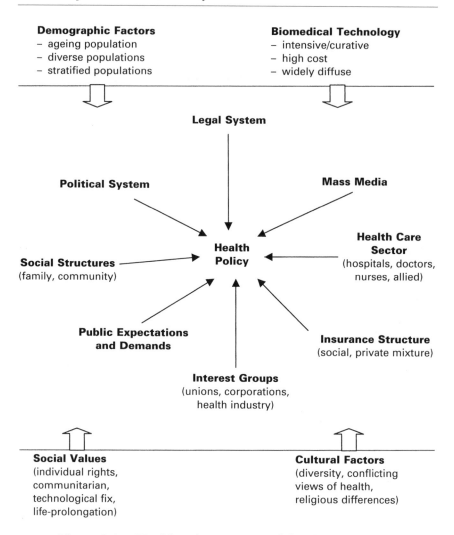

Figure 2.1 *Health policy context of developed nations*

demands that accompany it. For example, a survey of attitudes about length and quality of life among adults conducted by the UK International Longevity Centre in 2002 found significant differences between the French and the Americans and British. While 64 per cent of the Americans and 55 per cent of the British wanted to live as long as possible even if that entailed pain, nearly two-thirds of the French opted to live a shorter than average life if it meant dying without being in pain or dependent on others (Carvel, 2002a).

Moreover, the mass media and its coverage of medical stories clearly influence how medicine and health care policy are perceived by the public. Countries with 'tabloid' traditions are likely to emphasize the more sensational aspects of medicine and those with more investigative traditions are likely to look for faults in the health care system. In general, however, the mass media across these countries has tended to dramatize medicine, heighten expectations, and place more demands on health managers and politicians.

Public support for policy, of course, is an important factor in democratic societies and is critical in explaining how governments with similar problems cope differently. Interestingly, levels of public support for health services across countries seem to have little correlation with level of health spending or any objective level of services provided. Table 2.1, for instance, compares the public satisfaction with their health care system in each country with the percentage of GDP spent on health care, and it finds little relationship between higher spending and satisfaction. Spending more does not necessarily increase satisfaction levels.

Although, as discussed in Chapter 1, health care on one level might reflect universal challenges for all countries, the historical and cultural context of health and health care varies from country to country as well

Table 2.1   *Public satisfaction and percentage of GDP spent on health care*

	Satisfaction level[a]		*% GDP*	
	1991	*1996*	*1990*	*1998*
Australia	34	n/a	7.9	8.6
France	41	65	8.6	9.4
Germany	41	58	8.7	10.3
Italy	12	20	8.1	8.2
Japan	49	n/a	6.1	7.4
Netherlands	47	70	8.5	8.7
Sweden	32	58	8.5	7.9
UK	27	57	6.0	6.8
US	10	40	11.9	12.9

[a] 1991 measured by statement, 'On the whole, the health care system works pretty well, and only minor changes are necessary to make it work better' (Blendon, Leitman, Morrison and Donelan, 1990). 1996, percentage saying they were 'fairly or very' satisfied' with their health system (Blendon, Kim and Benson, 2001).

n/a = not available

Sources: Data from OECD (2001b); Blendon *et al.* (1990); and Blendon *et al.* (2001).

as within countries. A main argument in this book is that variation in health care policy from one country to the next can be explained only by understanding the unique combination of these variables and their interaction in each nation. After surveying the political structures and institutions of these countries, this chapter examines the policy implications of their varied demographic patterns. It then discusses the historical and cultural context of each country and analyses its importance for understanding differences in health policy. For instance, why do some countries view health as a public good and others as primarily a private matter? Why, as illustrated above, is it that some countries that spend and deliver considerably less on health services have higher public satisfaction rates? Why do some countries with such similar political systems have such divergent health systems?

National culture and history might help explain health policy, but as populations become more diverse through immigration many nations are finding health delivery increasingly problematic due to the new cultural diversities within their populations. Not only health care needs, but also perceptions of health itself, vary among cultures. This chapter, therefore, also examines a range of models of health including the holistic models strongly adhered to in some Eastern cultures and among many indigenous populations which are often at odds with the dominant Western medical model. It also asks whether particular types of health care systems (e.g., public, private, National Health Service, etc.) are more responsive to multicultural health needs than other systems.

Contrasting political systems

Although the political systems of no two countries are identical and each nation has a unique combination of formal and informal structures, the characteristics of political systems can be categorized along several overlapping dimensions (Lijphart, 1999). The major distinguishing factor is the extent to which political power is concentrated or dispersed. As a rule, *unitary* systems concentrate political authority in a central government while *federal* systems constitutionally divide powers between the central government and states, provinces or other sub-national governments. Although the central government in a unitary system might choose to delegate specific administrative functions and responsibilities to lower units, final authority rests at the national level. In contrast, states in a federal system have constitutionally-based powers that most often include health policy. Unitary governments include most European countries and Singapore, while Germany, the Netherlands, Australia and the USA are examples of the federal model.

Another institutional configuration that relates directly to the continuum of centralization is the distribution of power within each level of government. For instance, many democracies, such as New Zealand and the UK, concentrate power in Parliament where the distinction between executive and legislative power is obscured or virtually non-existent. Moreover, although many parliamentary systems have upper and lower houses (e.g., the House of Lords and House of Commons in the UK), in effect most power rests in the lower houses.

In stark contrast to other countries is the USA with its deliberate constitutional separation of powers among a separately elected president, two houses of Congress, and a relatively active judicial system. Despite a great deal of variation in dispersion of policy-making authority in parliamentary systems, when compared to the USA they all have considerably more concentrated bases of power. Figure 2.2 presents a rough distribution of our case countries in terms of centralization of institutional power along these dimensions. This distribution corresponds closely to the findings of Lijphart (1999: 189) who classifies Australia, Germany and the USA as 'federal and decentralised'; the Netherlands as 'semi-federal'; Japan and Sweden as 'unitary and decentralised'; and France, Italy, New Zealand and the UK as 'unitary and centralised'. Singapore, a city-state of 4 million people in which all political power rests in the central government, is by far the most centralized of the countries discussed here.

Figure 2.2   *Institutional power in political systems*

The implications of these formal government types for health policy are significant. Where power is centralized, the government has the formal capacity to make more rapid and comprehensive policy changes. Singapore, for instance, was able to initiate a major change in funding with little contest, and successive New Zealand governments introduced unimpeded a range of major restructuring initiatives of the health system during the 1990s. In contrast, the more fragmented the political authority, the higher the probability of deadlock and inaction or at best more incremental change. The USA is the prime example of a system where making even minor changes in health policy represents a long-term struggle. Even in a relatively narrow area such as payment of prescription charges for the elderly on Medicare where almost everyone agrees something must be done, nothing has been accomplished after over two years of political wrangling (Abrams, 2002). Australia and the USA are both federal systems, but their approaches to health care are quite divergent. Although not as static as the USA, however, reform in Australia over the years has been very measured compared to that of neighbouring New Zealand.

In Germany health policy making also tends to be highly incremental, to the extent that health policy is often locked into 'reform blockades'. As decision-making powers are dispersed among a multitude of mainly non-state actors (the insurance funds and provider organizations) across federal, state and local levels, the federal government has little direct influence on health care. This is particularly pertinent in the case of medical reform (Burau, 2001). Through the joint self-administration with insurance funds doctors are at the heart of health governance, and it is difficult to address the relationship between economic and medical rationality.

Moreover, in fragmented political systems where competing political parties are able to control particular institutions, there is more likely to be a divided government where one party controls one or several branches or levels and the other party controls others. Although this might contribute to a more deliberative policy-making process, it can also easily degenerate into stagnation and gridlock as has been common in US health policy. Conversely, it might be expected that a highly centralized system, as in the UK or Singapore, results in a policy arena characterized by more frequent and inclusive changes such as major restructuring, often to the detriment of programme stability. For instance, instability and insecurity have been major charges made by opponents of the near-continuous reforms of the New Zealand health system in the 1990s (Martin and Salmond, 2001).

Another dimension that Lijphart (1999) sees as important in distinguishing among democracies is the strength of judicial review (the extent to which a high court can overrule the elected representative bodies). Figure 2.3 demonstrates a wide range across our countries regarding the power of the courts to influence health policy. In recent decades, the German and American courts in particular have become highly activist, invalidating many laws on constitutional grounds, thus earning them the label of being an 'imperial judiciary' (Franck, 1996).

In contrast, the Netherlands, New Zealand, the UK and Singapore do not have systems of judicial review. In these countries, the will of Parliament, therefore, is supreme and cannot be challenged or overridden by a high court. The remaining countries have provisions for judicial review but for a variety of reasons the courts have exercised their power with restraint and moderation. The role of the European Court

Strong Judicial Review
Germany
USA

Medium Judicial Review
Australia
Italy

Weak Judicial Review
France
Japan
Sweden

No Judicial Review
Netherlands
New Zealand
UK

Figure 2.3 *The strength of judicial review*

Source: Extracted from Lijphart (1999: 226)

of Human Rights is likely to influence health policy in affected countries but its powers are still metamorphosing.

The comparative wealth of countries

One of the most straightforward determinants of health care funding and provision across all countries of course is wealth. Rich countries on average would be expected to put considerably more resources into health care simply because they have more discretionary funds. Unfortunately, very poor countries cannot compete with more wealthy countries in health care spending and cannot afford the kind of medicine affluent countries take for granted.

The most used comparative measure of wealth is the GDP per capita. In 2002, the average GDP per capita of all countries was $7,081, with a low of $498 in Sierra Leone and a high of $35,894 in Luxembourg. Twenty-six countries had per capita GDP below $1000 and an additional 40 between $1,000 and $2,000. From the data presented in Table 2.2, it is clear that all of our countries are relatively wealthy; in fact, they are clustered, except for New Zealand, at over $20,000. The variance in wealth among these nations might help explain minor economic limits on those nations near the bottom of Table 2.2 as compared to those at the top. However, the relatively small differences in wealth among these particular countries means that differences in health provision and spending found among them here are not likely to be explained simply by this one factor.

Table 2.2   *GDP per capita, 2002, in US dollars*

Country	GDP/capita
USA	35,831
Singapore	25,532
Japan	24,848
France	24,315
Netherlands	24,303
Germany	23,317
Australia	23,030
UK	22,801
Sweden	22,197
Italy	22,070
New Zealand	17,494

Source: Data from World Factbook (2003).

Population size and diversity

As noted above, health policy can be significantly influenced by the demographic characteristics of a country. Moreover, because these characteristics change over time, such as the ageing or the diversification of the population through immigration, the health system must adapt to those changes. To some extent, the reform efforts of countries over the last several decades represent attempts to deal with changing needs brought about in part by demographic trends, especially population ageing. One might expect, therefore, that some of the differences in health policy among these countries described in the following chapters can be traced in part to differences in the size of the respective populations, their age and ethnic diversity, and their degree of social stratification in terms distribution of wealth.

Table 2.3 summarizes key demographic variables across our countries. Most obvious is the vast difference in the size of population. It is not surprising that the USA struggles to devise a workable health system for almost 300 million people. The State of California alone, with over 33 million people, is larger than half the countries examined here. Certainly, it can be argued that countries with smaller populations ought to be better able to design a workable health policy. Since the total populations of New Zealand and Singapore are smaller than at least five metropolitan areas in the USA, perhaps it would be more appropriate to compare their systems with a large US city or a small state. Large population size might also contribute to efforts in the UK

Table 2.3   *Population characteristics, 2000*

	Population	% growth rate	Net migration	% over 65	% under 14
Australia	19,169,083	1.02	4.26	12	21
France	59,329,691	0.38	0.66	16	19
Germany	82,797,408	0.29	4.01	16	16
Italy	57,634,327	0.09	1.74	18	14
Japan	126,549,976	0.18	0.00	17	15
Netherlands	15,892,237	0.57	2.30	14	18
New Zealand	3,819,762	1.17	4.95	11	23
Singapore	4,151,264	3.54	26.80	7	18
Sweden	8,873,052	0.02	0.86	18	18
UK	59,511,464	0.25	1.07	16	19
USA	275,562,673	0.91	3.50	12	21

Source: Data from World Factbook (2003).

to decentralize decision making in the National Health Service (NHS) to health authorities, or (more recently) Primary Care Trusts.

However, population size is but one important variable for health policy. Population growth rates are crucial because they point to future health needs and relate to the composition of that dynamic population. A high growth rate calls for planning for expansion of services and, depending on where the growth is coming from (e.g., births, immigration), a change in types of services needed. In contrast, a low or negative growth rate might indicate difficulties in funding services even at the existing level. Singapore, New Zealand and Australia display the highest percentages of growth, indicating a need for expanded services just to take care of the increased numbers. However, most of the European countries demonstrate smaller rates of growth, and in Sweden's case near zero growth (Box 2.1). Combined with the ageing of their populations, these low growth rates signal difficulties in maintaining existing spending patterns without increasing the tax load on the shrinking proportion that is employed.

One way of counteracting low growth rates is to increase immigration rates, which at least several countries (Italy, Germany and the Netherlands) appear to be doing. Net migration per 1,000 ranges from zero in Japan to almost 27 in Singapore. Again, it is important to know more details about the immigrants before estimating their impact on health policy. Are they skilled or unskilled, destitute or

Box 2.1   Policies for older people in Sweden

Together with low rates of net migration and low growth rates of the population Sweden has one of the highest percentages of older people (see Table 2.3). Together, these factors make Sweden something of a test bed for coping with the challenges of ageing. In the area of care of older people Sweden has responded with a combination of decentralization, service integration and de-institutionalization and targeting. In 1992 municipalities became responsible for providing health and social care to older people living in institutions; and in half of the county councils this has been extended to home-based services. In addition, the number of long-term beds has been reduced significantly, while home-based services are increasingly targeted to highly dependent older people.

wealthy? Are they members of compatible cultures and religions or those likely to cause friction with the existing community? Although diverse cultures and ethnic groupings can strengthen countries in the long run, they can put severe pressures on health and social service system upon arrival (see Box 2.2). Often, they bring with them disease patterns that require shifts in resources. Just as infusions of immigrants of different backgrounds can produce challenges for the health system, countries that are more homogeneous are likely to have an easier time meeting the health needs of their population than highly ethnically diverse populations.

As will be discussed later in this chapter, diverse cultures can have

Box 2.2   Asylum seekers and the National Health Service in Britain

In 2000, Britain received the largest number of asylum applications in Europe (United Nations High Commission for Refugees, 2001). Asylum seekers impact on the NHS in two ways. In an already tightly cash-limited health service any increase in the number of patients puts considerable additional strain on existing services. This particularly applies to GPs as the first point of contact for patients. The NHS also struggles to cope with the scale and the nature of health problems of asylum seekers. In part, this reflects special needs arising from asylum seekers coming from countries with a high prevalence of infectious diseases, or having been tortured (Dunne, 2002). However, health problems are often exacerbated by the poor living conditions of asylum seekers once they arrive in the country (Casciani, 2002). Their vulnerable and very marginal position is also a major barrier to accessing health services.

Table 2.4 *Ethnic composition, 2000*

Australia	Caucasian 92%; Asian 7 %; Aboriginal and other 1%
France	Predominantly Celtic and Latin with Teutonic, Slavic, North African, Indochinese and Basque minorities
Germany	German 91.5%; Turkish 2.4%; other 6.1% (mainly Serbo-Croatian, Italian, Russian, Greek, Polish, Spanish)
Italy	Predominantly Italian with small clusters of German-, French-, and Slovene-Italians in the north and Albanian- and Greek-Italians in the south
Japan	Japanese 99.4%; other 0.6% (mainly Korean)
Netherlands	Dutch 91%; other 9% (mainly Moroccan and Turkish)
New Zealand	NZ European 74.5%; Maori 9.7%; other European 4.6%; Asian 7.4%; Pacific Islander 3.8%
Singapore	Chinese 77%; Malay 14%; Indian 7.6%; other 1.4%
Sweden	Predominantly Swedish, with indigenous Finnish and Lapp with small minority of foreign-born Finns, Yugoslavs, Danes, Norwegians, Greeks and Turks
UK	English 81.5%; Scottish 9.6%; Irish 2.4%; Welsh 1.9%; Ulster 1.8%; other 2.8% (mainly West Indian, Indian, and Pakistani)
USA	White 83.5%; black 12.4%; Asian 3.3%

Source: Data from World Factbook (2003).

vastly different views of health, health care and health service delivery. These differences can be heightened when the values of a group are in conflict with those of the medical profession (e.g., female genital mutilation). With the clear exception of Japan, the countries examined here all reflect relatively high degrees of ethnic (Table 2.4) or religious (Table 2.5) diversity, or in (many cases) both.

While religious diversity in some cases might be a significant factor beyond simply reflecting other cleavages in society, ethnic differences can be more crucial, particularly where newer immigrants are predominantly from minority groupings. Ethnic groups not only challenge the health system because they have varying prevalences of particular diseases and conditions, but also because they bring with them divergent views about the medical community, health and political authorities.

Table 2.5   *Religious composition*

Australia	Anglican 26.1%; Roman Catholic 26%; other Christian 24.3%; non- Christian 11%
France	Roman Catholic 90%; Protestant 2%; Jewish 1%; Muslim 1%
Germany	Protestant 38%; Roman Catholic 34%; Muslim 1.7%, other or unaffiliated 26.3%
Italy	Predominantly Roman Catholic with Protestant, Jewish and Muslim minorities
Japan	Shinto and Buddhist 84%; other 16%, including Christian 0.7%
Netherlands	Roman Catholic 34%, Protestant 25%, Muslim 3%; other 2%, unaffiliated 36%
New Zealand	Anglican 24%; Protestant 28%; Roman Catholic 15%; unaffiliated 33%
Singapore	Buddhist (Chinese); Muslim (Malays); plus minorities of Christian, Hindu, Sikh, Taoist and Confucianist
Sweden	Lutheran 87%; others include Roman Catholic, Orthodox, Baptist, Muslim, Jewish and Buddhist
UK	Anglican 66%; Roman Catholic 22%; Muslim 2.8%; other including Presbyterian, Methodist, Sikh, Hindu and Jewish
US	Protestant 56%; Roman Catholic 28%; Jewish 2%; other 4%; unaffiliated 10%

Source: Data from World Factbook (2003).

Although most countries studied here have a single dominant majority, except for Japan they have significant ethnic/racial minorities that complicate delivery of health care services. The problem is aggravated because health services often have not embraced diversity. An exception is Singapore, which seems to have been largely successful in integrating the Malay and Indian minorities into the health system. In contrast, blacks in the USA continue to be significantly less well served by the health care system than whites as measured by access or health outcomes (see Table 2.6). Similarly, the Maori minority in New Zealand has traditionally had a difficult assimilation into the health care system. As more asylum seekers are coming into specific European countries, they will complicate health delivery and will bring with them unique new health problems with which the health care systems must deal.

Table 2.6   *Health indicators by race, USA, 2000*

	White	Black
Low birthweight/1,000 births	7.1	14.8
Neonatal deaths/1,000 births	3.8	9.1
Infant Deaths/1,000 births	5.7	13.5
Life Expectancy (at birth)		
Male	74.8	68.2
Female	80.0	74.9

Source: Data from National Center for Health Care Statistics (2002).

Cultural/historical factors shaping health care

It is argued here that each country brings to health a unique combination of historical and cultural factors that are crucial in explaining its proclivities and characteristics. Political culture is the complex of beliefs, values and attitudes held by the public concerning the proper role of government. To what extent is health care a public as opposed to private good and, if a public good, on what grounds should health services be distributed to individuals? What is the perceived role of the state as opposed to the citizen? To focus on those elements of political culture which influence health policy, one must look at beliefs concerning definitions of health, the role of the government in the health arena, and the extent to which health care represents an individual right or a privilege granted by society. In order to provide a basis for more in-depth comparison throughout later chapters, we will look briefly at one of the key defining cultural characteristics that shapes health care across countries and then provide an overview of the most defining aspects in each country.

One key dimension focuses on how the individual in the society relates to the whole. Table 2.7 illustrates a rough distribution of these countries showing whether they are classified primarily as communitarian, egalitarian or individualistic cultures. Countries with communitarian traditions, based either in the family or other groupings, have designed various mechanisms to ensure the interests of the various communities. Germany, for instance, has a strong tradition of self-administration, the Netherlands guarantees empowerment of the various pillars to reach consensus, and Japan puts strong emphasis on the family and on tradition itself.

In contrast, egalitarian cultures such as those of New Zealand and

Table 2.7   *Distribution by type of health political culture*

Communitarian	Egalitarian	Individualistic
Germany	Sweden	USA
Netherlands	New Zealand	Australia
Japan	UK	Singapore

Sweden, although having divergent political systems, place emphasis on the entitlement to health care and on a societal commitment to provide health care on those grounds. Interestingly, countries such as the USA and Australia due to their rugged individualism have a tendency to elevate individual rights above the welfare of the community. For such countries, it is difficult to limit these negative rights to health care even for the common good. While rights and entitlements are often used synonymously, entitlements suggest a concern for equality that can be found only in the notion of positive rights, while the individualistic version of negative, self-centred rights lacks the social dimension found in egalitarian and communitarian societies.

Although they are placed in Table 2.7 as to their predominant orientation, some countries have tended to combine aspects of these types into unique hybrids. For instance, Singapore has merged communitarian and common good features with a very strong view of individual responsibility for health and health care. Similarly, the UK culture combines a pragmatic approach to collective action with a very generous entitlement philosophy reminiscent of egalitarian cultures such as New Zealand and Sweden. In Japan (and, to a lesser extent, Singapore), meanwhile, Western medicine has introduced a form of individualism foreign to communitarian culture and created friction between generations as well as among social classes, as illustrated by the discussion of traditional medicine later in this chapter.

Germany

Germany has a strong tradition of voluntarism, self-help and family support, embedded in Roman Catholic social teachings and the idea of 'subsidiarity'. The 1873 social health insurance, the first of its kind, built on these traditions and incorporated them in a statutory system of social solidarity (Freeman, 2000). The conservative underpinnings of this vision of social solidarity contrast with the egalitarian orientations characteristic of New Zealand and Sweden. The organization of health care in Germany is marked by profound continuity and is shaped by a number of principles, among them social solidarity, freedom of choice for patients and nearly full coverage of services (Greiner and Schulenburg, 1997).

In the social insurance context, access to health care is an entitlement that individuals 'earn' by virtue of paying insurance contributions. This, together with a strong legalistic approach typical of Germany, turns access to health care into the right of individuals to a defined range of services. Patients literally have 'ownership' of health services. This helps to explain why the freedom of patients to choose their doctors remains a fundamental principle of health care provision. Not surprisingly, Germany is one of the few countries, which does not operate a British-style GP gate-keeping system. The individualized right to health care also goes hand in hand with the expectation that the social health insurance system provides full coverage. In conjunction with the structural features of the health system this makes cost containment and restrictions of services covered by social insurance difficult.

The Netherlands

Another example of a communitarian country is the Netherlands, which resembles Germany in that private initiative has been a guiding principle in the organization of society. Dutch society has traditionally been organized in separate segments or pillars that represent different religious and political orientations (Maarse, 1997). According to the Roman Catholic notion of subsidiarity and its Protestant counterpart of sovereignty the different segments in society should be empowered to provide for their members (Björkman and Okma, 1997). However, the 'pillarization' of Dutch society began to weaken in the 1960s and state intervention in health care increased (Maarse, 1997).

This marked the modernization of the Dutch health system and a 'universalist turn'. The introduction of insurance for exceptional medical risks in 1967 is indicative here (see Chapter 3, p. 67). This insurance is compulsory for all employers irrespective of income and, together with relatively generous entitlements, such insurance has helped to establish a culture of care which gives preference to formal care. However, elements of universalism do co-exist with the legacy of pillarization. The provision of health care continues to be predominantly in the hands of private non-profit organizations and health policy making still requires the consensus of a large number of interest groups, to the extent that health reform almost becomes impossible.

Japan

Although for many Westerners Japan is an enigma, its health care context shares much in common with Germany and the Netherlands, because at its base Japan has a communitarian, extended-family-based culture with veneration for the elderly. For health care, this has meant that universal coverage for health care is widely accepted socially as a given, although long-term care has until recently largely rested with the family, particularly women (see p. 156). However, during the last half-century traditional Japanese values have come into conflict with the infusion of Western, largely American, individualistic culture, thus causing significant distress, particularly among the older Japanese population.

As a result, Japanese views of medicine are an amalgamation of Buddhist, Confucian and Shinto influence, combined more recently with Hippocratic and Christian influences (Macer, 1999). During the fifth and sixth centuries, for instance, the medical profession was restricted to the privileged classes. During centralization of government in the seventh and eighth centuries, a bureau of medicine was established creating an official physician class. After the Heian period in the ninth to fourteenth centuries, the government-sponsored health service was replaced by professional physicians, and in the sixteenth century, a code of practice similar to the Hippocratic code, the 'Seventeen Rules of Enjuin', was drawn up which emphasized a priestly role for a physician. Although modern Western medicine took hold in the nineteenth century and the rapid progress of medical technology challenged the way medicine is practised, there remains a very strong paternalistic attitude on the part of doctors and a lasting reliance on traditional practice (see later in this chapter, p. 55).

Sweden

Perhaps the clearest example of an egalitarian type of culture is Sweden, which is notable for the very early provision of medical care by the state dating back to the seventeenth century (European Observatory on Health Care Systems, 2001). Towns and cities employed doctors to provide public health care and municipalities also operated hospitals. In rural areas the central state paid physicians to provide basic care. State involvement in health care was consolidated in the middle of the nineteenth century with the setting up of county councils, which were mainly responsible for health care. However, a considerable expansion of health services only occurred in the post-war period, paving the way for the universal health care system as we know it today.

The historical legacy of public involvement in health care is combined with the principle of equality, which is deeply embedded in Swedish society. People have a right to health care regardless of income and where they live (Håkansson and Nordling, 1997). The right to health care is part of people's citizenship and not an individually earned entitlement, as in the case of Germany and the Netherlands. Public funding and provision of health care are key features of the health system in Sweden, as is a strong emphasis on public health and concern for equity.

New Zealand

Although its national health system compares most closely with that of the UK and its political culture retains many features of its Commonwealth heritage, like Sweden, New Zealand has a strong tradition of egalitarianism. This was clearly reflected in the Social Security Act of 1938 that promised an open-ended provision to all citizens based on need. It is also demonstrated by the strong belief in the public consultation process and the view that office holders are holders of the public trust, not above it. New Zealand's egalitarian foundation is also illustrated by the 'tall poppy' belief which holds that people who get too successful, wealthy or powerful must be cut back to size. New Zealand politicians embraced the New Right, market-centred philosophy in the 1980s and 1990s, but the public rejected attempts to restructure the health system in ways that were seen as destroying its egalitarian foundations. The result has been a series of rather bold attempts by governments of both parties to make major changes in the health care structure, only to pull back from more extreme and unpopular tactics once the public felt threatened and demanded a return to a more egalitarian system.

Britain

In comparison to Sweden, Britain not only has had a much shorter history of public involvement in health care, but the approach to collective action has typically also been pragmatic and empirical rather than principled (Johnson and Cullen, 2000). This also helps to explain why after the Second World War a universal health service was introduced in what was traditionally a liberal state regime. However, the NHS did not resolve the tension between *laissez-faire* liberalism and collectivism and instead a generous entitlement philosophy has co-existed with rationed service provision (Moran, 1999).

The NHS enjoys high public support. The generosity of the NHS entitlement philosophy contrasts with both the failure of the earlier National Insurance arrangements and the austerity of post-war Britain, and it is deeply entrenched in the public's mind. Not surprisingly, reforms have focused on the organization of health services, and even the extensive changes under the Conservatives in the late 1980s were prefaced with the assurance 'the NHS is safe in our hands'.

Universalism, together with a centralist political system, also generates expectations that health services are the same (or at least comparable) across the country. Concerns about inequities in access are prominent and are reflected in debates about the 'postcode lottery', whereby services vary significantly from one locale to the next.

USA

The USA has to be the prototype of an individualistic society. Although individual rights have some emphasis in all the nations examined here, in the USA rights have been elevated to a status of supremacy over collective interests. Moreover, by rights Americans mean 'negative' rights, meaning that Americans prefer to minimize government intervention and discount the notion of public goods and opt instead for a system where individuals fend for themselves. As a result, Americans are hesitant to sacrifice perceived individual needs for the common good: thus, there is no guaranteed universal coverage but also no limits on what health care individuals can buy if they can afford it.

This cultural tenet goes a long way to explain why the USA expends so much more of its GDP on health care than other countries, without providing universal access. As stated by Churchill, in health care 'demands are transformed by their cultural significance into needs . . . [and] our needs seem to be insatiable' (1994: 8). Not surprisingly, the USA is unwilling to institute policies that place limits on the amount of medical resources that an individual can acquire, or even which doctor they can see. Cost containment measures such as Health Maintenance Organisations (HMOs) that attempt to set limits on individual care have been widely attacked as counter to patient rights and led to a call for a 'Patients' Bill of Rights'.

In the USA, when individual rights and the common good conflict, the individual's claims take precedence. 'Our premium on individual rights and our emphasis on the differences between us is a far cry from the social beliefs that back the health systems of Europe, Canada, and Japan, in which more homogenous societies band together for the common good' (Kassler, 1994: 130). Moreover, in direct contrast to the UK and New Zealand, in the USA there is a strong aversion by the medical community to serve as gate-keepers and professional codes of ethics refuse to acknowledge the existence of scarcity of resources. The idea that limits on medical expenditures for an individual patient could be set in order to benefit the wider community contradicts the traditional patient-oriented mores of medicine so dear to the USA. Although Americans complain about high costs and high taxes, when their health or life is at stake they expect no expense to be spared and believe that medicine should not have a price tag (Ubel, 2001).

Box 2.3   Health care in the USA

It is sometimes said that the USA has the best *medical* system but one of the worst *health care* systems among developed nations. The heavy dependence on intensive and expensive diagnostic and life-saving interventions has resulted in a system where those with adequate third-party coverage have quick access to a broad range of technologies and specialists unmatched in any other country. It has, however, also spawned a system under which the control of costs has been elusive and over 40 million people have no health care coverage. The extreme contrasts of the system are illustrated by the expenditure of $5 million over 34 days to treat a 69-year-old patient who in the end died (Winslow, 2001) but the failure to guarantee pre-natal care for pregnant women.

American patients expect a different standard of care. In contrast to Japan, where physicians spend little time with patients, such conduct would be unacceptable in the USA. Moreover, one is struck by the comparatively Spartan conditions in hospitals in other nations. In the USA, amenities commonly include satellite television, DVD libraries, bedside phones, wide menu choices, and tastefully decorated rooms. These extras have little appreciable impact on health but add substantially to the costs.

This value setting has led to the inability to control health care spending. In 2001, over $1.42 trillion was spent on health care, an average of $5,035 per person. In that year alone, spending went up by 8.7 per cent, the biggest increase in a decade. Observers warn that this should lead to policy changes or private sector initiatives to put the brakes on spending growth, but given the US culture that is an unpopular task (Zwillich, 2003).

Reinforcing the predominance of negative rights, US culture is also predisposed towards progress through technological means (see Box 2.3). The result has been an unrealistic dependence on technology to fix health problems at the expense of non-technological solutions. High-quality medicine is equated with high-technology medicine and the best health care is that which uses the most sophisticated new techniques. This demand for medical technology is aggrandized by the dominance of medical specialists who extend the indications for use of new innovations, thus leading to a very aggressive form of medicine, under which, for example, the USA carries out four operations for every one performed in Japan (Drake, 1994: 138).

Australia

Although Australia shares the far South Pacific and a similar British heritage with New Zealand, the two cultures have diverged since independence in the ninteenth century, with New Zealand opting for a more egalitarian and collectivist political culture and Australia adopting a much more individualistic, US-type approach to defining the scope of public goods and role of government in promoting equality. Not surprisingly, the fragmented Australian health care system with its strong private component is closer to the USA than it is to its neighbour, New Zealand. The decentralized Australian health delivery system reflects the rugged individualism of Australian's need to survive in a hostile environment as much as it does the fragmented federal system that defines Australian politics.

Thus, while there has been an inevitable British influence in Australia since the beginning of the first prisoner settlements and this continues to be reflected in some aspects of its health care system, the 'tendency to look to North America as a source of technology, of funding and organisational initiatives and the inspiration for new policies has continued to the present time' (Palmer and Short, 2000: 6). Australian culture, then, represents a unique combination of its European heritage with a heavy dose of individualism more closely identified with the USA.

Singapore

Of all the countries, Singapore is the most difficult to classify as to cultural orientation, in part because, unlike other Asian countries, its history is short and it is thus a unique mixture of several blends of culture, East and West. Singapore has risen in the last 40 years from a Third World territory with appalling health and human conditions to a highly modern society that ranks high on health and economic measures. Its political leaders are rightfully proud of their success and angered by criticism by some Western nations that they have accomplished this by violating individual freedom. In fact, health officials argue that their health funding system based on personal savings accounts maximizes freedom of choice by focusing on the individual's responsibility for his or her own health care. Individual responsibility, not rights, is at the centre of the Singapore value system and is clearly exhibited in the health system. Thus, Singapore represents a hybrid form of individualism often at odds with that of the USA and Australia.

Singapore's health care philosophy is to build a healthy population through innovative preventive programmes and through promotion of healthy lifestyles which individuals have a responsibility to follow. As a result, the system de-emphasizes high-cost curative technologies, thereby explaining the low rates of intensive medical procedures performed in Singapore relative to other countries and the low proportion of its GDP that it spends on health care. Like Japan, Singapore's authorities are 'decisively in favour of preventive programs and have incorporated them as part of the nation's health policy' (Quah, 1988: 219). According to Yeo Cheow Tong, the then Minister of Health:

> Our medical system is based on individual responsibility . . . no Singaporean has enjoyed or expects to enjoy health services for free. When hospitalised he pays part of the bill . . . His Medisave is his own money. This gives him the incentive to be healthy, minimise[s] the need for medical treatment, and save[s] on medical expenses. (Quoted in Blank, 1994: 118)

*   *   *

As noted in Chapter 1 (p. 20), the convergence theory suggests that any subsequent differences in health policy will tend to fade over time as health systems of all shapes face the same problems. While this theory might or might not be borne out in the substantive discussions that follow, the presumption here is that the underlying values and beliefs of a population will be reflected in how they view health, health care and the distribution of health care resources. In that regard, we see considerable variation across these countries and it will be interesting to see how it will play out in the analysis of health care systems in the coming chapters.

Legal systems

Figure 2.1 also suggests that the legal framework can have significant influence on health care. It can do this in many ways, ranging from regulating the medical professions to influencing the distribution of health care resources, to constructing liability systems that impact on both. While some countries have opted for no-fault accident compensation systems and for sanctions by medical bodies, others turn to the courts to various degrees to determine liability and the allocation of medical resources, and to punish wrongdoers in the medical professions.

Not surprisingly given its emphasis on negative rights, the USA has the most extensive civil liability system imaginable and health care is no exception. In early 2003, some 43 states were considered to have a crisis with medical malpractice insurance affordability or even availability, and doctors in Florida, New Jersey, West Virginia and other states had work stoppages or slowdowns to protest (Reiss, 2003). Insurance rates for the riskiest medical specialities skyrocketed again. In Florida, annual insurance coverage for obstetricians averaged over $210,000 and for general surgery had increased by 58 per cent since 2000; they now stand at $174,000. Consequently, physicians are leaving the state to practise elsewhere or leaving medicine entirely (Reiss, 2003).

The crisis has been blamed on larger claims and more lawsuits: the average jury award increased from $700,000 to over $1,000,000, or 43 per cent from 1999 to 2000 alone (INSWorld, 2002). The doctors' argument is that medical liability awards for the elusive categories of pain and suffering and punishment awards, which often reach tens of millions of dollars, must be capped (a usual figure given is $250,000) as they have been in California, which has escaped the crisis. However, trial lawyers and consumer groups argue that the real problem is the failure of the medical profession to discipline bad doctors. Furthermore, they argue that any attempt to limit awards would run counter to the rights of individuals to redress wrongs against them in a court of law (Public Citizen, 2003). The only thing that all sides agree on, though, is that the current system is most inequitable and that it is not sustainable. Most patients who go to court lose and get absolutely nothing while in some cases persons who have suffered little or no harm get huge monetary rewards.

There can be no doubt that the civil liability system in the USA contributes heavily to the inflated health care costs there although the two sides offer substantially different estimates. The system adds to the costs in two ways. The direct cost increases come from the cost of malpractice insurance itself, most of which is passed on to patients and private and public providers, including the government (the total cost in 1994 was estimated to be $12 billion). In addition to the direct impact of increased malpractice insurance rates on the cost of health care, their indirect impact is even more profound. Moreover, as well as to the added cost of maintaining legal counsel in medical facilities, virtually every medical decision is made within a legal context and under threat of litigation.

This environment, in turn, leads to what is termed defensive medicine, 'a waste of resources that results from physicians changing their practice patterns in response to the threat of liability' (Danzon, 1985: 12). Under defensive medicine, doctors will order all available diagnostic tests and therapeutic measures, even those that are of marginal or no benefit. They do this not because they believe it best for the patient but rather to avert a lawsuit (e.g., the doctor did not do everything possible) or, if sued, to provide documentation that in fact all that was possible was done for the patient. Although there are no reliable cost estimates for defensive medicine, it represents a significant portion of overall health spending in the USA and helps explain why US costs are so out of line with other countries.

Other countries have tended to depend on alternative systems to deal with medical misadventure and compensation. New Zealand, for instance, created an accident compensation system specifically to avoid the problem of costly litigation. Under this system, individuals suffering harm, medical or otherwise, are compensated by an Accident

Compensation Commission (ACC) according to a standardized formula. In return, legal action is severely limited, although in recent years the possibility of legal action has increased. Moreover, over the past several decades as more people have pursued medical misadventure claims, the ACC cost for health care has multiplied, as has compensation (Blank, 1994: 131).

Although accident compensation systems are more successful in ensuring that all victims are compensated, often the compensation is small in comparison to the possible awards granted in a liability-based system. As noted above, most claimants in the USA get nothing, a very few get big settlements, and the lawyers always come out ahead. It makes sense that countries with national health services would wish to avoid an unpredictable but costly liability system and opt for a predictable less costly system even if critics argue it violates the rights of individuals to go to court. That these health systems tend to be in countries with traditions of solidarity and community rather than individual rights gives them legitimacy they would not enjoy in the USA.

In the absence of civil liability, accident compensation systems normally are linked with stricter professional self-regulating systems for medical negligence. Medical societies are given responsibility to sanction and, where appropriate, prevent such members from practising. European countries in general have traditionally put emphasis on preventing medical malpractice and disciplining problem doctors, both through professional self-regulation. In Germany, for example, professional chambers at state level are responsible for licensing doctors, controlling medical ethics, organizing disciplinary processes and offering specialist training. The chambers are public bodies regulated by law (Moran, 1999).

However, the case of Britain shows the limitations of this approach. In recent years, there have been a number of high-profile cases of medical malpractice. One involved a pathologist who had removed entire organs from the bodies of dead children during post-mortem examinations without the prior consent of parents (Boseley, 2001b). In another case, a GP was convicted of murdering 15 of his elderly patients and a subsequent inquiry suggested that the actual number of victims exceeded 200 (Carter, 2002). Both cases strongly throw into doubt the ability of the General Medical Council (GMC), the doctors' professional body, to protect patients from medical malpractice. Mounting pressure from the government and the public, as well from within the medical profession, have led to substantial reforms of the Council (Batty, 2001). The Council has been reduced in size and lay membership has been increased to 40 per cent; fitness to practice procedures have changed and revalidation has been introduced.

At the same time, liability claims in the UK have risen sharply.

According to the National Audit Office, NHS hospitals in England face massive liabilities totalling £3.9 billion. The rate of new claims rose by 72 per cent between 1990 and 1998, and as of March 2000, around 23,000 claims of clinical negligence were outstanding (Woodman, 2001). The average value of settlement in 2000 was £87,000, excluding brain damage and cerebral palsy where courts have at times awarded more than £1 million. The report found that the current system for handling litigation is 'fraught with delays', and often lawyers benefit far more than do the patients (Woodman, 2001). Despite divergent legal systems, then, the problems facing the UK are reminiscent of the malpractice debacle in the USA.

Different approaches to defining health

A critical question for health care policy is what is meant by the term 'health'. There are several competing models, each of which has important implications for how we organize health care. The prevailing Western medical model is primarily founded on defining health as the *absence of disease or illness*. People are healthy under this definition if they are not suffering from an illness or disease. The goal of curative medicine is to diagnose an illness and restore the health of the patient, who by definition is unhealthy. Inherent in medicine is the continual expansion of categories of disease to account for a broadening range of conditions deemed unhealthy. Such labelling of a condition as a disease has tended to ingrain in medicine the notion that disease is the enemy (Seedhouse, 1991: 43).

A competing definition of health is the *coping* model where health is essentially an ability to adapt to the problems life gives us (Seedhouse, 1991). Under this definition, individuals can be healthy even if they are diseased or ill so long as they have the personal strength and resilience to cope with life. The tension with the not-ill theory is manifested in a concern that the latter interferes with individuals' ability to cope with their internal states and environment. Under this definition people without identifiable disease or illness are still unhealthy if they are unable to cope.

The third definition of health, that of the World Health Organization (WHO), defines it as 'a state of complete physical, mental and social well-being and not merely the absence of disease or infirmity' (1946). This ambitious ideal has been widely criticized because, if taken literally, it means that individuals are unhealthy if they are unhappy with their lot in life or even if they just feel unfulfilled. Moreover, in conflict with the coping theory, individuals with any defined disease, illness or disability cannot be healthy. Although this definition is so broad as to make it meaningless, this is unfortunate because it does incorporate the need to expand the definition of health beyond the situation where a person has a medically defined illness or disease. To the extent that it does broaden ill health beyond the notion of biological dysfunction, the WHO definition is useful despite its operational problems.

One problem with all of these definitions is their failure to bring in the social and cultural dimensions of health and ill health explicitly. Health has both a personal and a public dimension. Although pain, suffering, disappointment and regret are personal under the WHO definition, their effect on the lives of others might be severe. Moreover, because health and illness are social constructs and culturally defined, health and disease have to be considered within a cultural context. For Callahan (1990: 103), illness itself is as much social as individual in its characteristics because tolerability will depend on the kind of care and support provided by others and by the social meaning of the disease. Good health, therefore, requires social networks and systems that are obscured by all of these definitions of health.

Even within particular social systems health can be a very relative term. Seedhouse (1991: 40), for instance, sees disease and health akin to the analogy of weeds and flowers. As with plants, what we perceive as undesirable in one case might be desirable in another. Pneumonia in an otherwise active 20-year-old is undesirable and it is appropriate to say she is suffering from a disease. In contrast, pneumonia in a 90-year-old victim of a severe stroke might be welcomed as offering an easier death. Although in clinical terms pneumonia in both cases is termed a disease, the ambiguity of the disease label requires clarification of the specific context.

Increasingly, it is evident that health must encompass not only the physical and mental aspects of personal well-being but also the social (Babcock and Belotti, 1994: 209). Although there are many models that incorporate this broader view of health, one useful model that illustrates cultural differences is that of the indigenous people of New Zealand, the Maori. Like other highly-integrated Eastern world views, the Maori refuse to segment the world into discrete parts and this is reflected in their view of health. Durie (1994) describes this model as a construct of a four-sided house *(whare tapa wha)* whereby each wall of the house represents a different dimension: the spiritual, the mental, the physical, and the extended family (Table 2.8). Like a house, unless there is balance among the four dimensions, it will collapse.

For the Maori, the most essential requirement for health is the spiritual, which implies a capacity to have faith and the capacity to understand the links between the human condition and the environment. Without a spiritual awareness and a *mauri* (a spirit or vitality, sometimes called a life-force), an individual cannot be healthy and is more

Table 2.8　*The Maori model of health*

	Taha Wairua	Taha Hinengaro	Taha Tinana	Taha Whanau
Focus	Spiritual	Mental	Physical	Extended family
Key aspects	Capacity for faith and wider communion	Capacity to communicate think, feel	Capacity for growth and development	Capacity to belong, care and share
Themes	Health is related to unseen energies	Mind and body are inseparable	Good physical health is necessary for optimal development	Individuals are part of wider social systems

Source:　Adapted from Durie (1994: 70).

prone to illness. The spiritual dimension might involve religious beliefs and practices and a belief in a god, but it is most clearly manifested in relationships with the environment. Interestingly, while the spiritual dimension of health is not apparent in modern medicine, it is an integral part of twelve-step programmes and some alternative medicine.

The second dimension is about the expression of thoughts and feelings that in Maori nomenclature derive from the same source within the individual and are vital to health. Poor health is regarded as a breakdown of harmony between the individual and the wider environment. This dimension of health goes beyond the Western view of mental health as the absence of mental illness and instead merges with physical health since mind and body become inseparable. This dimension is implicit in the coping definition but not in the not-ill definition of health.

The third dimension of this model of health is the extended family or social structure. This dimension addresses the contention that health is a social characteristic and must be defined in that setting. For Maori people the family is the prime support system, providing not only physical but also emotional and cultural support. A failure to turn to the family when warranted is regarded as immaturity not strength, because the problem is beyond the individual and social in nature. Interdependence not independence is the healthier goal. This dimension addresses findings of studies that have demonstrated the importance of kinship structure for good health status. Mechanic, for example, argues that Mormons and other groups with good health indices share a strong kinship structure that emphasizes the importance of the family, parenthood and family relationships. Mormons have good health not simply because they value health and abstain from smoking and drinking, but also because of the presence of a 'well-knit group structure that demands a person's loyalty and commitment' (1994: 123).

Although acknowledging physical health as a critical dimension (one of the four walls), the Maori model of health requires a relative de-emphasis of the dominance of the physical aspects of health and the preoccupation with biological constructs so central to Western health care. Individual health is a natural part of a wider system. Similarly, the divisions between temporal and spiritual, thoughts and feelings, and the mental and physical are no longer acceptable. Good health, therefore, cannot be gauged solely by medical indicators such as blood pressure, cholesterol levels and absence of physical disease, and must include spiritual and emotional factors.

Putting health into this broader context also raises the question of why we value health in its narrow sense as freedom from disease. Although health should be highly valued since it is central to the completion of one's plan of life, health is better viewed as a means to broader goals and purposes in life. Good health is not a substitute for a good life, and good health does not guarantee a good life. Good health in itself cannot guarantee achievement of our goals, give us a reason to live, or maximize our potential to the highest order. Good health in the physical sense but without the other three dimensions of health, then, is unlikely to ensure contentment. One area in which these ideas take form is in what is often termed 'alternative' or 'holistic' medicine.

Culture and traditional medicine

Although the Western medical model enjoys dominance in all of the countries examined here, traditional values continue to shape how it is practised. Therefore, although most attention in this book centres on the analysis of the similarities and differences of these countries within that broader framework, it is imperative to examine features that might be unique to, or more dominant in, particular countries. One area that offers useful insights is the extent to which various forms of traditional medicine continue to be practised alongside modern Western medicine.

Until 1875, when Western medicine became the official form of medicine in Japan, kampo and acupuncture were dominant. Kampo means 'Han Method' in Japanese because it was the Chinese who introduced the use of herbal products for medical therapy during the seventh to ninth centuries at the time of the Han Dynasty. The Japanese health care system remains an amalgamation of modern Western medicine and traditional Eastern practices, and kampo is still an important feature of medical practice. The great majority of Japanese physicians (72 per cent of all Western-style doctors in an October 2000 survey) use at least some kampo formulae in their practice. Moreover, almost all pharmacies have staff trained in traditional methods of prescription and most health insurance companies recognize and support its use (Kenner, 2001). From 1974 to 1989 there was a 15-fold increase in kampo medicinal preparations in comparison with only 2.6-fold increase in the sales of mainstream pharmaceutical products in Japan (WHO, 1996). Acupuncture and other holistic practices are also integrated into the Japanese health system, in part a reflection of its Shinto/Buddhist roots.

Similarly, while Singapore's health care services are based in Western medicine, it has been common practice among the various ethnic groups to contact traditional practitioners for general ailments. Although Western medicine is the main form of health care, a variety of traditional practices continue to serve as complementary forms of medical care (for implications of this clash of 'ethos' see Quah, 2003). Given the large proportion of Chinese in Singapore, traditional Chinese medicine (TCM) has been of special importance. TCM is an important part of Singapore's heritage and enjoys considerable popularity. Although its practice is confined to outpatient care, two acupuncture clinics are affiliated with public hospitals. The Ministry of Health estimates that about 12 per cent of daily outpatient attendance is through TCM practitioners, the majority of whom are trained locally by specialist TCM schools (Singapore Ministry of Health, 1995). In its report, the Ministry concluded that there should be no forced integration of TCM and Western medicine and that only those persons properly trained to practise TCM should be allowed to do so. Therefore, some government regulation of TCM was necessary to safeguard patients' interests, which meant legitimizing it as a facet of health care.

Perhaps because of their location in the South Pacific and ties to Asia the health care systems of both Australia and New Zealand, although emerging out of significantly different political systems, have heavy links to holistic medical practices. In Australia, for instance, where TCM has been practised since the nineteenth century, it has been estimated that over 48 per cent of the population use at least one form of alternative medicine (Maclennan *et al.*, 1996). Between 1992 and 1996, imports of Chinese herbal medicines increased four-fold in Australia, accounting for approximately A$1 billion of business (Bensoussan and Myers, 1996). In 1995, the Australian State of Victoria, in response to the 'rapid expansion of the practice of and demand for TCM in this country', created a Ministerial Committee on Traditional Medicine (Victorian Department of Human Services, 1996). In 1998, the

Committee issued an extensive report on the risks and benefits of TCM and a wide range of other traditional approaches used in Australia, and a consideration of the need for regulation. A major recommendation of the Committee to the Australian Health Minister's Advisory Council was that occupational registration of the profession of TCM 'proceed as a matter of urgency' (Victorian Ministerial Advisory Committee, 1998: 1).

As in Australia, oriental medicine is well established in New Zealand with schools of acupuncture, TCM and holistic healing. Many general practitioners are trained in acupuncture and the use of herbal products, including New Zealand native plants, is common. Although Chinese and other Asian traditional approaches are available, the most unique influence on New Zealand health policy comes via Maori and Pacific Island cultures, as noted in discussing the Maori model above. Considerable effort in the past decades has been directed at accounting for cultural differences in the perception of health and health care between the European and Maori populations and to integrate this into the health delivery system.

In contrast with these systems, the dominance of the American Medical Association and other mainstream medical organizations has largely minimized the scope of alternative medicine in the USA. Although recently some insurance carriers and HMOs have begun to partially reimburse selected non-traditional treatments, this practice remains the exception. Moreover, unlike even Australia and New Zealand, few medical practitioners in the USA have training in acupuncture or other alternative regimes. The predominance of the medical model even as portrayed in the media has resulted in a very closed notion of health care among most Americans. As a result, when they feel unwell they expect to be seen post-haste by a medical specialist, thus again driving up expectations and costs.

Although conventional medicine remains at the centre of the health service in Britain, there are moves to integrate complementary and alternative medicine into the NHS. In 2000 a report by the House of Lords called for patients to have access to unconventional medicine and to be given more and better information about existing therapies (Boseley, 2000). Here, tighter regulation was identified as a key issue and the report argued that only those therapies which were properly regulated should be accessible through the NHS. In response to this report, there have been moves to strengthen the regulation of alternative practitioners and to standardize the myriad of training schemes in alternative therapies that currently exist. The Department of Health is also providing funding to develop the research capacity in alternative medicine as part of the drive to towards evidence-based health care practice.

The context of health care

This chapter attempted to place health care within its broader context in each of our countries. It presumed that one cannot understand why a health care system took the form it did without an understanding of the political and legal institutions and practices of the country and of a basic knowledge of the cultural and historical environment from which it emerged, including the size and mix of the population, its ethnic, racial, and religious composition, and, as seen in Chapter 1, its age characteristics, which all help shape the health care system of each country. Each of these countries has its own character, a certain combination of features that sets it apart from its neighbours. Although far from an in-depth analysis of each country, this overview demonstrates that each of these countries provides a unique setting for the emergence of a health care system over time.

Chapter 1 (p. 2) suggested that there are strong forces that might be leading by necessity to a convergence of policies across countries. In this brief overview of the context of health policy in these countries, it is obvious that although they are all affluent, developed countries, they bring with them a divergent set of structural and value systems that will be useful for comparative purposes in the following substantive chapters. While these factors certainly cannot explain all the differences or similarities among the countries, they can help us understand some of the anomalies that will arise out of the more in-depth analysis of these health care systems that follows.

Chapter 3

Funding, Provision and Governance

Health care is often thought of as a system. A health system is a highly complex entity and consists of a range of sub-systems. Among these, the sub-systems of *funding, provision* and *governance* are central for understanding health policy comparatively (see Figure 3.1).

The sub-system of *funding* is concerned with raising financial resources and allocating monies to the providers of health care. Health care can be funded from a range of sources, from taxes and social insurance contributions to private insurance premiums and out-of-pocket payments by patients. Funding, however, is about more than the technicalities of raising and allocating financial resources; funding is also a pointer to power, and control of funding is a major resource in health policy. The sub-system of *provision* focuses on the delivery of health services. Health systems provide a range of services, and patients have varying levels of choice when using health services, such as among individual doctors or among different care settings. The delivery of health services is in the hands of different types of providers including public and private, profit or non-profit, hospitals. The mix of providers makes the provision of health care more or less publicly integrated. The sub-systems of funding and provision form the basis of the sub-system of *governance*. Governance describes the modes of co-ordinating health systems and their multiple actors. Governance is underpinned by

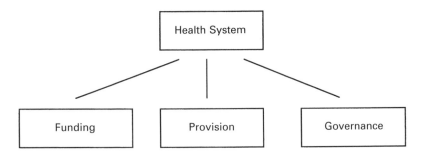

Figure 3.1   *The sub-systems of health care*

tensions between public and private as well as between the centre and localities. As governments tend to play an important role in health systems, governance can also be thought of as government capacity or authority.

In a comparative context, health systems are often grouped under specific typologies of health systems, as discussed in Chapter 1 (p. 23). The typologies present models of funding, providing and governing health care in the form of distinct ideal types. The implicit assumption is that certain models of funding are directly associated with certain models of provision. For example, the funding of health care from taxation is said to make for public provision of health care. As the analysis below shows, this is the case in the health systems in some countries. In others, however, individual health systems combine different models of funding and provision, and even rely on a mix of several models of funding or provision. This directs the attention to the country-specific political contexts in which health systems are embedded, as introduced in Chapter 2.

For example, in Britain and Sweden, where health care is predominantly publicly funded and provided, government looms large in the governance of health systems. At the same time, the specific features of health governance also reflect the fact that the wider political system and health governance in Britain is much more centralized than in Sweden. The factors which lead to differences between countries co-exist with common pressures across health systems including ageing populations, advances in medical technology and increasing demands from patients. This chapter provides an overview of the funding, provision and governance of health care in our nine countries and how this is shaped by country-specific contexts as well as by universal pressures. An important aim will be to assess the relative usefulness of the typologies of the different types of health systems.

Comparing funding of health systems

Funding offers a good starting-point for looking at health systems comparatively. Funding provides a first indicator of the relative size of health systems and the role of governments in health systems. Not surprisingly, there is some variation among these countries. Table 3.1 ranks the countries according to their per capita expenditure on health care. The USA is in first place and spends over four times as much per head as Singapore, which is the lowest spender in our group of countries. However, this is not typical of the entire range because these two countries are outliers. The upper midrange is represented by Germany, France, Japan, the Netherlands and Sweden, which spend between

Table 3.1   *Per capita expenditure on
health care in US dollars, 1998*

USA	4,165
Germany	2,697
France	2,324
Japan	2,242
Netherlands	2,172
Sweden	2,146
Australia	1,718
Italy	1,702
UK	1,636
New Zealand	1,132
Singapore	876

Sources: Data from OECD (2001b) and Singapore
Ministry of Health (2000).

US$2,146 and US$2,697 per capita on health care. Australia, Italy,
Britain and New Zealand are in the lower midrange and spend an average of $1,547.

The picture is similar when looking at health care expenditure as a
percentage of GDP in Table 3.2. The majority of countries spend
between about 7 and 9 per cent of their GDP on health care. The clear
exception is the USA with 12.9 per cent, followed by Germany with
10.3 per cent. Health spending has increased since the 1970s, although
less dramatically in some countries than in others. For example, in the
Netherlands health spending increased from 7.0 to 8.7 per cent between
1973 and 1998, while in the USA health spending almost doubled over
the same period of time. However, over the last two decades this growth
has generally slowed down, and also in Sweden and to a lesser extent in
Italy, the Netherlands, Singapore and the USA the percentage of GDP
spent on health care actually fell in 1998, although in the USA it has
since risen sharply (a 9.6 per cent increase in 2002 alone).

Besides the overall level of funding, the sources of funding give an
initial indication of the kinds of health system with which we are dealing. Table 3.3 suggests that all the health systems are predominantly
publicly funded. As before, Singapore and the USA are the clear outliers
with only 26.0 and 44.8 per cent of spending respectively coming from
public sources. For the remaining countries, however, public expenditure as a share of total health care expenditure ranges from 67.3 per
cent in Italy to 83.8 per cent in Sweden. Looking at figures from the
early 1970s onwards, continuity is the most striking feature, although

Table 3.2   Changes in health care expenditure as a percentage of GDP

	1973	1978	1983	1988	1993	1998
Australia	5.6	7.3	7.4	7.4	8.2	8.6
France	6.0	7.1	8.0	8.4	9.5	9.4
Germany	7.4	8.7	9.0	9.4	9.7	10.3
Italy	5.9	5.9	7.1	7.6	8.5	8.2
Japan	4.7	6.0	6.9	6.4	6.6	7.4
Netherlands	7.0	7.7	8.3	8.2	9.0	8.7
New Zealand	5.5	7.1	6.0	6.5	7.2	8.1
Singapore	n/a	n/a	n/a	2.8	3.1	2.9
Sweden	7.1	8.8	9.2	8.4	8.6	7.9
UK	4.7	5.3	6.0	5.9	6.9	6.8
USA	7.2	8.1	9.9	10.8	13.2	12.9

n/a = not available

Sources: Data from OECD (2001b) and Singapore Ministry of Health (2000).

Table 3.3   Changes in public expenditure on health care as a percentage of total expenditure on health care

	1973	1978	1983	1988	1993	1998
Australia	62.5	62.5	64.6	68.4	66.5	70.0
France	75.3	77.5	77.9	74.7	78.0	77.7
Germany	77.0	78.7	77.3	77.2	77.5	75.8
Italy	89.2	88.8	78.9	77.9	73.1	67.3
Japan	68.8	76.0	72.8	75.2	79.2	78.5
Netherlands	64.6	69.0	70.8	67.0	74.2	68.6
New Zealand	74.0	76.9	88.6	85.6	76.6	77.0
Singapore	70.1	n/a	68.0	n/a	n/a	26.0
Sweden	86.1	91.5	91.5	89.4	85.7	83.8
UK	87.6	90.0	87.4	84.3	85.9	83.3
USA	37.8	40.7	40.7	39.6	43.1	44.8

n/a = not available

Sources: Data from OECD (2001b) and Singapore Ministry of Health (2000).

there have been interesting changes in some countries. In Australia, Japan and the USA the share of public funding rose between 7 and almost 10 per cent, while Sweden and Britain saw a slight fall in the percentage of expenditure from public sources. The reduction in public expenditure was more significant in Italy, where it fell by over 20 per cent. Singapore demonstrates an even more dramatic decrease in public funding as they moved to the Medisave scheme, thus shifting to an individual funding base (see later discussion).

With the exception of the USA and Singapore, therefore, the health systems examined here are all predominantly publicly funded. However, a closer look at the exact sources of funding reveals important differences. Table 3.4 distinguishes between public expenditure by governments and compulsory social security schemes, and private expenditure from out-of-pocket payments, private insurance and other private funds. Government expenditure can come from general taxation or earmarked taxes, whereas out-of-pocket payments are payments made directly by patients themselves. Out-of-pocket payments come in a variety of forms (OECD, 2001b). As part of a social or private insurance patients may have to cover part of the cost of medical treatment (co-payments).

Table 3.4   *Sources of funding as a percentage of health care expenditure, 1998*

	Public funding		Private funding		
	Government	Social Security	Out-of-pocket payments	Private insurance	Other funds
Australia[a]	70.0	n/a	16.2	7.9	5.9
France[a]	2.4	73.7	10.2	12.5	1.0
Germany	6.4	69.4	12.8	7.1	4.3
Italy[a]	67.2	0.1	23.5	n/a	n/a
Japan[a]	8.6	69.9	17.1	n/a	4.5
Netherlands	4.1	64.5	8.0	17.5	5.9
New Zealand[a]	77.0	n/a	16.3	6.4	n/a
Sweden	n/a	n/a	n/a	n/a	n/a
UK	73.5	9.8	11.1	3.5	2.1
USA[a]	30.3	14.9	15.6	33.5	6.1

[a] For reasons unknown the figures for these countries do not add up exactly to 100 per cent.

n/a = not available

Source: Data from OECD (2001b).

Alternatively, patients may have to pay a fixed amount before the insurance company gets involved (deductibles). Out-of-pocket payments may also occur as a result of self-medication. This includes over-the-counter prescriptions and medical services not covered by the health insurance.

Looking at the public sources of funding, is it striking that countries seem to rely predominantly either on social security, as in the case of France, Germany, Japan and the Netherlands, or on government funding, as in the case of Australia, Italy, New Zealand and Britain. As for private funding, most countries rely on out-of-pocket payments by patients, although the percentage ranges from 11.1 per cent in Britain to 23.5 per cent in Italy. The exceptions are the Netherlands, France and the USA, where private insurance is the main source of private funding. Considering the earlier figures on public expenditure, it is not surprising that the sources of health care funding are more diverse in the USA. Here, one-third of health care expenditure comes from government funds, one-third from private insurance, while the remaining one-third comes from social security and out-of-pocket payments. The reasons for the differences in the sources of funding are analysed in more detail in the following sections.

National health services and the commitment to public funding

National health services are the archetypal example of a publicly funded health system. Health care is predominantly funded from taxation and is available to every resident in the country. Public funding results in universal access. Britain, New Zealand and Sweden, together with Italy as a latecomer, are classical examples of this type of public funding.

In the British NHS over 90 per cent of funding comes from public sources, over 80 per cent from general taxation and the rest from contributions to National Insurance, which is a specific tax levied on incomes. Co-payments by patients account for about only 2 per cent of funding (European Observatory on Health Care Systems, 1999: 33). Prominent areas of co-payments include: drugs, where payments by patients have risen over time, although they remain low in comparison to other countries; dental services, where patients have to cover 80 per cent of the costs up to a maximum; and ophthalmic services, which have been widely deregulated. Another source of funding is private insurance. The market for employment-based private insurance schemes expanded dramatically in the 1980s in response to tax incentives, but has since levelled off. An important reason for taking out private insurance is to compensate for the perceived low quality of NHS services and for the long waiting lists for elective surgery. The situation in Sweden is similar. Public funding is central and comes from income tax raised by county councils, the regional tier of government, and is complemented by state grants and reimbursements from National Health Insurance. Private funding from co-payments and supplementary private insurance play a marginal role.

The universality typical of national health services leads to the socialization of funding, although it is never complete (Freeman, 2000). Whereas over 90 per cent of funding in Britain and Sweden comes from public sources, other national health services rely to a greater extent on private sources of funding. In New Zealand, the percentage of public health expenditure has fallen over the last 20 years and is now clearly below that of Britain and Sweden. In 1999 about 77.5 per cent of health expenditure was public, which was down from 88.1 per cent in 1980 (New Zealand Ministry of Health, 2001). The remaining funding comes from private health insurance (6.2 per cent) and individual out-of-pocket payments for primary care, dentistry and drugs (16.4 per cent: New Zealand Ministry of Health, 2001).

Although the National government considered moving to a largely private system of finance for New Zealand in 1991, it opted to retain a system based on public finance through taxes and access to those services based on need. With the exceptions of primary care, where a fee-for-service system operates, and individual co-payments for drugs, most health services in New Zealand are provided free of charge. In 2000, about 37 per cent of the population was covered by private health insurance of some kind, much of this supplemental. Although its proportion of total health expenditure grew from 1.1 per cent in 1980 to 6.2 per cent in 1999 (New Zealand Ministry of Health, 2001: 13), it remains limited and has been static over the last decade.

Private sources of funding have also played an important role in Australia, which had the distinction of being the only country to have introduced universal national health insurance and then dismantle it. By 1981, most Australians relied on private insurance coverage. In 1984, however, Medicare, a compulsory national health insurance administered by the Commonwealth, was introduced. It is primarily funded from general tax revenue, supplemented by a 1.5 per cent identified income tax levy, state revenue and co-payments (Hall, 1999: 96). Private insurance accounts for 11 per cent of total health care expenditure while 19 per cent comes from co-payments by individuals. Medicare reimburses 75 per cent of the scheduled fee for inpatient services and 85 per cent of ambulatory services. While about one-third of the population has private insurance to cover the gap between Medicare benefits and scheduled fees for inpatient services, this represents a substantial decrease in private insurance from the over 80 per cent in 1970 and the 64 per cent just prior to Medicare in 1983 (Palmer and Short, 2000: 13).

Public funding through social insurance

Social insurance is another form of public funding. Social insurance is a hybrid and combines two very different principles of organizing health care: the insurance is paid for by independent institutions but is publicly mandated (Freeman, 2000: 54f.). In contrast to private insurance, social health insurance is based on the principle of social solidarity. Contributions are paid as a percentage of the salary rather than according to the specific health risks of the individual and are often shared by employers and employees. This represents a redistributive policy between high and low risk patients as well as between high and low earners. Dependants of employees (i.e., is non-earning spouses and children) are also covered, thus in effect ensuring universal coverage of the population.

The German health system was the pioneer among its kind. Health care is funded by contributions paid equally by employers and employees as a fixed percentage of the monthly salary. Membership is compulsory on everyone with annual earnings below a certain ceiling, which in 2000 was 40,000 Euro (European Observatory on Health Care Systems, 2000: 39). Employees earning above the ceiling (and the self-employed) are free to make their own arrangements and can choose to stay with the social health insurance or join a private health insurance scheme. However, only 12 per cent of the population opted for private insurance (European Observatory on Health Care Systems, 2000: 39). Other sources of private funding are co-payments. Co-payments have a long tradition in relation to drugs, but have increased considerably in the 1990s and now stand at 10 per cent of expenditure on pharmaceuticals (European Observatory on Health Care Systems, 2000: 46). With greater cost pressures, co-payments in other areas have also been added. The social health insurance is administered by private, non-profit funds, which operate under public law.

A close variant of the classical German model is the health system in the Netherlands (and France). An important difference concerns the diversity of sources of funding, which reflects complexity at organizational level. The Netherlands social health insurance consists of two schemes. The insurance for acute risks covers ambulatory and hospital medical services and is compulsory for all employees whose earnings are below a certain ceiling. Although the insurance contributions are shared by employers and employees, employees have to pay an additional flat-rate contribution directly to their insurance fund. In 1995, this constituted 10 per cent of the total health care expenditure (Ven, 1997: 91). The insurance for exceptional medical risks covers long-term nursing care, psychiatric care and costs for outpatient prescriptions, and it covers all employees irrespective of income and is funded by contributions from employees. The Dutch social health insurance puts greater emphasis on payments by employees. This burden is compounded by the fact that one-third of employees have to take out private insurance to cover acute health risks (Maarse, 1997: 150). At the same time, co-payments are limited to the social health insurance of exceptional medical risks and the private health insurance.

Another, although more remote variant of the social insurance model is the Japanese health system, which is built on the German model but is a unique combination of private and public components of funding and provision. The social insurance consists of three parts: insurance schemes for employees and their dependants; a community-based insurance for the self-employed, unemployed, pensioners and dependants; and an insurance pool to cross-subsidize the costs of health care for the elderly. These three groups comprise more than 5,000 independent insurance plans, thus subsuming the private sector under a government regulatory umbrella. The sources of funding vary between insurance schemes, but all schemes are characterized by co-payments of between 10 and 30 per cent of charges designed to constrain demand (Imai, 2002: 5). In comparison with the Netherlands, France and Germany, co-payments are high and clearly limit the scope of social solidarity. The emphasis on individual responsibility is partly offset by government subsidies for the community-based insurance scheme and the pool for health care for the elderly (see Box 3.1). Overall, insurance contributions account for 57 per cent of health expenditure, national government subsidies for 24 per cent, local government subsidies for 7 per cent and co-payments by patients for 12 per cent (Japanese Ministry of Health, 2000).

Private insurance and the emphasis on individual responsibility

Countries that predominantly rely on private insurance put considerable emphasis on individual responsibility. However, here, too, individual responsibility is never complete and private funding co-exists with some public funding, particularly for designated groups such as the poor and elderly. In some respects, the USA is the archetypal example of this system of funding and is characterized by high complexity (see Box 3.2). Private insurance covers 58 per cent of the population and accounts for

Box 3.1   The social insurance system in Japan

INSURANCE SCHEME	CONTRIBUTIONS	CO-PAYMENTS
A. Employees and their dependants 1. Government managed insurance for employees of small companies. 2. Society managed insurance for employees of large companies. 3. Mutual aid associations for government and private school employees, seamen, and day labourers.	Currently, 8.5 per cent of salary (half by employer and half by employee). Self-financing with government paying only the administrative costs of these plans.	Employees pay 10 per cent of inpatient and outpatient costs. Dependants pay 20 per cent inpatient and 30 per cent outpatient costs.
B. Community-based insurance for self-employed, unemployed, pensioners and dependants (National Health Insurance (NHI) is the principal plan).	NHI plan contribution based on individual income and assets. Government subsidizes approximately 50 per cent.	Both insured and dependants pay 30 per cent of inpatient and outpatient costs with 63,000 yen (approximately $475) per month maximum.
C. Health Service for the Aged Law of 1983 created an insurance pool to cross-subsidize the costs of health care for the elderly (over the age of 70 or over 65 with disabilities designated by government).	Paid by government with cross-subsidy among other insurance plans based on ratio of the elderly in the population.	Deductible payment of 1,000 yen (approximately $7.50) per month outpatient and 700 yen ($4) per day inpatient.

Source: Adapted from Powell and Anesaki (1990: 131).

34 per cent of total health expenditure (Health Care Financing Administration, 2000). Private insurance is provided by more than 1,500 non- and for-profit insurance companies. Private health insurance is largely funded as an employment-based system, as part of the job benefit and subject to negotiations. Normally, premium contributions

Box 3.2   Medicare in the USA – public insurance in a private system

Medicare is a public insurance for the elderly, administered by the federal government. Medicare consists of two parts. Part A is compulsory; it covers hospital care and is funded through earmarked social security taxes paid by all working citizens. Part B is voluntary anc covers other costs including doctors' bills and outpatient hospital treatment; it is funded by monthly premiums paid by enrollees and federal subsidies. Here, annual deductibles and some co-payments are required and neither part covers prescription cost. In contrast, a second public programme, Medicaid, is a joint federal–state health insurance programme covering certain groups of the poor and it is funded by a combination of federal and state funds. Although originally Medicaid was designed for children and single women and the indigent poor, at present over 75 per cent of its funding goes to supplement Medicare for the elderly poor (Iglehart, 1999). Outside programmes for the elderly, the US health system remains largely market-based. Co-payments are high and account for 15 per cent of total health expenditure. More importantly, 17 per cent of the population – that is between 40 and 50 million people – remains uncovered. (State Coverage Initiatives, 2002)

are shared by employers and employees. An additional 21 per cent of total health spending comes from co-payments or other private sources. The private insurance co-exists with a social insurance system, which accounts for 34 per cent of total health expenditure and covers 25 per cent of the population (Health Care Financing Adminstraion, 2000: see also Box 3.2). Other public expenditures constitute 12 per cent of total health care expenditure.

With its emphasis on individual responsibility, Singapore represents another, although rather unique, variant of private insurance (see Box 1.3, p. 27). At the centre of the health system is Medisave, a compulsory savings scheme, which is managed centrally by the Central Provident Fund, Singapore's mandatory pension fund. Under the scheme, each employee and self-employed person puts aside a percentage of monthly income into an account to meet future hospital expenses for inpatient care. Contributions are paid as a percentage of the total wage and rise with age, to 8 per cent at the age of 45. The insurance scheme puts individual responsibility centre stage and medical risks remain largely individualized. Solidarity is confined to the immediate family and accounts are transferable to one's spouse, children, parents and grandparents. The very limited redistribution, together with ceilings on contributions, also significantly limits the scope of Medisave, as does the reluctance of individuals to deplete their savings.

Medisave is supplemented by Medishield, a catastrophic insurance programme that pays for extraordinary hospital expenses for those under the age of 70. About half of the entire population and 88 per cent of Medisave account holders opt to participate in this scheme (Singapore Ministry of Health, 2001). Annual premiums are based on the contributor's age. A third source of funding is Medifund, a safety net that provides financial assistance to individuals who, despite the subsidies and payments from their Medisave accounts and the Medishield scheme, cannot pay their medical bills. Medifund is a government endowment fund built on surpluses each year. In 1999, some 69,000 individuals received financial support from the Medifund (Vasoo, 2001).

Control of funding and pressures for reform

As Figure 3.2 suggests, funding is about raising resources from a range of sources (such as taxes, social insurance contributions, private insurance premiums or out-of-pocket payments) and allocating these resources to the providers of health care.

Health care tends to be funded by a mix of public and private sources, reflecting predominant types of funding and other, country-specific factors. National health services with their commitment to universality of access get the majority of their funding from taxes.

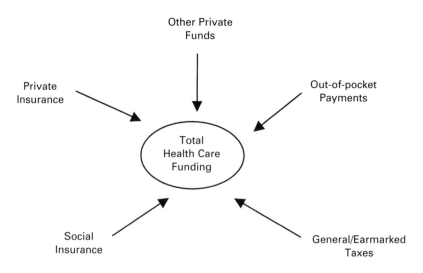

Figure 3.2 *Sources of health care funding*

Britain and Sweden are classical examples of this type of publicly funded health system. Australia and New Zealand combine tax funding with strong elements of private funding, and over 20 per cent of funds come from private insurance and out-of-pocket payments.

Social insurance systems are a hybrid as money is raised from independent insurance funds, but these are publicly mandated and here social solidarity is key. Germany is the classical example of this of type of funding, and social insurance contributions account for the majority of health care expenditure. In comparison with the health systems in the Netherlands and Japan, social insurance co-exists with strong elements of private funding, from private insurance and out-of-pocket payments respectively. Finally, health systems where private insurance dominates put individual responsibility first and largely rely on private funds. In Singapore, a highly individualized compulsory savings account is key, whereas the USA relies on a mixture between private and public insurance at the price of leaving over 17 per cent of the population uncovered.

However, funding is about more than raising and allocating financial resources. How funds are raised and allocated is also a pointer to power. Different types of funding result in different types of control, and different types of control lead to different types of pressures for reform. Public funding means public control (Freeman, 2000: 44). Public control can be expected to be strongest in national health services, which are largely funded by taxes. Taxes place control over funding in public hands, leading to concentration rather than fragmentation, and allowing for the control of (global) budgets. The prime example is Britain, where the total NHS expenditure is set by the Treasury and is part of the government's yearly general public expenditure planning process. Once the overall spending level has been set, the Department of Health determines the funds allocated to the regions, and the regions determine the funds allocated to health authorities. Public control over funding is further tightened by the fact that control resides primarily with central government and its agencies at regional level. In contrast, in Sweden public control of funding is more decentralized and rests with the county councils.

However, public control of funding comes at a price (Klein, 2001). Inevitably, the interests of government as the payer of health care will be reflected in its approach to raising and allocating funds, and cost efficiency and containment are likely priorities (Fattore, 1999). And, to paraphrase Moran (1999: 61), a uniquely generous entitlement philosophy often goes hand-in-hand with parsimonious practice.

In national health services, problems of controlling total expenditure are practically unknown. Instead the central challenge is to meet the growing demands for health care within a fixed and above all tight budget. For example, a recent WHO study ranked the British NHS eighteen in the world because of its lack of responsiveness to patients (Laurance and Norton, 2000). The political price of public control of funding rises when patients become less deferential and more demanding and the heightened mismatch between supply and demand manifests itself in long waiting lists for elective surgery. Centralization of control adds to the politicization of health care expenditure and in Britain responsibility for the negative consequences of inadequate funding falls back on central government. Health care reforms over the last 20 years can be read as attempts to make limited resources go further and have focused on increasing micro-efficiency and competition. Competition promises to provide more and/or better health services without spending more money (Freeman, 1998, 2000). The British NHS, for example, has gone through several waves of major reorganization (Ham, 1999). Interestingly, in Sweden organizational reform has been coupled with moves to extend patient choice (Saltman, 1998: 164).

In contrast with national health services, public control of funding is weaker in health systems that rely on social insurance and this typically manifests itself in problems of controlling total health care expenditure. A classical case is Germany where health reform has long been seen as an attempt to halt the 'cost explosion'. As a percentage of monthly salaries social insurance contribution rates make health care expenditure highly visible (Moran, 1999: 74). However, contribution rates have come under pressure not only from rising expenditure but also from falling funding. An increasingly lower proportion of GDP is used for wages, reflecting larger profits by employers, wage increases below productivity as well as high levels of unemployment. This has been exacerbated by unification, to the extent that shortfalls in funding now are the main reason for the financial problems of the health system (Busse and Howorth, 1999: 331). Traditionally, power over funding has been decentralized and fragmented. In part, this is typical of the organizational complexity of social insurance systems and in the case of Germany is compounded by federalism. Until the mid-1990s, there were over 1,000 different insurance funds, each raising its own funds and setting its own contribution rates. Health care resources were allocated from the bottom up and doctors were free to decide on the treatment of patients. Moreover, the federal government was limited to setting (and altering) the framework in which the insurance funds and providers operated.

However, even social insurance schemes allow for some control of funding. In the Netherlands, for example, the contribution rates for the two social insurance schemes are set by central government and the yearly surveys on current and future expenditures published by the Department of Health have acquired the status of spending ceilings

(Loo, Kahan and Okma, 1999: 574). Interestingly, private health insurance is also subject to extensive regulation and the government has introduced pooling and a standard insurance package for high-risk employees. Japan is another example of successful public control of a social insurance system where insurance funds and providers are all strictly regulated by government. Importantly, all health care payments are made on the basis of a national fee schedule with implicit limits on the increase in overall expenditure. In Japan, all billing and payment is centralized through the payment fund of the National Health Insurance, which reviews all bills submitted and has the power to reduce payments to minimize fraud.

Systematic and effective public control of funding is weakest in health systems that rely on private insurance. The USA is a case in point. Rising health expenditure has been a major problem and the USA continues to be the most expensive health system of all industrialized countries. As seen earlier, the USA now spends over 14 per cent of its GDP on health care, almost double the average of industrialized nations. It is not only the predominance of private funding that makes public control of expenditure difficult, but also the fragmentation of insurance funds and provider organizations, together with the federalist structure in the USA. The US health system is a amalgamation of over 1,500 private insurance companies and managed care organizations; over 600,000 doctors, most of whom are in private practice; over 5,200 acute care hospitals and 15,000 long-term care facilities. Moreover, the public sector health system includes over 3,000 counties that operate community hospitals and clinics; the 50 states which retain the primary constitutional roles of protecting the health of their respective residents and the training and licensing of medical personnel; and finally the federal government which funds Medicare and the joint federal–state Medicaid programme as well as specialized veterans' and research hospitals.

In the 1980s, the government attempted to control Medicare/Medicaid spending by initiating diagnosis-related groups (DRGs), a system under which each category of treatment has a scheduled payment. Furthermore, in order to constrain private sector costs the government encouraged the creation of HMOs and other managed care systems. Other attempts to control cost growth have included a combination of selective provider contracting, discount price negotiations, utilization control practices, and risk-sharing payment methods. After the levelling-off of health care expenditures following the initiating of DRGs and managed care in the late 1980s to mid-1990s, costs have begun to rise more rapidly, again far exceeding general inflation rates. This is especially the case for Medicare/Medicaid where, despite DRGs, real growth is now approaching double figures annually.

Singapore is an interesting exception to the rule. In 2000, the WHO ranked Singapore as the most effective health system in Asia and sixth in the world, despite spending only 3.1 per cent of its GDP on health care ('Singapore's Health System is Best in Asia', 2000). This success has been attributed to: (1) the creation of the savings account system where individuals are encouraged to use their savings parsimoniously; (2) the government's success in dampening demand for health care through education programmes designed to keep health care expectations modest; and (3) the government's encouragement of family responsibilities for care of elderly and ill members (Duff, 2001: 147). The Medisave scheme emphasizes individual responsibility and family networks and gives the individuals control of their accounts but, crucially, this freedom is combined with strong government regulation. The medical savings schemes are compulsory and caps on contribution rates, together with very high co-payments, have given government tight control of expenditure. The government also heavily subsidizes the primary care services and health promotion and disease prevention programmes, and emphasizes community health care over hospital care. The highly centralized political structure of Singapore and widespread regime approval ensures that government control is effective.

Health services and patient choice

Health services are first and foremost medical services, reflecting the prominence of doctors in the delivery of services and the allocation of health care resources. As Table 3.5 suggests, medical health services can be distinguished according to the specificity and the locality of care delivered (also see Chapter 1, p. 13). Primary care is typically less

Table 3.5   *Types and settings of health services*

	Ambulatory settings	Hospital settings
Primary Care	Services provided by GPs working in their own practices or in health centres	Services provided by GPs in long-term care nursing homes
Acute Care	Services provided by specialists working in their own practices or health centres	Services provided by specialists on wards or in outpatient departments in hospitals

specialized than secondary care. This distinction corresponds to different localities of care delivery. Typically, primary care services are delivered in ambulatory settings (such as doctors' practices or health centres) whereas acute care services are delivered in (inpatient) hospital settings or in outpatient departments of hospitals. In contrast, chronic care services have traditionally been less medically oriented and are delivered in a range of settings, from people's homes to day centres and nursing homes.

As Table 3.6 suggests, in all these health systems inpatient care accounts for the single largest share of health care expenditure, more or less narrowly followed by outpatient care. The definitions of inpatient and outpatient care are quite extensive, although they broadly correspond to care provided in hospitals and care provided in ambulatory settings. Interestingly, the difference between expenditure on inpatient and outpatient expenditure varies considerably between countries. Australia, France and the Netherlands spend about twice as much on inpatient care as on outpatient care, whereas in Japan and Germany the difference in health care expenditure is only about 5 percentage points. However, all countries are characterized by almost universal negligence of home health care services. This will be addressed in more detail in Chapter 6.

Patient access to different types of health care varies between countries, reflecting different levels of patient choice. Choice can mean different things, such as the ability to choose a generalist or a specialist doctor as the first point of contact or the ability to choose between different hospitals and ambulatory care settings. A broad distinction can be

Table 3.6   *Expenditure on medical services as a percentage of health care expenditure, 1998*

	Inpatient care	Outpatient care	Home health care services
Australia	43.3	22.0	0.2
France	44.6	23.0	0.4
Germany	34.0	28.9	4.0
Japan	37.6	32.8	0.2
Netherlands	52.8	20.2	n/a
USA	41.3	32.5	3.0

n/a = not available

Source: Data from OECD (2001b).

drawn between complete choice, extensive choice, and the GP model where choice is restricted. The level of patient choice reflects the way health services are organized, but also more explicit decisions about the appropriate level of patient choice.

Singapore is the only country that offers complete choice as long as an individual's Medisave account is active. Patients with savings accounts are free to go directly to the hospital (private or public) of their choice and choose the level of subsidy they receive in public hospitals. In relation to primary care services, patients are free to choose between private practices and government-subsidized health centres. Saving accounts can also be used to buy private insurance or Medishield coverage. The high level of patient choice concurs with the principle of individual responsibility, which is central to the health system in Singapore. Paradoxically, the high level of individual responsibility also limits choice when it comes to expensive or long-term care, because few patients are wealthy enough to afford such care and exercise free choice. Also, once a person's or family's Medisave account is exhausted, he or she must depend on the Medifund under which choice as to both providers and class of hospital care is limited (Massaro and Wong, 1996). In the end, the high level of individual responsibility constrains the choice of those persons most dependent on the health system, who have used up their Medisave funds. Although Medisave contributes to the 'cultural rhetoric' of personal responsibility for health care, Barr (2001) argues that at its core the Singapore system of health funding represents a 'strict rationing of health services according to wealth'.

The health systems in Germany and Sweden offer extensive individual choice. In Germany, patients are free to choose any doctor working in ambulatory care, but require referral for hospital care. This leads to extensive choice as both generalists and specialists work in office-based settings. In Sweden, this corresponds to the choice between using a health centre or going directly to a specialist outpatient department in a hospital. Interestingly, patient choice was extended further in the 1990s and patients can now freely choose the doctor and institution for medical treatment (European Observatory on Health Care Systems, 2001: 47). This reflects a strong commitment to equity and quality and contrasts with Britain and the Netherlands, where patients' choice was further curtailed in the name of efficiency (Saltman, 1998: 164).

The health systems in Australia, Britain, the Netherlands and New Zealand have adopted a GP model, which offers the lowest level of patient choice. Patients have to register with a general practitioner (sometimes in their area) and it is the GP who refers patients to specialist out- and inpatient services in hospitals. This gives GPs a strong gatekeeping function. The predominance of the GP model is surprising. With the exception of Britain, the health systems in these countries share a commitment to individualism, as reflected in significant components of private funding. A possible explanation is that patient choice is expensive and therefore likely to be restricted, especially in times of cost containment. This can also account for the fact that in the USA one of the main characteristics of HMOs was to introduce a gate-keeping role for GPs, thus limiting the wide choices of specialists inherent in the traditional insurance system. As noted earlier, not surprisingly, this has led to widespread condemnation of HMOs by US patients and doctors.

Welfare mixes in the provision of health care

Health systems allow for different levels of patient choice, reflecting the ways in which heath services are organized as well as specific decisions about the appropriate level of patient choice. This partly corresponds to the principles underpinning different types of health systems. The principles of equity, social solidarity and individual responsibility also inform the welfare mix in the provision of health care: that is, who the providers of health care are (see Box 3.3).

The differences in welfare mix apply primarily to hospitals, whereas the situation in ambulatory care is more uniform. In most countries,

---

Box 3.3   Welfare mix: mixed meanings and policies

As a *concept* welfare mix refers to the diverse ways in which health services can be provided. Welfare mix is concerned with the division of labour between the public, private, voluntary and informal sector. In as much as the provision of health care is always mixed to a greater or lesser extent, welfare mix is also a *descriptor* of how services are delivered in individual health systems. Finally, as a *political programme* welfare mix challenges the notion that public provision is always best (Evers and Svetlik, 1993). By some, welfare mix is seen to serve better the needs of increasingly diverse societies. Others argue that a more mixed provision of health services is more cost efficient. Different health systems typically have different welfare mixes. Public funding through taxes often accompanies public ownership, leading to a highly publicly integrated provision of health services. Social insurance combines social solidarity with a commitment to individualism/subsidiarity. Public and private providers tend to exist side-by-side, creating complex and less well-integrated structures of health provision. The same is often true for health systems that predominantly rely on private insurance. In both social and private insurance systems, the welfare mix in health care provision comes naturally, whereas in national health services the welfare mix has been closely associated with market-oriented reforms.

doctors working in ambulatory care are independent practitioners, who either practise privately or who are contracted to provide publicly-funded medical services. Reflecting their independent status, doctors are typically paid on a capitation or a fee-for-service basis (see Chapter 5 for details, p. 137). The only exception is Sweden, where doctors in ambulatory care are salaried employees. This is a powerful indication of the high public integration of health care in Sweden.

The health systems in Britain, New Zealand and Sweden are typical examples of national health services, where public hospitals provide the majority of beds and where private hospitals are few. In New Zealand, for example, there are about 80 public hospital facilities, which operate under the direction of 21 community-focused District Health Boards, the regional administrative tier of the Department of Health (New Zealand Ministry of Health, 2001). Public hospitals derive their entire income from government funding agencies. A few private hospitals provide acute health care services and costs are met by individuals or by private insurance. Significantly, only a few District Health Boards have contracted with private hospitals to provide services. In comparison, the boundary between public and private provision is more blurred in Britain. Consultants are allowed to practise privately and the NHS has the largest number of private beds, which offer a lucrative source of income (Baggott, 1998: 166). In special cases NHS patients are treated in independent hospitals, and with the Private Finance Initiative independent hospitals will be built as part of NHS hospital developments. Australia is unusual in that it combines public funding through taxes with a strong element of private provision of services. In 2000, over 40 per cent of acute hospitals were in public hands, although the private hospitals tend to be smaller and less likely to provide complex, high-technology services. Nevertheless, the private hospital sector accounts for about 30 per cent of all admissions and 25 per cent of total hospital bed days (Hall, 1999: 98).

The provision of hospital care has traditionally been more mixed in social insurance systems. In Germany, for example about half the hospital beds are in hospitals in public ownership, almost 40 per cent in hospitals in private, non-profit ownership and the rest in hospitals in private for-profit ownership (European Observatory on Health Care Systems, 2000: 37). The high degree of welfare mix reflects the principle of subsidiarity, whereby public provision is a matter of last resort, as well as the fact that historically the German health system was built around existing provision structures. The number of private, non-profit hospitals is even higher in the Netherlands. This echoes the traditional division of Dutch society into distinct religious and political segments, giving private initiative a prominent role in the delivery of health services (Maarse, 1997: 136). The situation in Japan is similar as the majority of hospitals are run on a private, non-profit basis by doctors working in ambulatory care (Nakahara, 1997).

Market-based health systems are also characterized by high levels of welfare mixes and, compared to social insurance systems, private for-profit hospitals play a more prominent role. For instance, in the USA there are 245 federal government hospitals and 1,163 state and local government hospitals compared to 3,003 private non-profit hospitals and 749 for-profit hospitals (American Hospital Association, 2002). Singapore is unusual in that most beds are provided in publicly run hospitals. The eight public hospitals and five public speciality treatment centres together comprise 84 per cent of available beds (Singapore Ministry of Health, 2002b). This reflects the unique combination of individual responsibility for funding and a strong role of government in regulation and the provision of hospital care in Singapore.

Models of contracting health services

Health systems are about funding and provision, and the two can be linked in different ways. In national health services, funding and provision have traditionally been integrated with both being in public hands. In contrast, funding and provision are separate in social insurance systems and contracts provide the key link between the payers and the providers of health care. Private insurance systems operate in a similar way, although contracts are not subject to direct public regulation. The last two decades, however, have seen interesting changes in many countries. National health services have experimented with the public contract model, often in an attempt to introduce market-style dynamics into their health service. Likewise, competition has been an important element of reform in social insurance systems, changing the nature of the more established public contract models. In its various versions the public contract model, with its separation between public funding bodies and providers who relate to each other through contracts (OECD, 1992), is now the dominant model of organizing and reforming health services. Interesting variations exist in relation to the degree of government control of the contract process.

The Netherlands is a typical example of the social insurance variant of the public contract model. Social health insurance is administered by private non-profit insurance funds, which operate under public law. The insurance funds negotiate rates and fees with providers (i.e., hospitals and doctors working in ambulatory care). However, the rates and fees are regulated by the Health Tariffs Act and have to be approved by the Central Agency of Health Care Tariffs, although the early 1990s saw some deregulation. Insurance funds can now contract selectively with providers and are allowed to negotiate lower fees and rates, and doctors can set up their practices anywhere in the country (Ven, 1997: 92). Both measures have encouraged some competition between providers. This has been complemented by competition among purchasers, as patients have a free choice concerning insurance funds. The public contract model in Japan is even more state-centred. Providers are contracted under the uniform fee system, which the government's Central Social Medical Care Council negotiates with representatives of providers, payers and public interest groups (Ikegami and Campbell, 1999: 63). However, in contrast to the Netherlands and Japan insurance funds and provider organizations enjoy more autonomy in the public contract model in Germany. As discussed in the next section, the public contract model is embedded in an extensive system of statutory joint self-administration, reflecting subsidarity at procedural level (Altenstetter, 1997).

Among the national health services, Britain has gone furthest with the implementation of a public contract model. Health authorities (and now Primary Care Trusts) are the purchasers of health care. They are corporate bodies that operate under the general direction of a chairperson appointed by the Secretary of State. As non-departmental public bodies, health authorities receive funds from the regional offices of the NHS Executive, which is part of the Department of Health. In comparison to insurance funds, health authorities enjoy less autonomy as they are in effect sub-central tiers of health administration and 'creatures of statute' (Paton, 1997: 23) The same applies to hospitals, which are non-profit trusts within the NHS. Their room for manoeuvre has been further curtailed by recent moves towards national priorities and performance management (Ham, 1999: 158f.). Health authorities and trusts negotiate and complete service agreements with providers, but they are not legally enforceable. In contrast to insurance funds, the role of health authorities goes beyond paying for services since they are also responsible for ensuring that the heath needs of the population are met (Ham, 1997b: 58). The public contract model was introduced in the early 1990s under the banner of an 'internal market', but has since evolved into a system of 'managed competition' with strong elements of planning and regulation. Increasingly, this is complemented by elements of partnership and Light (1997) suggests that the NHS is moving to a system of 'managed co-operation'. The experience in New Zealand has been similar (see Blank, 1994). Cumming and Scott (1998) contend that the reforms in New Zealand were aimed at improving accountability and strengthening the purchasers' roles relative to providers. In the latest round of reforms in 2000, however, the Labour government moved to consolidate the funding/provider roles in one agency, the District Health Boards, thus amalgamating the roles again.

In contrast, Sweden is an example of a national health service where the purchaser–provider split was never introduced comprehensively. County councils, an independent, secondary level of local government, are responsible for the funding and provision of health care and are also free to develop their own management systems (Rehnberg, 1997: 69). In 1994, for example, only 14 out of 26 county councils had experimented with different models of the purchaser–provider split, a decision which above all reflected local traditions (Anell and Svarvar, 1999: 710). Also, the emerging market was very different from that in the UK and New Zealand because competition was combined with patient choice, thus limiting the extent to which purchasers could selectively contract with providers (Jacobs, 1998: 12f.). However, the insights into the downsides of the market, combined with a renewed emphasis on social solidarity in the mid-1990s, led to moves away from competition-based model and back to the basics and models based on co-operation (Saltman, 1998: 171).

Health governance between centre and locality

As we have seen, health systems are about the funding and provision of health care. Health systems are funded from a range of sources that result in different levels of public control. Health systems consist of a range of services that are delivered by different providers to which patients have different levels of access. The different ways in which funding and provision are organized lead not only to different policies and pressures for reform, but also to different politics, different relationships between central and local government, among government and provider organizations/payers, and among payers and providers themselves.

Governance, for its part, includes the regulation of areas such as medical practice and pharmaceuticals, but is broader than that. Governance is concerned with modes of co-ordinating health systems and their multiple actors (Freeman, 2000). Governance is underpinned by two sets of tensions: between public and private (ie., between the state and the market); and between centre and locality. Government looms large in most health systems and governance can be thought of as government authority/capacity. Government authority/capacity is reflected in the degree of institutional integration in health systems: that is, in the power of the national government (executive integration), in the extent of government authority over private interests such as doctors, hospitals and insurers (public integration), and in the extent to which policy-making authority is concentrated at national rather than regional or local levels (central integration) (see Freeman, 2000). Executive and public integration are discussed in the next section. This section focuses on central integration that concerns the relationship among the different levels of governance.

Some health systems are more decentralized than others, reflecting the respective political systems in which they are embedded. However, over the last two decades many health systems have attempted to decentralize governance. This is about convergence, but offers equally strong indications of persistent differences. The health systems in Sweden and Britain (and New Zealand) illustrate this point. In both countries, health care is publicly funded and provided and this results in health systems that are characterized by a high degree of public integration and control. At the same time, important differences exist in relation to the levels of governance. In Sweden, responsibility for funding and provision rests with the county councils, leading to decentralized health governance. Sweden has a strong tradition of local government and, importantly, a type of local government that defines itself by democratic decision making (Håkansson and Nordling, 1997: 194). This contrasts with Britain where the publicly funded and provided health service is embedded in a highly centralized political system. The centrality of central government is compounded by a tradition that sees local government first and foremost as a provider of services. Not surprisingly, the NHS has been described as a 'command and control system' (Moran, 1999). In many ways New Zealand resembles Britain. The unitary political system of New Zealand ensures that a relatively high degree of control over the health system is centralized in the Ministry of Health, although this has varied considerably from one government to the next.

The differences in the degree of central integration can also help to explain differences in moves towards decentralization. In Britain, decentralization occurred as part of the introduction of a quasi market in health care that was inspired by the new public management paradigm. The actors at local level are hospital trusts and health authorities which are not only creatures of central government, but which also continue to operate within a highly hierarchical system of health governance. Not surprisingly, the autonomy of trusts and health authorities is confined to managerial responsibility. The complex division of labour between different levels of governance has highlighted problems of accountability (Iliffe and Munro, 2000: 322).

This contrasts with Sweden, where in the early 1980s county councils were given complete control over funding and delivery of services. Here, decentralization was a genuine devolution of power that built on traditions of sub-central government, and not simply a refocusing of central control as in the case of Britain. This further strengthened the directly democratic character of managerial decision-making (Saltman, 1998: 164). However, there are limits to local autonomy. The central government has become increasingly involved in setting national priorities and quality standards to maintain equity across different counties. More bluntly, central government can control total expenditure by putting taxation limits on county councils as it did during the recession in the early 1990s (Rehnberg, 1997: 66).

Funding from social insurance results in institutional complexity and often limits the degree of central integration of health systems. For example, in Germany a statutory, joint self-administration of insurance funds and providers is at the centre of health governance and this form of corporatism operates at different levels. At the local level, providers and insurance funds relate to each other through contracts, which specify the services to be provided and the prices to be paid, including the financing mechanisms. However, local contracts are embedded in a complex system of framework agreements at state and federal level (again between providers and insurance funds) and these, in turn, are embedded in federal legislation; the Social Code Book. Corporatism is a particular approach to policy making and has several aspects to it (Schwartz and Busse, 1997: 104). Corporatism hands over certain rights of the state to corporatist self-governing institutions, including the insurance funds and provider organizations. As corporatist institutions, they have mandatory membership and enjoy the right to raise their own financial resources as well as the right to negotiate and sign contracts with other corporatist institutions. In Germany, institutional complexity is underpinned by corporatism as a form of procedural subsidiarity and is compounded by federalism, which taken together results in decentralized health governance.

However, as the Netherlands and Japan illustrate, decentralized health governance can co-exist with strong elements of centralism. In the Netherlands, the central government enjoys extensive powers in relation to the determination of contribution rates, the setting of hospital budgets, and the approval of fees set as part of the negotiations between insurance funds and providers. And crucially, corporatism is also confined to the national level (Lieverdink and Made, 1997: 132). This more centralized form of corporatism is underpinned by a decentralized, yet unitary political system, where municipalities and provinces often act as implementation agencies of national policy programmes. Similarly, Japan combines central government control with strong elements of decentralization. Health governance is highly decentralized across 47 regional prefectures and thousands of municipalities, and provides a mixture of delivery levels reflecting a basic principle underlying national policies (Nakahara, 1997: 107). Despite this, the central government maintains strong control over all aspects of health care through the rigid and centrally controlled fee structure.

In contrast to Germany, the role of federalism in health governance is ambivalent in Australia and the USA, and the two countries illustrate how modes of governance can vary between sub-systems of health care. In Australia control over health funding is more highly centralized than in the USA where only the elderly and poor are covered by federal programmes. Over the past two decades, Australia has moved to centralize effective control and this has reduced substantially the proportion of funding derived from private sources while the US system of finance continues to be highly fragmented. Both countries, however, have strong traditions of decentralization and individual state autonomy in the provision of health care services and of robust and powerful private sectors. Although the central governments in both the USA and Australia have substantial and growing roles in funding, governance of provision remains highly decentralized, distributed among myriad state, local and private sectors.

The authority of governments in health policy

Looking at the roles of centre and locality in health governance provides a powerful indication of the complexity of health systems and the importance of political contexts for shaping health systems. Ultimately, health governance always happens at different levels: health systems as *systems* require direction from the centre while the provision of health care inevitably involves localities. However, the relative importance of different levels varies among health systems as well as among different sub-systems within the same health system. The variation among and within systems reflects how health care is provided as well as specific political contexts. For example, health governance is highly centralized in Britain, whereas it is more decentralized in the USA. This reflects the fact that the British central government is key to the public funding and provision of health care, whereas in the USA mixed funding and provision naturally decentralizes governance. The differences between the two countries also point to the importance of political contexts. As the comparison with Sweden shows, however, public funding and provision alone do not make for centralized governance, but a unitary, centralized political system plays an important role. Similarly, decentralized health governance in the USA is underpinned by federalism. Differences among systems co-exist with differences within the same health system. Japan and the Netherlands are a case in point: both countries combine centralized governance of funding with decentralized governance of provision.

Executive and public integration provide further evidence of the complexity of health systems. The power of national governments and the power of governments over private interests are closely related and offer key indications of the relative authority of governments in health policy. This issue has been implicit throughout the chapter when discussing the sub-systems of funding and provision. The basic assumption is that public funding and provision result in public control – that is, government authority – as the government is the principal public actor in health policy. Public control of funding can be measured in terms of the extent of public funding, the relative importance of taxes and social security as different types of public funding as well as the power of government to control funding. Public control of provision can be measured in terms of the share of public provision of health care. On this basis, Figure 3.3 characterizes the health systems in different countries.

		Provision		
		High	**Middle**	**Low**
Public Control of Funding	**High**	Britain Sweden		Japan Netherlands
	Middle	Australia New Zealand	Germany	
	Low	Singapore		United States

Figure 3.3   *Public control of funding and provision of health care*

The summary of the modes of governance and the extent of government authority in different countries demonstrates the sheer diversity of health systems. Health systems are all confronted with pressures from ageing populations, advances in medical technology and periodic economic down turns, and these pressures often manifest themselves in pressures to control and contain costs. However, the institutional contexts of health systems and the capacity of governments to address these pressures continue to vary considerably between countries. For example, public control of funding and provision is high in Britain and Sweden, whereas it is low in the USA.

Significantly, the picture is more complex than the typology of health systems introduced in Chapter 1 (p. 23) would suggest. The typology assumes that certain models of funding are directly associated with certain models of provision to the extent that high public control of funding goes hand in hand with high public control of provision and vice versa. This is true for the health systems in some countries such as Britain, Sweden, Germany and the USA, which are closest to the ideal types of national health service, social insurance system and private insurance system, respectively. In the health systems in the remaining countries, government authority varies between the sub-systems of funding and provision. For example, Japan and the Netherlands combine relatively strong (central) public control over funding with relatively low public control over provision, reflecting the predominance of non-public providers. This makes government authority over funding comparable to Britain and Sweden, whereas in relation to provision government authority is closer to the USA.

Differences and similarities are specific to individual sub-systems of health care and as such point to the importance of country-specific political contexts. Examples of country-specific political contexts include the semi-federal political system in the Netherlands that often helps to concentrate authority in the hands of central government, and the legacy of a private insurance system combined with federalism in Australia that weakens government authority over funding to some extent. However, acknowledging the uniqueness of individual health systems does not mean abandoning cross-country comparisons; instead, it requires removing the blinkers of ideal types of health systems and exploring what Moran (1999) calls the 'political embeddedness' of health systems. Chapter 4 continues this quest by examining the implications of these health system characteristics in the actual allocation of health care resources in these countries.

Setting Priorities and Allocating Resources

Chapter 3 demonstrated that health systems display variation in the sub-systems of funding, provision and governance that impact on the health policy and health care of these countries. It also illustrated that these sub-systems are dynamic, not static, and that many of them have undergone significant changes in recent decades. In order to better understand the impact of these sub-systems and of differences among them on health care, it is important to go beneath the institutional and structural dimensions and examine the goals, objectives and priorities of each health system. This chapter, therefore, examines the criteria various health care systems use to allocate medical resources and the implications of these policies for their respective populations.

The goals of health policy

Every policy is founded on goals and objectives which should be clarified early in the policy-making process. Two levels of goals are discernible. The first are broad stated goals that often function symbolically and are often more in the realm of political rhetoric than reality. The second are specific programmatic goals that frame a particular policy. Both are critical in evaluating the success or failure of a policy. Although some goals can be specified and measured with accuracy, others are more problematic; generally, the broader the goal, the more difficult it is to measure. Analysis becomes even more difficult when the goals themselves conflict, when they are defined differently by the various participants, or when they shift over time. In spite of these problems it is critical to examine the stated goals of health policy.

Theoretically, a successful health policy in a democracy would provide high quality services for all citizens on an equal basis. Moreover, it would be an efficient system with little waste and duplication and high levels of performance in all sectors. In addition to the goals of universal access, quality and efficiency, other goals might include maximizing the choice of patients, ensuring high accountability of the health care personnel, or guaranteeing rapid diffusion of the

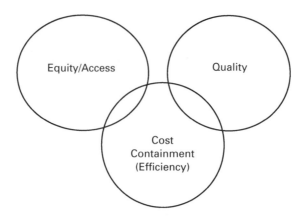

Figure 4.1   *Competing goals of health care*

newest medical technologies. As will be discussed in Chapter 7 (p. 174), goals also can vary as to whether the health of the population as a whole or the health of individual patients is primary. Although the goals of health care are many, Figure 4.1 displays the main ones for discussion here that are at the core of health policy.

For the two decades following the Second World War, the predominant goals of health policy initiatives in all developed nations were *equity* or *access* and *quality* of health care. Even though the actual policies varied significantly from country to country, together the goals of access and quality shaped health care priorities. The variation can largely be explained by how much emphasis each nation put on subsidiary competing goals of freedom of choice for consumers, autonomy of the health care providers and insurers, and various notions of common good or solidarity. The actual mix of these policy goals has been shaped by the variations in national cultures, politics, and institutional structures discussed in Chapter 2. In the USA, for instance, with its strong emphasis on individual freedom from both patients and the health care community, universal access and equity were never given the prominence they enjoyed in other countries. In contrast, New Zealand and the UK, with their stronger egalitarian roots and tradition of common good, enthusiastically established comprehensive national health services to deliver on the central goals of universal access and free care at the point of service.

Despite variation regarding universal coverage, however, health policy in all developed nations in the post-war period placed priority on ensuring all citizens had access to an expanding array of medical intervention. During this period, new hospitals were built and many beds were added to existing structures, significantly expanded investments were made in medical education and biomedical research, and the supply of medical personnel was increased and the boundaries of medicine extended by the addition of many new medical specialities. Furthermore, new institutional mechanisms for ensuring access to these resources were initiated, thus issuing in the era of technological medicine as the new centre of health care. This post-war boom of medicine, in turn, was met by heightened expectations and demands from the public for greater access to an ever-expanding arsenal of new medical innovations.

Equity and access: continuing problems

Two types of access were addressed by health policies of this era: financial access and physical or geographical access. Financial access was met by restructuring health care funding and provision so as to provide universal access to at least a minimal level of health care for all citizens based on individual need. This entailed either creating systems of direct public financing and provision of services or governmental regulation and co-ordination of private sickness funds with guaranteed coverage for those patients who fell through the gaps in the private system. Some, such as Germany and the Netherlands, chose to strengthen health systems that pre-dated the Second World War while others, such as the UK and Sweden, set up new systems to meet these goals. Except for the USA, which chose not to establish a national system, all countries examined here were largely successful in achieving universal levels of access, despite major variation in the means used to achieve that goal.

Recently, however, many countries with universal coverage have found themselves facing a problem of equity of access relating to the presence of a tiered system where persons with sufficient resources or private coverage are able to obtain services which are either unavailable or limited in the public system. Ironically, there is greater public awareness of these discrepancies in the countries with national health services (such as the UK and New Zealand) that have made the strongest claims for financial equity. For instance, while universality is at the centre of the NHS in Britain, pressures of cost containment have challenged this principle. Waiting lists limit access to elective surgery and lead to a two-tier system whereby patients with private insurance or sufficient financial means can get private treatment immediately. Further, it is up to health authorities to decide which specific services to fund, opening the way to local variation. This is also referred to as the 'postcode lottery'. A recent, widely publicized case was that of a woman who was denied the drug she had been taking for her Alzheimer's disease when she moved (Boseley, 2001a).

The second type of access has proven increasingly difficult to achieve as health care has become more specialized and capital intensive. Geographical inequities in health care, although initially reduced by regional reallocation schemes, have proved troublesome to resolve. Isolated, rural communities consistently are undersupplied in terms of skilled medical personnel and facilities. The disproportionate number of physicians located in urban centres is reinforced by the insufficient number of patients in many rural areas and by the resultant concentration of health care facilities in core urban populations.

Although most countries have created incentives to correct the geographical imbalances of physicians, financial inducements and other policies have not proved capable of resolving the problem (this is discussed in more detail in Chapter 5, p. 125). For instance, Germany has one of the highest numbers of doctors (OECD, 2001b) but they have been concentrated in urban areas. However, in 1993 the freedom to set up practice anywhere was replaced by manpower planning based on needs, and the number of additional doctors per speciality and region was limited in order to make rural regions more attractive to new doctors (Burau, 2001).

An important barrier to establishing physical equity is the fact that the delivery of health care services to rural areas is significantly more expensive on a per case basis, in part because of the high cost of capital equipment needed to supply state of the art medical care. As a result, many specialized services can be provided efficiently only in urban regional centres with a critical mass of population. This problem is especially acute in Australia, New Zealand and the USA where large proportions of the population live in urban centres, but a minority of the population live in remote rural areas. Only with the highly concentrated population of Singapore is this not a problem. In other countries, even when patients from isolated geographical locations have equal financial access to the same level of medicine as their urban brethren, travel costs, relocation costs and costs in wasted time produce substantial inequities in effective access.

Quality care: what is it?

The goal of high quality of health care, a hallmark of the 1950s and 1960s, has also proved problematic. The main difficulty with defining quality is that we lack an objective means of measuring what quality medicine is. Not surprisingly, international comparisons made by the OECD and other organizations seldom address this factor because it is much easier to compare cost figures, use figures, and other readily quantifiable factors. Even within single countries, quality is rarely monitored systematically because there is little agreement on what criteria should be used. Unfortunately, quality is frequently equated with the latest

Table 4.1 *MRI units per million population, 1995*

Country	MRI units
Canada	1.3
France	2.1
Italy	2.4
Australia	2.9
UK	3.4
Germany	4.8
USA	7.3

Source: Data from OECD (2001b).

technological developments, with curative medicine, the latest in diagnostic technologies, and with specialist services. This emphasis is misleading in that it makes the assumption that quality can be defined by the number of machines, the number of medical specialists, and the number of intensive medical interventions performed (see McClellan and Kessler, 1999).

Quality as defined by technology however is of questionable value when compared to health outcome as measured by a variety of indicators of the health of the population. Table 4.1, for instance, compares countries where data is available on the number of expensive Magnetic Resonance Imaging units per million people. Although the USA has the highest 'quality' if measured solely by availability of this type of care, it rates much lower than other countries on many measures of health outcome. Also, when quality is defined in this way it is likely to conflict with the goal of access, which by necessity requires constraints on disproportionate investments on a small number of users. While the goal of universal access assumes some minimal level of care available to those persons in need, it cannot permit unlimited amounts of resources to be expended on high-technology interventions. Despite these problems, however, quality, along with equity, was the most articulated goal of health policy until the mid- to late 1970s.

In the 1970s, however, escalating costs, in large part fuelled by the open-ended goals of access and quality, were aggravated by the global recession and oil crisis. One result was an unmistakable shift in emphasis from access and quality to *cost containment* and the need to constrain health care spending. Ageing populations, unbounded technological expansion and heightened public expectations solidified this goal in the 1990s. Moreover, its prominence was encouraged by the ideological shift towards neo-liberalism, which eschewed the welfare state and placed emphasis on efficiency of the market (see the discussion later in this chapter, p. 102). Although strategies differed, no country escaped the highly visible shift towards improving productivity, maximizing efficiency, and incorporating management procedures into health care due to the predominant goal of cost containment. Moreover, to date reform efforts in most Western countries, with the notable exception of the USA, have been effective to the extent that they have stopped or slowed the rate of increase of health care spending as a proportion of GDP (see Table 3.2 in Chapter 3: p. 62).

Interestingly, the emphasis on cost containment and system efficiency forced evaluation of quality (an effort that was conspicuously absent when quality was a stated goal) because it required priorities to be set in distributing health care resources in terms of value for money. Not surprisingly, this shift in goals has run into opposition from the health care industry, medical professionals and health care consumers who have 'grown accustomed to expensive care at low direct cost' (Harrop, 1992: 159).

Cost containment strategies

Cost containment strategies vary significantly across health systems. The objective might be to slow the rate of increase in costs, or to stop costs from rising in real terms, or to actually reduce the costs of health care in real terms. The health care sectors to which a particular cost containment strategy is targeted will vary depending on whether the health services are financed by the government: (1) on a direct budget basis; (2) through public contracts with independent providers such as physicians paid on a fee-for-service basis or hospitals paid per item of service provided; or (3) by the private marketplace. As seen in Chapter 3, countries with national health services, such as the UK and New Zealand, as well as several without, such as Singapore and Japan, exercise direct budgetary control, while countries such as Germany, France and the Netherlands rely more on the second, contractual-based approach. In contrast, the USA, and to a lesser extent Australia, depend upon a less effective mixture of approaches, including those based in the marketplace. The capacity for effective cost containment policies, therefore, varies considerably from one country to the next.

A good example of a country with effective controls is Sweden, which has a national health service and where the general rule of 'public funding makes for public control' applies. However, in contrast to Britain and New Zealand (but similar to Australia) the control over funding is decentralized, since health care is predominantly funded from taxes raised by the regional tier of government, county councils. 'Macro-level' measures of cost containment vary, because county councils decide on the rate of regional taxation, the majority of which goes to health care. Besides this, global budgets play an important role and county councils may allocate funds to districts using needs-based global budgets. Similarly, county councils or districts may fund health centres and hospitals using global budgets in conjunction with other forms of payment. The only true 'macro-level' measure of cost containment is when central government decides to control total expenditure by putting taxation limits on county councils, as it did during the severe recession in the early 1990s (Rehnberg, 1997: 66).

Cost containment strategies can operate on either the *demand* or the *supply* side of health care. Additionally, they can be carried out through a direct, regulatory edict (macro-management) or through indirect incentive systems aimed at providers and patients (micro-management). Furthermore, depending on the system, the major efforts can be initiated and implemented either by public agencies – national, state or local – or by the private sector. According to Reinhardt (1990: 107), European countries tended to emphasize macro-management strategies such as global budgets to control their health systems, while the USA, with its basic fear of centralized control, largely rejected regulatory macro-management opting instead to fine-tune financial incentives for health care. However, even in Europe this is changing with more moves to micro-manage some aspects (see Chapter 5 on doctors: p. 132).

Demand side

Demand-side cost containment strategies depend primarily on strategies designed to reduce consumer demand and increase patient consciousness of the costs of providing care. Usually this is accomplished by requiring some form of cost sharing by the users of health care. This might be done through user charges as a flat rate per unit of service (e.g., $50 per hospital night, $20 per doctor visit, $20 per prescription), some proportion of the cost (e.g., 20 per cent of outpatient costs, 30 per cent of inpatient costs), or some combination. Out-of-pocket costs are normally applied at the time of use with the explicit goal of discouraging user demand and, by extension, acting indirectly on physicians to reduce services through the knowledge that the patient must share in the cost. Another approach is to require deductibles or excesses (e.g., the first $100 per condition) which the consumer must pay, thereby discouraging demand.

Among our countries, the form of demand-side strategies varies significantly. In Germany, for instance, co-payments are the most common form of out-of-pocket payments. Co-payments have a long tradition, particularly in relation to drugs, but increased considerably in the early 1990s and are now at 10 per cent of the expenditure on pharmaceuticals (European Observatory on Health Care Systems, 2000: 46). With increasing cost pressures, co-payments in other areas have been added, including charges for inpatient days in hospitals, rehabilitative care facilities, ambulance transportation, and dental treatment as well as crowns and dentures.

In contrast, in the Netherlands out-of-pocket payments play a marginal role. Only co-payments for glasses have been a long established feature of the Dutch health system. In comparison to other countries, co-payments have not been extended significantly, thus reflecting entrenched expectations that all health care should be free at the point of use. However, this is different for the exceptional medical risks scheme, where in 1993 about 5.5 per cent of funds came from co-payments (Maarse, 1997: 150). The situation in relation to private health insurance is similar. In addition, since 1993 people covered by the social health insurance for acute risks have to pay a flat rate premium directly to their sickness fund. In 1995 this constituted 10 per cent of the total health expenditure (Ven, 1997: 91). The flat-rate premiums are set by individual insurance funds and are the key component for insurance funds to compete for customers, who have free choice of insurance fund.

Out-of-pocket payments in Sweden exist in form of direct, small patient fees that are paid for receipt of medical attention. The payments are a flat rate and are set by the county councils; however, the national Parliament sets ceilings on the total to be paid by patients annually (European Observatory on Health Care Systems, 2001: 28). There are separate co-payments for drugs, which are set by central government and are uniform across the country. In the UK, out-of-pocket payments take the form of co-payments. Prominent areas of cost sharing include: drugs, where co-payments have risen steeply over time; dental services, where patients have to cover 80 per cent of the costs up to a maximum; and ophthalmic services that have been widely de-regulated (Baggot, 1998; for a good European comparison of cost sharing arrangements, see Ros, Groenwegen and Delnoij, 2000).

The major assumption of demand-side cost containment measures is that use of services will decrease when market incentives are implemented which make patients bear a significant part of the costs. Studies have found that cost sharing through either supplementary insurance or deductibles does, indeed, reduce health spending. The European Observatory on Health Care Systems (1999: 41) refers to a study on the UK showing that, despite the existence of widespread exemptions, changes in prescription charges can have a noticeable impact on the number of prescriptions dispensed. The study estimates that even the modest increase in prescription charges from £3.75 to £4.25 per item in 1993 resulted in a reduction of 2.3 million in the number of prescriptions dispensed compared with the number that would have been dispensed if charges had not risen.

Similarly, in the USA a Rand Corporation study found that outpatient spending was 46 per cent lower among individuals enrolled in health plans that required 5 per cent co-insurance compared with those in free care plans. The 25 per cent co-insurance plans produced the largest difference from the free care plan. Likewise, outpatient spending was 30 per cent lower and inpatient spending 10 per cent lower under individual deductible plans. Moreover, cost sharing reduces adult hospital admissions by up to 38 per cent as compared to free plans (Thorpe, 1992: 260).

Despite these findings of cost savings, there is some question as to how genuine the benefits of demand-side cost containment are in the long run. The critical question is, does the reduced use of medical resources produced by these policies lead to lowered levels of health for those individuals who do not seek treatment due to cost considerations? In the Rand study, access to more services did not result in better health among consumers who were young, on middle incomes, and in good health. In contrast, access to more services did result in better health outcomes among the poor and those persons with initial clinical indicators of poor health. In other words, while many healthy people can reduce care without adverse health consequences, when ill people forgo needed services, health outcomes suffer. Part of this difference might be explained by the fact that relatively young, healthy and affluent consumers are able to carry supplemental insurance to cover charges, thus undercutting the strategy of cost sharing. Unless prohibited from doing so, those using insurance resources will counteract the apparent cost savings.

Other demand-side approaches to cost containment include the exclusion of certain types of coverage or the reduction of reimbursement for specific services such as glasses, dentistry, diagnostic tests, pharmaceuticals, transportation, and mental health or counselling services. As noted earlier, co-payments for pharmaceuticals represent a common demand-side strategy used by countries with national health services such as New Zealand and the UK, as well as the market driven USA. Moreover, some systems such as Australia and the USA allow extra billing, while others such as Japan and Germany have either prohibited or strictly limited extra billing because of its impact on equity and its overall inflationary effect.

While Germany, Japan, the Netherlands, Sweden and the UK allow no extra billing by office-based doctors working in ambulatory care, a clear example of extra billing is France. As in many other countries, doctors in ambulatory care are self-employed, independent practitioners, and they are paid on a fee-for-service basis in France. The majority of doctors contract with the social insurance system, but up to a quarter depart from the negotiated fee schedule in favour of extra billing, referred to as 'sector 2' (Freeman, 2000: 52). Patients are reimbursed by the statutory social insurance according to the national fee schedule, regardless of whether they choose a doctor who charges higher fees. Patients have to pay for the extra billing themselves, although over 90 per cent have additional non-statutory insurance to cover extra billing and other co-payments (Freeman, 2000).

Overall, demand-side approaches are limited by their adverse impact on access and their inequitable financial burden across groups in society. While the problems of inequity they raise theoretically can be reduced by providing subsidies or a safety net for those unable to pay or by providing exemptions to the co-payments (e.g., New Zealand's policy on GPs), this entails a complicated administrative and monitoring system that in turn adds to costs. According to the OECD, 'it is doubtful whether anything other than modest charges (with exceptions for poor and high users) will be either equitable or efficient' (1992: 139).

Supply side

Supply-side cost containment measures are generally more effective than demand-side measures, especially when they entail the imposition of direct, central controls on payments to providers. This effectiveness is reinforced because as providers make decisions for the users, the users are not necessarily informed and sovereign. In commenting on seven European countries, for instance, the OECD concludes that there is a 'strong suggestion that any cost-containment that was achieved came through direct action on the supply side such as the introduction of global budgeting or central regulation of fees and charges' (1992: 148). Other than the USA and Singapore, most countries have emphasized strategies to control the supply side by strengthening the hands of insurers and/or by imposing direct, central controls on payments to providers and on the capacities of their health systems. For instance, during the 1980s, France and the Netherlands introduced systems of global budgeting to replace the daily rates paid to hospitals, thus joining the UK which already had mechanisms for capping hospital expenditures (Hurst and Poullier, 1993: 5). The major instruments of this regulatory cost containment are fee and price controls, control over capacity of the system, and control over wages and salaries. Table 4.2 illustrates the wide range of possible short to long-term supply-side controls available.

Table 4.2 *Supply-side controls*

Short-term direct controls
Budget ceilings for hospitals
Controls on staff numbers in hospitals or clinics
Controls on levels of remuneration
Controls on prices (e.g., per bed day)
Controls on quantities (e.g., per prescription)
Short-term indirect controls
Changing relative value scales
A positive or negative list for pharmaceutical products or chemist
    substitution
Doctor profiles for excess use of diagnostic tests, visits per
    patient, prescriptions
Medium-term direct controls and incentives
Controls over construction or extension of hospitals
Controls over the installation of expensive equipment
Controls and incentives to develop substitutes to traditional
    hospital care
Long-term direct controls on manpower
Controls over number of students entering medical or dental
school
Controls over entry to specialist training

Source: Adapted from Abel-Smith (1984: 3–4).

The most direct supply-side strategy is to tighten controls over reimbursement or payment schedules. This is easiest to accomplish in an integrated system where the government has the capacity to set global budgets. Sweden and the UK are classical examples of integrated health systems where government sets global budgets, in the former case at the regional level.

In Britain, the total expenditure of the NHS is set by the Treasury and is part of the government's yearly general public expenditure planning process. Once the overall spending has been set, the Department of Health determines the funds allocated to regions, and the regions determine the funds allocated to the health authorities and Primary Care Trusts respectively (European Observatory on Health Care Systems, 1999). In contrast, hospitals are funded through contracts: the 'sophisticated block' form of contract, with contracts specifying service requirements relating to the admission, care and discharge of patients, has become particularly common (Baggott, 1998: 193). As such, the UK payment system can be described as a mix of global budgets with elements of cost-per-case payments.

The situation in Sweden is more complex as funding arrangements vary among county councils (see earlier discussion above, p. 81). Some county councils/districts use global budgets to pay hospitals and health centres, while others have introduced a purchaser–provider split. Here, 'contracts are often based on fixed prospective per case payments, complemented with price and volume ceilings and quality components' (European Observatory on Health Care Systems, 2001: 74).

Another approach is that of Germany where cost containment policy means limiting insurance funds' expenditure to a level where it matches income so that contribution rates remain stable. To achieve this, the 1990s have seen the introduction of sectoral budgets or spending caps. The budgets are based on historic spending patterns rather than any needs-based formula (as in the UK). Some of the budgets limit the expenditure of individual funds while other budgets do not impose these kind of limits. For example, the hospital budget is divided between insurance funds according to the actual utilization of their members. At the level of the individual hospital, this has coincided with the abolition of the full-cost cover principle and, instead, fixed budgets are calculated for each hospital. These budgets are targets in relation to service number and per diems and are made up of prospective case and procedure fees, introduced in 1996, as well as the old, prospective per diem charges (European Observatory on Health Care Systems, 2000: 101f.). Furthermore, since 1989 fixed regional budgets exist. This means that the fees for individual services are not fixed, but vary depending on the total budget negotiated with the insurance fund and the total volume of services delivered within the regional association of insurance fund doctors.

Global budgets for hospitals are more effective than price or volume controls alone because they cannot be avoided by raising volume when prices are fixed or prices when volume is fixed. Usually, although not always, discretion is given to local managers to spend within the prospective budget. Budget caps work provided there is the political will to enforce them, but they can be politically risky because they make the central government responsible for the failure of micro-decisions. In other words, global budgets allow hospitals to blame the government policy makers for shortfalls in service due to lack of adequate funding levels. Because hospitals consume the majority of health spending, this single approach is effective; however, budget caps are less effective when the government grants additional funds to those hospitals that overspend and require supplements to their budgets in order to keep operating. According to the OECD, the analysis of per capita health expenditure across all OECD nations suggests that hospital global budgets reduce total national health expenditures by about 13 per cent (1992: 141).

One problem with global budgets is that they might effectuate cost containment by forcing hospitals to cut corners, thus providing a lower quality of care. Because they do not readily distinguish as to the quality or intensity of care, there are often no rewards for *good* economical treatment. Although this problem can be minimized by close auditing of quality, global budgets themselves are not sufficient to protect consumers because the focus is on lowering the costs per case. In terms of the goal of containing costs, however, any form of prospective payment will succeed by relating rewards to planned workload and encouraging awareness of cost per case. In contrast, any system with open-ended retrospective reimbursement for hospitals, such as traditional private insurance in the USA, will have higher expenditures per capita (Blank, 1997).

Although global budgets are more easily implemented if there is one central authority, single-source funding is not essential. Germany and the Netherlands, for example, have been successful in securing cost control in systems composed of many payers. As noted above (p. 98), Germany has accomplished this by the combination of changing the payment to providers and centralizing control of funding. The 1990s saw the partial introduction of a system of prospective payments in hospitals. In ambulatory care, a maximum ceiling for fees per patient was introduced, co-existing with fixed sectoral budgets. At the same time, the autonomy of insurance funds over raising and allocating funds has been curtailed, with contribution rates now linked to the income of insurance funds rather than expenditure. The federal government also has become more interventionist and in 1997, for example, mandated that contributed rates had to be reduced by 0.4 percentage points. Similarly, the federal government sets upper limits for negotiated sectoral budgets for ambulatory and hospital care (European Observatory on Health Care Systems, 2000: 109).

In the Netherlands, cost containment has been achieved by a combination of integrated control over funding and measures of expenditure control. The contribution rates for the two social insurance schemes are set by central government. At the same time, the yearly survey published by the Ministry of Health of current and future expenditure has acquired the status of de facto spending ceilings (Loo, Kahan and Okma, 1999: 574). This has been complemented by regulated competition both between insurance funds for employees and between providers for selective contracting with insurance funds as well as by micro-level measures to increase efficiency.

Similarly, Japan has been most successful in controlling a network of private insurance funds and local providers by instituting a rigid uniform fee structure and prohibiting extra billing. These countries' policies demonstrate that control over medical spending can be accomplished without centralized global budgeting. Although direct price and quantity controls may be less effective than global budgets or direct caps, they are applicable to all segments of health care, including pharmaceuticals, and thus are potentially more comprehensive.

Lacking the centralized regulatory control over health care found in other countries, the USA implemented a prospective payment system in the mid-1980s in the one area it could control, the Medicare programme. As noted in Chapter 3 (p. 73), diagnosis-related groups were introduced to constrain costs of Medicare spending by setting prospective limits per diagnostic category on a fixed schedule. It was hoped that the private sector would follow the lead to reduce overall costs, but this did not happen. There is evidence, however, that this approach alone can not constrain costs in the long run and that it has resulted in a 'revolving door' through which patients are readmitted for new a DRG when the previous one runs its course (Blank, 1997: 142). For instance, while hospitals under the DRG system initially were found to have reduced costs per day by 9.8 per cent and average length of stay by 6.5 per cent, the effect on total costs was offset by an 11.7 per cent increase in admission rates (Culyer, Brazier and O'Donnell, 1988). Moreover, once the initial savings were realized, health care costs in the USA resumed their escalation, surging to nearly 15 per cent in the late 1990s after the one-time savings from managed care began to dissipate.

Other supply-side approaches include controls over construction of hospitals, the purchase of expensive and often duplicative equipment, and the numbers of medical students entering particular specialities. Encouragement of outpatient over inpatient facilities and a reduction in the oversupply of acute hospital beds are likely to constrain costs, as is the shift from more expensive hospital beds to nursing homes or home care (see Chapter 6). The changes in Germany are an example of a shift towards this strategy. Traditionally, the monopoly of office-based doctors over the delivery of ambulatory care has hindered the development of outpatient facilities. However, in the face of cost pressures, hospitals are now allowed to offer day surgery, pre-admission diagnostic procedures, and post-discharge treatment. Furthermore, the role of the outpatient departments of university hospitals in the provision of highly specialized care has been recognized through special contracts with insurance funds.

Meanwhile, in the Netherlands there has been a reduction in the capacity for inpatient care and day surgery has expanded (Maarse, 1997: 141). This has gone hand in hand with increasingly tight government regulation of hospitals. For example, the Hospitals Facilities Act regulates the number of hospital beds and specialist units. Moreover, all major investments in hospitals and hospitals need the formal approval of the Minister of Health if any additional facility is to be reimbursed through social health insurance (Maarse, 1997: 142).

Throughout the 1990s, Sweden saw a substantial decline in the number of hospital beds that was more drastic than in other countries (European Observatory on Health Care Systems, 2001: 49). At the same time, the position of ambulatory care was strengthened. The 1995 Primary Care Act for the first time acknowledged primary care as a separate level of care and defined primary care as the basis of the organization and health care. This is significant, because compared to other European countries primary care in Sweden has traditionally been less developed. For example, 46 per cent of all outpatient visits in Sweden are made at hospitals instead of health centres (European Observatory on Health Care Systems, 2001: 38).

As in other countries, at least at the level of rhetoric there has been a turn away from hospitals. Instead, ambulatory care settings seem to hold the promise of both tailored and cost-effective care. Both points are particularly relevant in the context of the British NHS where patient demand often appears to remain unmet and where successive governments have been interested in making existing funds go further. In the NHS, this is epitomized in the vision of a 'primary care-led' health service where GPs have become key players, not only in the provision, but also in the organization of health services. Following the purchaser–provider split in the early 1990s, GPs were given the option of becoming 'fund holders' and receiving funds to purchase a range of diagnostic and elective procedures. The health reforms under the New Labour government in 1997 built on these developments. GPs' practices have now become so-called 'Primary Care Trusts'. As part of these trusts, GPs are responsible for the commissioning of all health care services in their areas while remaining responsible for the provision of ambulatory health care services.

A final supply-side strategy to cost containment is the creation of competitive market conditions under which the more efficient providers will thrive and the relatively more costly ones will be driven out of existence. One such approach entails separating the funding and providing functions and thus, it is assumed, opening up competition among providers. In the UK internal market, introduced in the early 1990s, for instance, self-governing public hospitals, together with private sector hospitals, were envisaged as competing for contracts with the health authorities that funded secondary health. Because of the controversy surrounding these moves to incorporate marketplace mechanisms and their breadth over the past decade, it is important to look at role of market and health care in more detail.

The government and the marketplace

One trend in many public health systems is towards inclusion of market or quasi-market mechanisms to provide incentives to improve efficiency (see Ranade, 1998). This trend has been fuelled by ideological shifts towards neo-liberalism across Western democracies since the 1980s. According to neo-liberalism, public sector monopolies provide few incentives for system efficiency and are likely to contain perverse incentives which in effect punish efficiency (see Heywood, 1997: 48ff). Despite this paradigm shift, evidence suggests that a totally free market in health insurance can produce neither equity nor efficiency. Therefore, even in the USA, clearly the most market-oriented system, the government exerts considerable regulatory influence over the workings of the market and, despite this, it remains the least successful effort in controlling costs. As with other aspects of health policy, the approach a particular government takes is dependent upon the ideology of past and present governments and the predominant models of health care finance and delivery.

Generally, governments can take one of two main routes in regulating health care systems, although as Saltman (2002) suggests the two approaches often exist side by side. The first approach involves regulation in the more conventional sense of setting constraints on the non-public sector. This detailed command-and-control type of activity is generally designed to supplant and override market forces and institutions. This can be effected by specifying coverage of insurance policies, regulating membership and premiums, controlling the quantity and quality of prices, mandating set fee structures and schedules, fixing wage rates, and controlling planning capacity.

For example, although the Japanese health system is largely non-public, over 5,000 independent insurance plans and the largely private providers are highly regulated by the government through the universal fee structure, centralized billing and payment, standard co-payments, and prohibition of extra billing. Despite the predominance of the private sector in the USA, providers, especially hospitals, face many constraints as a result of the regulation by local, state and national government. In fact, some observers argue that the major problem in health care even in the USA is overregulation (Califano, 1992). If the competitive market were left to operate on its own, they contend, medical care dilemmas would dissipate.

The second approach a government can take is to foster an environment for promoting self-regulation by the health-care community. Such measures are generally included under the rubric of pro-market or pro-competitive policies. The goal of these policies is to maximize autonomy for insurers, providers and consumers through the operation of traditional marketplace principles. The government's role here is to provide an appropriate balance among the various stakeholders such as it would in other areas of the economy. Furthermore, the government has a responsibility to ensure proper incentives for the provision and consumption of health care resources. The major assumption of this approach to regulation is that a free market for health care can regulate itself if given the opportunity by the government. Supporters of this strategy generally contend that the health care system is in effect a large business and that, if left alone to operate according to the principles of supply and demand, it will best serve the consumer public. Regulation, it is contended, interferes with the effective operation of the marketplace and creates artificial inequities in the system.

The fallacy of this approach is that the health care market contains none of the self-selecting mechanisms that work to check market excesses. In order for an efficient, market-based health care system to work, several conditions are essential. First, all decisions must be the consumer's. Second, consumers must know the value and costs of the goods they are contemplating purchasing. Third, consumers must pay the full cost and receive the full value of the goods they choose to buy.

Importantly, not one of these conditions is present in the market for health care services. First, no medical decisions are solely that of the patient. Although some discretion is possible, ultimately the individual patient's choice is heavily conditioned and constrained by the providers of health care. Second, most patients have a difficult time judging the value of the care they get. As a result, health care providers have enormous discretion in deciding both the type and cost of care provided. The specialized knowledge required for the dispensation of health care, in conjunction with the emotional and often urgent nature of medical decisions, undercuts the patient's ability to be a rational shopper. Furthermore, it does not follow that more informed consumers of health care will buy for lower cost. In fact, evidence suggests that knowledge often leads to higher costs because patients with more knowledge tend to be more demanding in terms of the drugs, tests and treatments they want for themselves (Ubel, 2001).

The major reason that patients are unlikely to be frugal consumers as assumed by marketplace models, however, is the failure to meet the third condition. Third-party payment, whether public or private, ensures that the potential consumer who receives the value pays only a fraction of the costs, if any. Under this incentive structure, it is well known that people consume more when they do not pay the full cost of something than they would consume if they did (Ubel, 2001: 32). Also, while health economists might put cost containment first, politicians are likely to emphasize access and thus drive up the expectations of the public for an ever-expanding array of services.

In addition to the asymmetry of knowledge and power between patients and health care professionals, the inability of health care consumers to judge the value of the services they receive, and the general failure of traditional marketplace mechanisms to produce efficiency, risk spreading through insurance is essential. Although private insurance can spread the risk and the burden of payment, private insurers have an incentive to exclude, or at least raise premiums against, high-risk individuals. Typically, private health insurance is most affordable to people who are healthy while most health care is consumed by sick people unable to get reasonable private insurance. Income redistribution based on market principles is therefore not possible without intervention that negates those very principles of supply and demand. To some extent, then, a social insurance mechanism is critical to resolve this problem.

Health insurance, either social or private, is accompanied by over-consumption because neither the patient nor the physician has an incentive to economize when an amorphous third party is paying the bill. This *moral hazard* problem is by no means unique to private insurance, and in fact is inherent in any third-party payment system (see Box 4.1). However, without strict controls and a restructuring of the traditional market functioning, both equity and efficiency are lacking. Pure market solutions are bound to fail in the long run because they serve to reaffirm claims to unlimited resources by those persons who can afford it or are covered. Although there are steps that can be taken by governments to modify the marketplace (e.g., move from retrospective to prospective payment systems), adequate regulation requires inclusion of bureaucratic controls in order to shape the diverse demands of the health care marketplace. While this does not negate any role for the market, alone it is insufficient to deal with the peculiarities of health care.

There are ways of controlling the non-public sector, however. As noted earlier, although Japan's health care system is dominated by the private insurance sector and providers compete for patients, all sectors are strictly regulated through a centralized national fee schedule. While universal coverage guarantees access to available health care, in large part, the uniform fee schedule has been effective in containing total health care expenditures and has a critical role in setting allocation priorities. It serves as an allocation mechanism by providing a financial incentive structure for the provision of selected services (i.e., primary care) by setting the fee allowed higher than the actual costs. In contrast it can discourage medical applications deemed undesirable by setting the allowable fees lower than the actual costs. For Ikegami (1992: 691) the schedule is a 'powerful tool' for promoting certain services and thus shaping the distribution of health care resources.

In addition to Japan, other countries actively intervene in private health care markets with detailed regulations of the command and

---

Box 4.1   What is moral hazard?

You have just finished a meal with a group of five of your friends at a fancy restaurant, and the waiter rolls by with a cart of desserts at a price of £6 each. You are hesitant to order because you are full and do not think you can get £6 worth of pleasure from the dessert. Then in a flash of brilliance, you remember that you are splitting the bill six ways, meaning the cost of the dessert to you will be only £1. Surely, you will be able to get a pound's worth of pleasure so you go ahead and order. Unfortunately, your friends, reasoning the same as you, all order a dessert. As a result, each of you pays the full price for a dessert that none of you would have spent £6 on. 'Health care insurance, like the single check in a restaurant, distributes expenses across many people, creating an incentive to buy health care services that cost more than they are worth, a phenomenon health economists refer to as moral hazard' (Ubel, 2001: 31).

Moral hazard, then, is the term used by economists when referring to the behavioural changes that occur when people are put in a position to spend or risk the funds of others (Havighurst, 2000). The bottom line is that unless there are strong incentives not to do so, people will generally want more when someone else is paying for the service. A major objective of moves towards managed care in the USA and elsewhere is to curb this moral hazard by limiting services that the insured can purchase at the plan's expense. Other attempts to rein in moral hazard are co-payments, the medical-necessity test, and medical savings accounts as found in Singapore.

---

control type. In the Netherlands, for instance, private insurers are mandated to provide basic insurance at set premiums for certain high risk individuals who are not eligible for public insurance. In contrast, in the UK, where private insurance plays only a supplementary role, there is little regulation of the private insurance market, while in the USA regulation is widespread but largely unco-ordinated, confusing and often counterproductive.

Although many traditionally public health systems have undergone reforms aimed at increased reliance on market or quasi-market mechanisms, in all cases the governments have maintained firm control. Germany, the Netherlands, New Zealand, Sweden and the UK have introduced or strengthened competition among the providers in their health systems without sacrificing cost control and universal coverage.

In Sweden, New Zealand and the UK, the so-called 'purchaser–provider split' was introduced in an attempt to mimic market mechanisms and to stimulate competition among providers. In the UK, the initial internal market with its emphasis on regulated competition has been replaced by a public contract model, which aims to build on long-term co-operation (Ham, 1999). For example, contracts have been replaced by long-term service level agreements and purchasers have become commissioners: that is, organizations that are concerned not only with paying for services but also with planning. In contrast to the UK, the introduction of the purchaser–provider split has been much less widespread in Sweden, reflecting the high degree of decentralization in the health system.

Meanwhile, in Germany and the Netherlands, the introduction of market mechanisms has focused on competition among purchasers (rather than providers): that is, the insurance funds. This was brought about by allowing employees a free choice of insurance fund, thus breaking with the tradition of occupationally-based health insurance. In Germany, the insurance funds compete for employees on the basis of the contribution rate. To mitigate the unequal distribution of health risks, a risk adjustment mechanism has been established so that in theory at least differences in contribution rates reflect the efficiency with which insurance funds manage their finances (Lieverdink and Made, 1997). However, in the Netherlands, the flat-rate premium which employees have to pay directly to their insurance fund is the key component for purchaser competition.

Although cost containment, accompanied by market mechanisms, became a central tenet of health policy reforms of the 1980s and 1990s, by itself it has not proved to be a sensible objective as evidenced by the USA. The major goal of health policy should not be to save money, but rather to promote the health and welfare of the population. To the extent that these cost-containment measures undermine this broader goal, they invite condemnation. On the other hand, it is evident that without successful initiatives to constrain costs, health care systems face severe funding crises, and perhaps breakdown, in the not too distant future. Because of these counterpressures, the problem of priority setting in health care will become an even more incendiary an issue than it now is. Central to this is the issue of rationing medicine.

Allocation and rationing: the need to set priorities

Allocation decisions are necessary at several levels: allocation to health care; allocation within health care; and rationing at the individual level. The first level, macro-allocation, requires a decision as to how much of its resources society is willing to devote to health care: 5 per cent of GDP, 10 per cent of GDP or 15 per cent of GDP? What priority does society place on spending for medical care as compared to education, housing, social welfare, national security, and leisure or recreation?

Also, would increased allocation to medical care actually improve the health of the population if the funding came at the expense of education, welfare and housing? (See Chapter 7 for expanded discussion of this issue: p. 205.)

Once society faces this issue, it must decide how these resources are to be allocated among the various competing categories of spending within health care, to particular forms of treatment, and to specific disease categories. Should priority be placed on preventive medicine, health promotion and primary care, or on more individual intensive high-technology medicine? Should treatment of diseases of the elderly or care of young mothers and children be given higher priority? Similarly, should priority be put on extending life or improving quality of life; the marginally ill or the severely ill; high-incidence diseases or rare diseases; AIDS or cancer or heart disease? At some stage, allocation within health care requires consideration of tradeoffs that can be more or less transparent, centralized or decentralized, fair or unfair, but always controversial.

Finally, assuming that we are unable and unwilling through our allocation policies to meet the health care needs of all persons due to limited resources, rationing decisions at the individual level are unavoidable (Blank, 1988). The ubiquitous nature of scarcity driven by the trends discussed in Chapter 1 makes it likely that the demands of individuals and groups will exceed the available resources, thus requiring the rationing of these resources. Rationing is generally defined as the denial of a treatment to a particular patient who would benefit from it. This could be any type of treatment, but most often it is an expensive procedure or drug. Whatever specific form it takes, rationing policy always results in the situation where potentially beneficial treatment is denied identifiable persons on cost grounds.

Although the term 'rationing' engenders strong emotions, all health systems ration medicine because no country can provide completely unlimited health care resources for all its citizens (Coulter and Ham, 2000; Ham and Robert, 2003; Maynard and Bloor, 2001). Furthermore, despite the recent heightened pressures on health care systems, rationing has always been a part of medical decision making. Table 4.3 illustrates the wide range of ways in which health care can be rationed. Whether imposed by a market system where price determines access, a triage system (see Box 4.2) where care is distributed on the basis of benefit as defined by the medical community, or a queue system where time and the waiting process become the major rationing device, medical resources have always been distributed according to a set of criteria that inherently contain varying degrees of subjectivity. In almost all instances, rationing criteria are grounded in a particular value context that results in an inequitable distribution of resources based on social as well as strictly medical considerations.

Table 4.3   *Forms of rationing medicine*

Form	Criteria used
Physician Discretion	Medical benefit to patient Medical risk to patient Social class or mental capacity
Competitive Marketplace	Ability to pay
Private Insurance	Ability to pay for insurance Group membership Employment
Social Insurance	Entitlement Means test
Legal	Litigation to gain access and treatment
Personal Fundraising	Support of social organizations Skill in public relations Willingness to appeal to public
Implicit Rationing	Queuing Limited manpower and facilities Medical benefits to patient with consideration of social costs
Explicit Rationing	Triage Medical benefits to patient with emphasis on social costs and benefits
Controlled Rationing	Government control of medicine Social benefit over specific patient benefits Costs to society

Source: Adapted from Blank (1997: 93).

Although a combination of these types of rationing is present in every country, different health care systems place emphasis on particular forms. Countries with national health systems, such as New Zealand, Sweden and the UK, have an easier time using more explicit rationing mechanisms through their control of the supply of resources. This is because they have not usually explicitly defined their services, as is common in social and private insurance systems where the contributor has in effect a contract for specific services. In national health systems, the services are purposely kept vague by the government so as to provide more room for manoeuvre. Also, in countries with socially determined health budgets, constraints in one area can be justified on grounds that the money will be spent on higher-priority services in

> ## Box 4.2 Medical triage
>
> Triage, meaning 'choice' or 'selection', is used when many patients simultaneously need medical attention and medical personnel cannot attend to all. The rule is to first serve persons whose condition requires immediate attention without which they will progress to a more serious state. Others, whose condition is not as serious and who are stable, are deferred. This sort of triage is often necessary in busy emergency departments. A second sort of triage is indicated in disasters where the most seriously injured may be left untreated even at risk of death if their care would absorb so much time and attention that the work of rescue would be compromised. As applied to rationing, triage means that some patients will not be treated if the use of resources on them would be futile and would divert resources from those patients who would benefit more.

another area. According to Wiener (1992: 15), this closed system of funding provides a 'moral underpinning for resource allocation across a range of potentially unlimited demands'. In contrast, in a fragmented US health care environment or Singapore's individual responsibility system funded by Medisave accounts it is considerably more difficult to refuse additional services for patients because there is no certainty the funds will be put to better use elsewhere. The lack of a fixed budget, either for government funding or overall national health care spending, makes it impossible to say where money 'saved' from rationing will go.

Not surprisingly rationing is both easier and more difficult in social insurance systems. Legislation and/or contracts explicitly spell out the coverage of the publicly funded health system. In principle, this makes rationing easier as it merely involves excluding certain treatments and procedures from the list of reimbursable services. An obvious leverage is the assessment of medical technology discussed below. In the Netherlands, for example, the coverage of social health insurance has come under scrutiny and homoeopathic drugs have been excluded, while the standard dental package has been considerably reduced. However, the explicit way in which coverage is defined also makes rationing more difficult because it makes any exclusion of services highly visible and therefore potentially very costly in political terms.

Cost containment in both the Netherlands and Germany has focused on supply-side measures, such as reducing the number of hospital beds, setting sectoral budgets and contribution rates respectively, or restricting the increase in the number of doctors. This supply-side rationing is traditionally practised by national health services and depends upon setting strict limits on medical facilities, equipment and staffs. In these systems the availability of resources inevitably affects clinical decisions.

	UK	NZ	Germany	Japan			Australia	USA
Sweden				France	Italy		Singapore	

No Price Rationing   **High Price Rationing**

Figure 4.2   *Degree of price rationing*

As noted in Chapter 3, general practitioners often serve as gate-keepers and deflect patients from overloading the system.

Market-oriented systems must depend on some form of demand-side rationing, however, which is more contentious. The USA, for instance, begins with excess hospital capacity and an oversupply of specialists for patients who have direct access. As a result, the system has the capacity to perform any available procedure, including those that the public system does not cover. Persons with adequate insurance or resources, therefore, are unlikely to accept artificially imposed constraints on their access to medical specialists. Moreover, demand-side rationing in this environment is susceptible to constant personal appeals for coverage and is difficult to sustain politically.

Another distinction is between *price* and *non-price* rationing (see Figure 4.2). Price rationing is common in the USA and denies health care resources only to persons who cannot afford them or who have inadequate third-party coverage. In contrast, non-price rationing, which is common in public health systems, depends on limiting the availability of certain health services, and thus denies medical resources even to persons who have the means to afford them. Of course, one option open to patients in countries with strict non-price rationing is to go elsewhere for treatment and pay for it out-of-pocket.

Another aspect of rationing is that some forms can be carried out only by government action, either direct or indirect, while others fail to distinguish clearly between public and private sector choices. Certainly, as one moves to the more explicit forms of rationing at the bottom of Table 4.3, a more systematic government role is required and thus it is no surprise that these types are found primarily in national health systems. Other forms of rationing, such as public relations and market, often occur outside the public sphere. A related question regarding the government role in rationing and broader allocation decisions centres on where in the government are they carried out: are these decisions made by government, by a department or ministry, by regional health boards, or by individual hospitals? Are these decisions highly centralized or decentralized, bureaucratized or ad hoc?

Furthermore, if resources are to be focused on the provision of appropriate health care, who defines what 'appropriate' is and how is it defined? And what are the criteria for rationing: total lives saved, life years saved, or quality of life years saved? Because there are no clear answers and because rationing is so entangled with problems of cost containment and efficiency, its implementation is potentially very divisive. As a result, each system will use a different combination of mechanisms (Drummond *et al.*, 1997). Although unavoidable, rationing remains a highly charged and controversial concept in all developed nations, and is most often met with contempt. Ultimately, conflicts in rationing health care can be managed only when societal goals and priorities are clarified and acceptable mechanisms are identified.

Some of the approaches to rationing that are widely used are 'first come, first served' systems of queues, triage systems based on medical urgency, and, more recently, systems based on computation of quality adjusted life years (QALY) used to compare patient and treatment priorities (for a good summary of QALY, see McKie *et al.*, 1998). Jennett (1986) offers a set of criteria used to determine if treatment is inappropriate. Treatment should be withheld if it is likely to prove unsuccessful, unsafe, unkind or unwise. According to the Australian National Health and Medical Research Council, however, even if these criteria were applied universally, 'there would remain insufficient funds for the care of those who are not excluded by these "tests" ' (1990: 9).

Rationing is also often proposed as a means of guaranteeing every citizen a basic level of health care by excluding from coverage those treatments outside this package. The tradeoff here is between universal access to those services deemed basic on the one hand and unequal access to the full range of technically feasible services on the other. In many countries, a *basic* level of health care focuses on low-technology, primary care and excludes high-technology services such as multiple organ transplants, fertility treatments and cosmetic surgery. If basic care is broadened to include unlimited access to intensive and expensive curative regimes, this will undermine the objectives of universal coverage and cost containment that are at the core of most developed countries' health care policies.

It is not surprising that health systems such as New Zealand, the UK and Japan are more successful in providing universal coverage and in maintaining lower per capita costs than the wide-open US system. However, they do so only as long as they somehow limit the availability of high-technology medicine. Once they try to provide similar levels of medical care to the USA, they lose this advantage.

One approach to rationing is to develop a set of funding priorities or list of core services to be funded. In 1992, New Zealand set up the Core Services Committee with the objective of implementing a comprehensive core services strategy to ration health services. The Committee promulgated four principles for assessing a service: benefit; value for money;

fairness; and consistency with the community's values and priorities (New Zealand Core Services Committee, 1992). After extensive public consultation and research on a range of specific treatment regimes, however, the Committee concluded that a specific list of funding priorities with exclusion of specific treatment categories was untenable and opted instead to continue services already funded. Exclusion of treatment categories was not only politically explosive, but also raised questions of fairness and did not account for variation among specific patients within a category.

Another approach was offered in the 1991 Dunning Committee report advising the Dutch government on priorities in the social health insurance (Ham, 1997b: 51). Similar to New Zealand, the Committee proposed a comprehensive approach that would include health technology assessment, the use of guidelines for the adequate provision of care, and the identification of criteria for prioritizing patients on waiting lists. The aim was to provide politicians with tools to decide on a basic health care package. Such explicit priority setting was considered necessary in order to be able to continue guaranteeing access to essential care for all. Interestingly, however, since the publication of the Committee's report, initiatives have focused on assessing the cost-effectiveness of health technologies (and developing guidelines) rather than on choices between services (Ham, 1997b: 54). Again, this reflected professional and public resistance to the removal of certain services, such as contraceptives, from public funding.

The Swedish Parliamentary Priorities Commission, which reported in 1995, was distinctive not only in its cross-party membership but also in its emphasis on ethical considerations of priority setting (Ham, 1997b: 51). As such, the Commission offered different ways of thinking about priority setting to front-line practitioners and decision makers. The primacy of ethical considerations meant that human dignity was more important than the principle of need or solidarity, whereas cost efficiency was subordinate to all three principles. In contrast to the Netherlands and the UK, in Sweden human dignity and the rights of the individual were central. 'Applying this approach meant that discrimination based on age, birth weight, lifestyle and whether illnesses were self-inflicted would not normally be allowed' (Ham, 1997b: 59).

Unlike the Netherlands and Sweden, the UK has not conducted a national inquiry into priority setting. This reflects the fact that in the UK priority setting happens at the local level, often the level of the health authority (Locock, 2000). However, in response to a comprehensive review by a parliamentary committee, the government has articulated its view on the issue. While explicitly excluding services from the NHS was not seen as necessary, it was felt that resources should be concentrated on the most effective type of treatments. This plea for evidence-based

based medicine has been echoed by recent developments in health technology assessment, particularly the setting up of the National Institute for Clinical Excellence, or NICE (p. 118).

Interestingly, the most detailed prioritization system was adopted in the State of Oregon in the 1990s (Box 4.3). Oregon generated a list of prioritized health care services in order to extend Medicaid services to all persons on public support. The criteria used to rank over 700 diagnostic and treatment categories were: the cost of the procedure; its potential to improve quality of life; and the number of years the improvement is expected to last. Treatments were originally put in

---

Box 4.3   Rationing and technology assessment in Oregon

Under Oregon's politically courageous plan, the state would create a list of disorders ranked in descending order from those most to least economically worthwhile. The planners reasoned that by limiting the number of services normally covered under Medicaid, they would be able to extend access to individuals who previously were ineligible. Thus, instead of excluding certain members of the population from having any access, Oregon attempted to ration care according to a priority list of services. Because the priority list limited the number of services normally mandated for inclusion in state Medicaid programmes, Oregon had to apply to the Federal Health Care Financing Administration (HCFA) for a waiver, which it received in 1992.

One problem with the Oregon system that raised charges of discrimination was its use of quality measures. In order to measure cost-effectiveness of treatments, a Quality of Well Being (QWB) scale defined 24 distinct states of health. One thousand patients were surveyed and asked to assign a numerical score to each of these states of health, from a scale of zero (as good as dead) to 100 (perfect health), and each of these states of health was assigned an overall numerical weight. These QWB scores were used to calculate the cost-effectiveness, and therefore the priority ranking, of the condition-treatment pairs. The result of this process was a series of 'league tables' of condition–treatment pairs ranked in descending order of priority.

In order to provide data by which to implement its rationing plan, Oregon initiated its Medical Technology Assessment Program designed to address technology usage and diffusion throughout the state. A Technical Advisory Panel of experts conducts the technical aspects of the assessment and the Health Resources Commission conducts the social policy aspects 'including projecting the overall state cost of providing the technology and assessing the likely net health, social, and economic consequences of the application and use of the technology in Oregon' (Mendelson, Abramson and Rubin, 1995: 87).

broad categories and efforts were made to ascertain community opinion regarding their relative importance. Under the implementation of the Oregon Plan, the procedures to be funded in a given year depend on the total amount budgeted by the state legislature, thus explicitly tying specific treatment to level of health care funding.

Although not as transparent as these attempts to prioritize health care services, the universal fee structure of Japan has a clear prioritizing function through its control over the diffusion of new technologies. More expensive innovations are discouraged because the charge allowed for a new treatment is computed by comparing it to the cost of the nearest existing treatment. Therefore, while one might explain the low rate of organ transplantation in Japan by cultural veneration of the dead and dislike of invasive technologies (Miller and Hagihara, 1997), expensive medical interventions are constrained through the government's strong role in fixing prices. Rationing decisions, then, are made through the broader incentive structure determined by societal priorities reflected in the fee levels. Moreover, the government ensures equity in financing among the multitude of private and public plans and equality of service since providers are always paid the same amount for a service no matter what insurance plan the patient has, even if on public assistance. Although the system has problems with multiple diagnoses and increased volume to make up for fee constraints, overall Japan has created an effective system for eliminating the necessity of making patient-specific rationing decisions at the individual level.

In Germany, priority setting is both implicit and explicit (R. Busse, 1999). In comparison to the Netherlands and Sweden it is implicit, in that there has been little public debate, let alone a formal review of the issue. At the same time, priority setting is quite explicit in that it is part of the contractual and fee negotiations between providers and insurance funds. For example, broad priorities can be expressed by defining the coverage of the social health insurance through a positive list (as in the case of care by non-physicians) or through evaluating the effectiveness of new diagnostic and therapeutic methods. Fine-tuning of priorities is also possible through defining the relative value of an individual treatment as part of the fee schedule. For example, the fee schedule introduced in 1996 reduced reimbursements for the more technically oriented specialists in an attempt to reward generalist office-based doctors (R. Busse, 1999: 78).

These diverse efforts at rationing represent rather primitive initial attempts to face systematically the problems of setting health care priorities within the context of scarce resources. Although none of these efforts has been fully successful, they have helped lay the groundwork for fair and workable rationing approaches. The real problems facing core services initiatives or other prioritizing schemes occur when services that have traditionally been supported are eliminated from the list. Explicit priority-setting efforts will also have to withstand pressures for dramatic, often lifesaving, interventions for specific individuals identified as needing them and the claims that a narrowed core services agenda will magnify the inequities between those with private insurance and those without.

Rationing and the individual

Any rationing of health care resources is complicated because, as noted in Chapter 1 (p. 18), the distribution of these resources is skewed towards a very small proportion of each population. With the shift towards sophisticated curative care, health spending has become concentrated on a relatively small number of patients in acute care settings. It is also important for public policy to know that the high users of health care are predominantly individuals who have unhealthy lifestyles or, as discussed earlier, the very elderly. Ten key risk factors including alcohol and drug abuse, heavy smoking, obesity, sedentary lifestyles and unhealthy diets are particularly prominent among high users of medical care (see Table 4.4). In addition to having more

Table 4.4   *Lifestyle and self-inflicted diseases*

Lifestyle	*Self-inflicted diseases*
Alcohol abuse	Cirrhosis of the liver, encephalopathy
Cigarette smoking	Emphysema and chronic bronchitis, lung cancer, coronary artery disease
Drug abuse	Suicide, homicide, overdose, malnutrition, infectious diseases
Overeating	Obesity, hypertension, diabetes, heart disease, varicose veins
High fat intake	Arteriosclerosis, diabetes, coronary artery disease
Low-fibre diet	Colorectal cancer
Lack of exercise	Coronary artery disease, hypertension
Failure to wear seat belts	Higher incidence of severe injury and death
Sexual promiscuity	Sexually transmitted diseases, AIDS, cervical cancer

Source: Adapted from Leichter (1991: 77).

frequent episodes of ill health, patients with these lifestyles and behaviours require greater repeated hospitalizations for each episode, thus increasing the 'limit cost' of the illness.

There are several serious implications raised for rationing by these data. First, they suggest that any efforts to reduce health care costs must be directed at high users simply because they collectively consume such a high proportion of the funds. Second, they demonstrate that considerable redistribution of societal resources is necessary if these individuals, many of whom are poor and/or on benefts, are to obtain the health services they need. The patterns of health use also raise serious questions concerning the extent to which society can afford to support individuals who knowingly engage in high-risk behaviour. This is a particularly salient issue when these needed services include extensive and expensive interventions such as liver, heart and lung transplantation.

Due to the costs, health systems are under heightened pressure to become more actively involved in personal lifestyle choices. Whether out of concern for fairness, paternalism, strict economics, or a blame-the-victim mentality, momentum has increased for aggressive efforts to effect changes in individual behaviour deemed dangerous for health. This is clearly evident for smoking and drinking. Attempts to prohibit smoking in public places and discourage its use through exceedingly high taxes and to remove the drinker from the highways are being approached with near missionary zeal in many countries. Anti-obesity programmes are likely to follow in some countries (e.g., in May 2003, the UK government announced a controversial plan to deny obese patients NHS care unless they lost weight).

However, what should happen when efforts to change behaviour fail and we are faced with patients who need treatment for self-imposed illness? Should smokers get heart transplants or even by-pass surgery? Should alcoholics who drink themselves into liver failure be candidates for liver transplants? If so, should they go to the top of the organ waiting lists if they are the most urgent cases? Is it fair for those who try to live healthy lives to pay the enormous costs of those who do not? In other words, can it ever be fair to ration medical resources away from those individuals who cause or contribute to their own ill health? The answers to these questions, of course, are in part to be found in the cultural frameworks discussed in Chapter 2, but they also reflect the economic realities of limits.

In an age of scarce resources in which medical goods and services are rationed, the debate over lifestyle choice increasingly will focus on the extent to which lifestyle ought to influence rationing decisions in all countries. More than any other issue surrounding the rationing of medical resources, this aspect of lifestyle promises to be the most

> ## Box 4.4   A $900,000 bill and climbing
>
> Gregory Goins is a 'frequent flyer', a label that many emergency rooms give to their regular visitors. Developmentally disabled and unwell in large part because he refuses to take his blood pressure medicines, between 1996 and 2001 he called '911' and was taken to the emergency room by ambulance over 1200 times. His emergency room visits, ambulance rides and hospital stays have cost the taxpayers over $900,000, with no end in sight. According to the staff, Goins enjoys his notoriety and the treatment he receives which he takes for granted – 'last year they told me my bill was a quarter-million dollars. I said so what? I'm sick. Take care of me.' Is there a moral obligation to treat such patients indefinitely or should society set limits? If so, who should implement these limits?
>
> *Source:*   Extracted from Foster (2001).

poignant. When should lifestyle criteria be expressly entered into the rationing equation? Who is responsible for establishing the criteria? What impact will this selection process have on the practice of medicine? What limits, if any, are there on the care of persons who continually harm themselves? (See Box 4.4.)

The other highly controversial aspect of rationing centres on the heavy use of health care resources by the elderly, especially those near the end of life. Although logically the elderly offer a prime target for rationing and some authors (such as Callahan, 1987) have suggested this, any attempts to explicitly ration medical care on grounds of age alone is unlikely given the political influence of the elderly. In effect, however, a similar outcome might occur if social priorities allocate resources away from high-technology medicine and towards prevention and health promotion, because the elderly are the prime beneficiaries of intensive medicine.

Efforts to control new technologies

As noted in Chapter 1 (p. 9), the rapid diffusion of biomedical technologies is a one factor that works to push up health care costs in all countries. Although the patterns of introduction, diffusion and rationing of new technologies vary across countries, in general those with centralized funding and controls require that new technologies be accommodated within the existing systems of resource allocation. Because tradeoffs must be made between the innovations and current treatment for that particular condition as well as other existing conditions, there is an explicit need to establish priorities. Analysis of the marginal costs and benefits and comparison with existing treatments is critical, and a new procedure might not be accepted unless it is clear that it will have a major impact on health outcomes and/or reduce costs. This section reviews the major medical technology assessment and review mechanisms in our countries.

Health technology assessment has been particularly well established in Australia, Sweden, the Netherlands, the UK and the USA, whereas in other countries it is still in its infancy. MacDaid (2001) offers possible explanations for this. In Germany and Italy biomedical and clinical research has been dominant, whereas the status of health services research and economic evaluation has been low. In the case of Germany this is exacerbated by reliance on decisions obtained through consensus and expert opinion. The importance of economic evaluation also seems to be related to the strength of health economics training, which has a long tradition in France, the Netherlands, Sweden and the UK.

In the Netherlands, when the implementation of the Dunning Report which provided guidelines for the exclusion of some medical services from social insurance coverage proved too controversial, attention turned to health technology assessment instead. The initial evaluation of the effectiveness of 126 existing technologies was undertaken as part of the investigative medicine programme run by the Health Insurance Funds Council (Ham, 1997b: 62). In this move towards evidence-based medicine, particular emphasis has been placed on the role of professional bodies and specialist associations.

In 1987, Sweden established a public agency, the Swedish Council on Technology Assessment in Health Care, which is responsible for promoting the cost-effective use of health care technologies. The Council reviews and evaluates the social, ethical and medical impact of health technologies and then distributes the information to front-line decision makers, including officials in the central government and county councils as well as doctors (Werkö, Chamova and Adolfson, 2001).

Similarly, in recent years, health technology assessment in the UK has received high public attention with the creation of NICE in 1999 (Butler, 2002). The Institute is responsible for evaluating, at the request of the Department of Health, new technologies and care guidelines with regard to their clinical and cost-effectiveness. The Institute's guidance on the effectiveness of specific drugs has attracted particular public attention, among them Beta Interferon for multiple sclerosis sufferers, the flu drug Relenza, and new types of drugs for breast cancer patients. The establishment of NICE accompanied the development of National Service Framework, which set out patterns of care for specific diseases, disabilities and patient groups and the establishment of the Commission for Health Improvement which, in turn, is responsible for monitoring and improving standards at local level (Dillon, 2001).

The Australian Health Technology Advisory Committee advises the Commonwealth government on the costs and effectiveness of targeted medical technologies. The Committee has representatives from the Commonwealth as well as the state governments which have a major provision role and representatives of the medical profession, insurance funds, hospitals and consumers. The Australian Institute of Health and Welfare has also established a health technology division to monitor technological developments and advise the government on whether and under what conditions technologies should be used in Australia. Of the specific major areas studied, including MRIs, various organ transplant procedures and laparoscopic surgery, the recommendations have led to introduction of these new techniques, although on a controlled basis (Palmer and Short, 2000: 207–8).

In the USA, assessment of medical technology has been widespread in both the private and public sectors, but there has been little co-operation, co-ordination or even exchange of data among the many assessment efforts. In 1984, Congress passed legislation that extended the mandate of the then National Center for Health Services Research to include not only considerations of safety and efficacy, but also cost-effectiveness, and changed its name to the National Center for Health Services Research Assessment/Health Care Technology Assessment (NCHSR/HCTA). The law also instituted a Council on Health Care Technology under the sponsorship of the National Academy of Sciences, with partial governmental support. After considerable problems in soliciting long-term private support to match federal grant monies and in gaining co-operation from groups in the private sector, the Council was ultimately abandoned. Its demise again reflected the uncertain attitudes both in the private and public sectors regarding limiting the diffusion of medical technology in the USA.

In part because of a lack of effective national guidance in the USA and largely driven by rapidly expanding Medicaid costs, individual states have begun to 'reevaluate their once-limited role in the assessment of medical technology' (Mendelson, Abramson and Rubin, 1995: 84). In a few states, detailed assessments are being conducted on selected technologies. Leading the way are Minnesota's Health Technology Advisory Committee, Washington State's Health Services Effectiveness Advisory Committee, and the Oregon Medical Technology Assessment Program (see Box 4.3). Whether the assessment effort these states will be successful depends on adequate funding as well as private and public co-operation. More critically, the jury is still out on whether such efforts will in fact achieve the primary goal of containing costs.

Medical technology assessment in Germany has tended to lag behind other countries and until recently was focused on the licensing of pharmaceuticals and medical devices (Perleth, Busse and Schwartz, 1999). Beyond that, the assessment of medical technology is linked to the coverage specified in contracts with health care providers: that is, hospitals and office-based doctors. In the case of ambulatory care, where regulation has developed furthest, the federal committee of doctors and insurance funds has to decide on the effectiveness of new technologies to be covered by health insurance. In 1997, the remit of the committee was extended to include the evaluation and re-evaluation of existing technologies. The evaluation itself is based on the criteria of benefit, medical necessity and efficiency. As assessments are sector-specific, overall the system of medical technology assessment is rather fragmented (R. Busse, 1999). However, following the 2000 health reforms, the German Institute for Medical Documentation and Information has been charged with establishing a database with relevant research results and related decisions by the joint self-administration and other bodies.

Trends in priority setting

This discussion of health care goals and priorities demonstrates that while there has been convergence in some areas, by and large the countries have adopted different strategies to deal with the problems facing them. For instance, while there has been a shift in goals in all countries towards cost containment, the emphasis on an array of demand- and supply-side approaches shows much diversity across these countries. Also, while the inclusion of efficiency or cost containment as a goal appears universal, there remain wide differences among the countries as to the degree of access and equity in their respective health care systems. Similarly, although all countries have integrated some aspects of the market into their systems through recent reforms, the wide variation in both form and degree would argue against the conclusion that they are converging to a market-driven health system. Far from it! Unlike the USA, other countries continue to maintain relatively robust regulatory controls over the market forces.

In regard to the allocation and rationing of health care resources, about the only perceivable convergence is the fact that all countries must increasingly ration medicine because, in the light of the endless technological possibilities, no country is able to serve all the health needs of their population to the full. Countries with global budgets or other effective supply-side controls are likely to depend on non-price rationing mechanisms and to make harder choices at the macro-allocation level. In contrast, countries that rely more heavily on price rationing forgo setting broad limits, thus risking any chance of equity and any systematic rationing policy. The result is that rationing in national health systems differs greatly from that in social insurance systems and especially the private-dominated systems.

In the end though, all countries are going to have to face the issue of rationing of health resources away from the high users of medicine, including the elderly and individuals with high-risk behaviours. Evidence in other areas here suggests that there will be little hope of consensus across these countries as to whether or how to do this. Finally, because the diffusion of new medical technologies is such a critical factor in cost containment and central to any debate over rationing (it is generally expensive technologies or drugs being rationed), the initial efforts at technology assessment and review outlined here must be strengthened. The process must also be more amenable to the determination of explicit tradeoffs required when a decision is made to fund expensive new technologies: where specifically will the money come from, and what other programmes might be cut. This leads us back to the medical profession which, as we shall see in the next chapter, continues to wield considerable power and have a substantial stake and interest in cost containment, rationing and health policy in general.

Chapter 5

The Medical Profession

The power of the medical profession stems from the fact that health care is largely defined as medical care. Doctors are responsible for diagnosis and as such define patients' health care needs. Doctors also provide treatment, but more often than not this involves (either directly or by referral) other health practitioners, such as medical specialists, nurses, physiotherapists, laboratory technicians or dieticians. This puts doctors in a key position regarding the allocation of health care resources. Health systems and policy cannot be understood without doctors and vice versa. Doctors often enjoy considerable power and are seen as the archetypal example of a *profession*. Autonomy and dominance are at the heart of medical power and refer to the ability of doctors to make autonomous decisions concerning the contents and the conditions of medical work (see also Box 5.1).

In as much as doctors are embedded in specific sub-systems of funding, provision and governance, professional autonomy will always be contingent and relative, and this also points to the complex relationship between doctors and the state. Significantly, professional autonomy and power are part of the implicit contract between doctors and the state. The state grants professional autonomy in return for doctors providing services that are central to the legitimacy of modern states. Medical practice, by virtue of the specialized knowledge on which it is based, also gives legitimacy to the (potentially problematic) allocation of health care resources. However, inherent in this interdependent relationship between doctors and the state is conflict, such as that between medically defined need and the finitude of financial resources. For the medical profession, the challenge is 'to manage the relationship with the state so as simultaneously to appropriate public authority without surrendering to public control' (Moran, 1999: 99).

What are the implications for understanding doctors in the context of health systems and policy? Power emerges as a central theme, as does the complex nature of medical power. Far from being absolute, the power of doctors is relative and varies between different specialities, points in time and countries. This comparative analysis highlights how medical power is contingent upon the specific sub-systems of funding, provision and governance. At the same time, the power of doctors is intrinsically changeable as it is tied up with states and their agendas. Analysing how health care reform affects doctors and their power is key.

Box 5.1   Understanding professions

The understanding of professions has changed over time. Early approaches defined professions by specific traits (such as formal knowledge, long training and high social status) and by a positive role in society. However, these approaches have been criticized for taking the self-image of professions at face value and for remaining largely uncritical. Instead, later approaches focus on the social organization of power. Freidson (1994) for example, defines professions as being primarily concerned with attaining and maintaining control. Control consists of autonomy (that is control over professions' own work) and dominance (that is, control over the work of others). Medical power is highly complex and has both an individual and a collective dimension, comprising the freedom of individual doctors to practise as they see fit as well as activities of doctors' professional organizations. Here, Light (1995) further distinguishes among clinical and fiscal autonomy, practise and organizational autonomy, and organizational and institutional control. Elston (1991) adds cultural authority to her understanding of medical power. Cultural authority refers to the dominance of medical definitions of health and illness.

At the same time, analysing professions across different countries has become an important concern for recent studies on the organization of expertise (Burau, Henriksson and Wrede, forthcoming). This builds on earlier historical analyses that emphasized the diversity of the phenomenon called 'professionalism' and that exposed the Anglo–American centredness of many ideas about professions. For example, Johnson (1995) suggests that professions and the state have tended to be perceived as separate entities, which relate to each other as autonomous professions and the interventionist state. This makes it difficult to understand professions in Continental and Nordic countries, which have traditionally been 'state interventionist'.

Equally, as much as doctors are entangled with health systems, changes in the regulation of medical work also give an indication of wider changes in health systems (Moran, 1999).

This chapter explores the issues of embeddedness, power and change. The first section provides an overview of the medical profession in our countries using OECD statistics. The second section locates the practice of doctors in the context of the respective health system while the third directs attention to recent reforms and how they have affected doctors. The fourth section examines how doctors are paid and what this says about the relative power of doctors. This is followed by an analysis of the political organization of doctors and the role of doctors in the policy process. The concluding section summarizes relations between doctors, health policy and the state.

Who doctors are

Doctors are often thought of as a homogeneous group. The notion of *profession* suggests a cohesion that allows for dominance and autonomy. This corresponds to the idea that medical professionalism is a universal phenomenon (see Box 5.1). However, even a cursory look at statistics reveals considerable diversity among doctors across and within countries, for example, in terms of the number of specialists or the percentage of female doctors. The analysis of statistics naturally remains on the surface, but as an overview provides a useful starting-point for comparison. Through highlighting similarities and differences, statistics raise 'why' questions which demand more detailed analysis. The number of doctors presented in Table 5.1 provides a first indication of the variety that exists between our countries.

In many countries, the trend in the number of doctors per 1,000 inhabitants since the early 1960s tells the familiar story of welfare state expansion, together with a shift towards curative, specialized medicine. In the majority of countries, the number of doctors has more or less doubled. The only exceptions are Germany, and particularly France and Sweden, where the number of doctors has roughly tripled. Beyond the commonality of growth over time, the current number of doctors ranges from 1.4 doctors per 1,000 inhabitants in Singapore to 5.5 in Italy. However, Italy is a clear outlier. The remaining countries fall into

Table 5.1   *Practising doctors, as numbers per 1,000 inhabitants*

	1961	1966	1971	1976	1981	1986	1991	1996
Australia	1.1	1.2	1.2	1.5	1.8	2.0	2.3	2.5
France	1.0	1.1	1.3	1.6	2.0	2.3	2.7	3.0
Germany	1.4	1.5	1.7	2.0	2.3	2.7	3.1	3.4
Italy	n/a	n/a	n/a	n/a	2.9	4.0	4.9	5.5
Japan	1.0	1.0	1.1	1.1	1.3	1.5	n/a	1.8
Netherlands	1.1	1.2	1.3	1.7	2.0	2.3	2.6	n/a
New Zealand	1.1	1.1	1.1	1.3	1.6	1.8	1.9	2.1
Singapore	n/a	n/a	n/a	n/a	0.8	1.1	1.3	1.4
Sweden	1.0	1.1	1.4	1.8	2.3	2.8	2.9	3.1
UK	0.8	0.9	1.0	1.1	1.3	1.4	1.4	1.6
USA	1.4	1.6	1.6	1.8	2.0	2.3	2.5	2.6

n/a = not available

Sources: Data from OECD (2001b) and Singapore Ministry of Health (2002c).

roughly three groups: Britain, Japan and Singapore with less than 2 doctors per 1,000 inhabitants; Australia, New Zealand and the USA with between 2 and 2.6 doctors; and France, Sweden and Germany with 3 to 3.4 doctors per 1,000 inhabitants. The variation is significant and, while there is no ready explanation for it, it may reflect differences in the levels of health care expenditure. It might also reflect government restrictions on the number doctors in the form of limits on the number of medical students or the number of doctors allowed to set up practice outside hospitals.

The differences in the number of doctors also disguise regional variations in the distribution of doctors. This is particularly pertinent in large, unevenly populated countries. Australia is a case in point. There are no legal restrictions on the ability of doctors to establish a practice wherever they wish in Australia. This has resulted in a geographical maldistribution of doctor/patient ratios, which are much higher in the capital cities than in the remainder of each state, especially among specialists (Palmer and Short, 2000: 196). Successive Commonwealth governments have attempted to address the shortage of doctors in the bush, but the imbalance in the distribution of doctors has proved to be persistent, in part reflecting lifestyle choices of doctors (Hamilton, 2001). For example, there is one GP for every 1,000 residents of Australian capital cities while small communities have a ratio of 1:1,700 (Birrell, 2002). Hamilton (2001) argues that even though most doctors receive much of their income in the form of Medicare payments, the government has little control over where they practise. In 1996, the government did require graduating doctors without their full qualifications to take part in programmes designed to address this imbalance. As a result, the number of doctors practising in rural and remote areas has increased from around 5,400 in 1996 to 6,200 in 2000, though rural areas remain underserved (Wooldridge, 2001).

The situation is similar in the USA. Rural areas tend to have physician shortages while urban areas have high concentrations of doctors, especially specialists. Despite incentive programmes through Medicare's massive subsidy for hospital-centred residency training of doctors, isolated areas find it difficult to retain doctors (Medicare and Graduate Medical Education, 1995). The fact that the USA is heavily skewed towards specialists compounds this problem because specialists are least likely to practise in rural areas (Medicare and Graduate Medical Education, 1995). In recent years, rural communities have come to depend heavily on foreign-trained doctors to fill the void (C. Busse, 1998).

Countries differ not only in terms of the number of doctors but also the diversity of the medical profession itself. One feature of this diversity is the fact that doctors are increasingly female and, as Table 5.2

Table 5.2   *Female practising doctors, as a percentage of practising doctors, 1996*

Australia	27.4
France	33.8
Germany	35.9
Italy	27.5
Japan	13.3
New Zealand	29.4
Sweden	35.9
UK	31.3
USA	21.2

Source: Data from OECD (2001b).

shows, in the majority of countries about a quarter or more of practising doctors are women. This can be attributed to cultural and economic developments which have changed the position of women in society and also to more specific state-initiated measures which have strengthened the position of women doctors (Riska and Wegar, 1995). For example, the end to discriminatory practices has helped to increase the number of medical students, as has the establishment of new medical schools with their emphasis on community and primary care medicine. Only in Japan and the USA with 13.3 and 21.2 per cent women doctors respectively, do women account for less than a quarter of all doctors. The traditional dominance of males in medicine in Japan has been resistant to change although an increasing number of young women have entered medicine in recent years. The reason for the smaller proportion of female doctors in the USA is less clear, but it might be linked to the fact that medical education in the USA tends to be considerably longer than in other countries (4 years of medical school after 4 years of university). Also, the strong emphasis on medical specialities instead of general practice might be less attractive to potential women candidates.

Another indication of the diversity of the medical profession is the division between generalist and specialist doctors. As Table 5.3 illustrates, in half the countries there are about twice as many specialists as generalists. One possible explanation is that in specialist practice and in relation to acute care that the medical model of health and illness can excel. The ratio is even higher in Sweden, where the number of specialists per 1,000 inhabitants is over three times as high as that of generalists. This reflects the fact that hospitals have long been dominant in the provision of health care, with patients having direct access to specialists

Table 5.3   *Generalist and specialist doctors, as numbers per 1,000 inhabitants, 1996*

	Generalist doctors	Specialist doctors
Australia	1.1	0.9
France	1.5	1.5
Germany	1.1	2.1
Italy	0.9	n/a
Netherlands	0.4	0.9
New Zealand	0.8	0.6
Singapore	0.8	0.6
Sweden	0.6	2.2
UK	0.6	1.4
USA	0.7	1.4

n/a = not available

Sources: Data from OECD (2001b) and Singapore Ministry of Health (2002c).

in outpatient hospital departments. In contrast, the provision of ambulatory care has been patchy. The other exception is France, where the numbers of generalists and specialists per 1,000 inhabitants are the same. Data for Japan are unavailable in part because, unlike Western countries, in Japan the generalist/specialist distinction is almost meaningless. Medical practitioners are all doctors of medical science, which includes some speciality. Significantly, there is no nationally recognized or formal system of speciality training or registration, and instead numerous academic societies have established their own training systems.

Types and settings of medical practice

In many ways medical practice goes to the heart of what doctors are about. It is here that doctors relate to patients and make decisions about the allocation of health care resources. This occurs at the micro-level of individual clinics, doctors' surgeries and ward rounds but it is also embedded in the respective health system. The sub-systems of funding, provision and governance frame the practice of doctors. The settings of medical practice describe the institutions in which medicine is organized and relate to what Moran and Wood (1993) call the 'regulation of

Table 5.4   *Types and settings of medical practice*

	Ambulatory settings (in either solo or group practice)	Hospital settings
Generalist/Specialist Practitioners[a]	Generalists only Australia, Britain, Netherlands, New Zealand, Sweden Singapore	Mostly specialists Ausgralia, Britain, Germany, Netherlands, Sweden, Singapore, USA
Private/Public Practitioners	Mostly public Sweden Mostly private Australia, Britain, Germany, Japan, Netherlands, New Zealand, Singapore, USA	Mostly public Australia, Britain, New Zealand, Sweden, Singapore Mostly private Japan, Netherlands, Public and private Germany, USA

[a] It is difficult to include Japan in this category as there is no clear distinction between generalist and specialist practitioners.

market structures'. This section focuses on the settings where different types of doctors work and the implications this has for the power of the medical profession.

As Table 5.4 illustrates, hospitals and ambulatory practices are the typical settings for doctors. Ambulatory settings can be further distinguished into solo and group practices. Different settings are closely associated with different types of medical practice (ambulatory settings with general practitioners and hospitals with specialists), although there are exceptions. As discussed in Chapter 3 (p. 74), in the majority of countries, patients have direct access to general practitioners, but need a medical referral to see specialists. In contrast, there is more diversity in terms of the public/private distinction, reflecting the public/private mix of the health systems in which medical practice is embedded.

Hospital doctors are either public or private practitioners, depending on the ownership of hospitals. Further, as providers of specialist care, hospitals are complex organizations that rely on the division of labour between a wide range of health practitioners. This means that specialist doctors depend to a great extent on the work of others when they practise in hospital settings. As complex organizations, hospitals also need management structures that co-ordinate the different parts of the labour process. In addition to being an organizing force, hospital managers personify the rationality of economics, which has come to the fore with concerns about cost pressures and containment. Not surprisingly, potential and real conflicts between managers and doctors have become a prominent issue, and have highlighted the contingency of medical power.

Here, the introduction of market mechanisms and corresponding managerialist reforms are the key. In New Zealand, for example, until the health reforms of the late 1980s and early 1990s, hospital boards were run by triumvirates composed of medical staff, nursing staff and administrators, with the medical staff being predominant on most boards. In large part, the reforms were an effort to wrest control from these boards, which it was felt were self-serving and, thus, not efficient or concerned with cost control. Beginning in 1983 with the government's setting of hospital budgets and culminating in the replacement of hospital boards with area health boards in 1989, a series of steps was taken to create a structure for hospitals that would enable them to 'avoid capture by the medical community' (Blank, 1994). The continual erosion of the influence of the medical community over decision making and the shift in authority to managers and outside consultants has been a contentious issue that at times has resulted in near open warfare between the parties.

Similar developments have taken place in Britain. An important juncture in the rise of hospital managers in the NHS was the introduction of 'general management' in 1987, replacing professionally-based consensus management structures. The underlying idea was that health service management required first and foremost generic skills, particularly those to be found in the private sector, rather than professional judgements by doctors. This, together with the introduction of an 'internal market' in the NHS in 1992, inevitably led to conflicts about the relative power of hospital managers and doctors (Harrison and Pollitt, 1994).

Conflicts between doctors and managers can be expected to be less prominent in Japan. Here, a majority of hospitals (though not usually the high-tech medical centres which are in the public sector) are owned and operated by individual doctors, most getting started as expansions of private ambulatory practices. These hospitals rely on outpatient primary care for a large proportion of their revenues. Furthermore, in Japan the chief executive of all hospitals must be a physician (Nakahari, 1997).

The situation is different in ambulatory settings, because they are not only smaller, but doctors also tend to work there as independent, private practitioners. Solo practice, the traditional way in which doctors have worked, promises greatest independence, whereas group practices are more likely to circumscribe independence. In Germany, Japan and the Netherlands the majority of doctors work in solo practices. The independence associated with solo practice is especially pronounced in Japan. Doctors operate out of so-called 'clinics', about 40 per cent of which have some inpatient accommodation (Nakahara, 1997). Clinics can keep a patient for up to 48 hours and are legally defined as having fewer than 20 beds. The clinics reflect the fact that office-based doctors do not have access to hospital facilities, although most doctors have some degree of specialization.

In contrast, in the USA, Britain and Sweden, most office-based doctors work in group practices. The potential significance of group settings is particularly apparent in Sweden. Office-based doctors work in multi-disciplinary health centres where the role of doctors is not necessarily pre-eminent. This reflects the fact that the provision of health care has long been dominated by hospitals and that the initiative to set up health centres came from political-administrative circles (including the Ministry for Health and Social Affairs) rather than the medical profession (Garpenby, 2001: 264).

However, operating in a group setting can also strengthen the position of doctors as the emergence of regional independent practice associations (IPAs) of office-based doctors in New Zealand and Australia demonstrates. The IPAs act as collective negotiators, contract and fund holders for office-based doctors who are overwhelmingly generalists. In New Zealand, for example, IPAs were originally established to provide GPs with a critical mass for negotiating with the Regional Health Authorities (Finlayson, 2001). A major role of IPAs is to act as umbrella organizations for general practioners in negotiations with purchasers and to manage any resulting fund-holding relationships (Crampton, 2001: 208). Approximately 70 per cent of New Zealand GPs are members of an IPA (Malcolm, Wright and Barnett, 2000). The increasing membership in IPAs has strengthened the negotiation power of GPs and protected their professional status (Malcolm and Powell, 1996). IPAs are also contracted to provide continuing medical education for GPs.

Regardless of the relative size of the practice settings the status of independent contractors is likely to give office-based doctors considerable autonomy. Nevertheless, it is in specialist practice that the medical model with its emphasis on acute illness and specialist knowledge can excel. This makes hospitals the most prestigious setting within which doctors work. A notable exception is Japan, which places heavy emphasis on preventive medicine and primary care in ambulatory settings. The hospital admission rate is about one-third that of the USA and the surgical procedure rate is only one-quarter of the USA's (Ikegami and Campbell, 1999).

In the majority of countries, hospitals are the only places in which specialist doctors practise. Germany and the USA are unusual in this respect. In Germany, hospital work is seen as transitional and is used as a springboard to set up a specialist practice in ambulatory care. In the USA, many specialists practice as office-based doctors. However, as a result of managed care, demand for general practitioners is growing because of their increased use as gate-keepers and to encourage the use of primary care doctors in lieu of more expensive specialists. These moves have raised opposition by a US public which is used to being able to consult a specialist directly rather than having to be referred by a GP (Blank, 1997).

The practice of doctors is embedded in the specific context of hospitals and ambulatory care and their relative position in the sub-systems of funding, provision and governance. This is a truism but nevertheless highly relevant to understanding medical practice. In the case of Germany, for example, hospitals have traditionally been less well integrated in health governance, reflecting not only the mix of public and private non-profit providers, typical of social insurance systems such as those found in Japan and the Netherlands, but also the absence of a system of self-administration. Instead, health governance has been fragmented into contracts between individual hospitals and insurance funds, and into co-existing competencies between the federal and state governments. The fragmentation of health governance (also typical of other federalist countries such as Australia and the USA) strengthened the position of the provider side and left hospitals and hospital doctors relatively untouched by health reforms in the 1980s (Schwartz and Busse, 1997). However, this has been changing as the funding of hospitals has moved away from prospective payments and as the self-administration has been extended to hospitals. A Committee for Hospital Care, consisting of the representatives from the hospital association, doctors and insurance funds, is now responsible for maintaining and extending the benefits catalogue for hospital care (European Observatory on Health Care Systems, 2000).

The situation is different in national health services such as those in Britain, New Zealand and Sweden, which have traditionally been characterized by a greater degree of public integration. Britain is a typical example of a system where the degree of integration of ambulatory care has actually increased over the last ten years. As part of the introduction of the internal market, many general practitioners chose to become 'fund holders' and were given budgets to purchase diagnostic procedures and elective surgery for their patients. GPs thereby extended their managerial responsibilities beyond their own practice and moved closer to the mainstream of NHS management. The reforms under the New Labour government in 1998 took this development a step further.

General practices became part of 'Primary Care Trusts', which are responsible not only for the provision of primary care but also for the commissioning of all other health services within a certain area (Peckham and Exworthy, 2003). GPs now work within an organization that is directly funded by and accountable to government. The Minister for Health appoints the chief executives of Primary Care Trusts and the Trust is subject to government guidance in the same way as hospital trusts are. For example, the Primary Care Trusts are subject to the national guidance on service priorities, which is much wider in scope than previous guidance.

Reforming medical practice

Positioning doctors in the context of health systems provides a sense of the type of settings where doctors work. More importantly, this also gives an insight into the relative permeability of medical practice when it comes to reform. Considering the centrality of doctors in the allocation of health care resources, any reform will, directly or indirectly, affect the practice of doctors. Measures to control expenditure at macro-level have been increasingly complemented by measures to control the allocation of health care resources at micro-level, and it is these measures that can be expected to affect doctors most directly. Reforms directed at the micro-level have included changes to how doctors are paid (discussed in the next section), restrictions on available treatment, and measures of quality management such as medical audit, clinical standards and, more recently, evidence-based medicine.

In any publicly funded health system, available treatment is naturally restricted in terms of both the range and the volume of services (see Chapter 4, p. 96). By virtue of being contract based, social insurance systems such as those in Japan, Germany and the Netherlands have traditionally spelled out more explicitly what services are covered while the commitment to comprehensive coverage has remained more vague in national health services. In Germany, for example, the Social Code Book Five defines the scope of social insurance, which is complemented by the more specific provisions of self-administration. In contrast, the national health services in Britain, New Zealand and Sweden are based on the duty of government to provide services as opposed on the right of patients to receive them. As Harrison (2001: 279) observes in relation to the British NHS, '[t]his enables governments to "cash limit" (that is, cap) increasing proportions of the annual NHS budget'.

However, concerns about cost pressures and containment, together with the move to a public contract model in national health services, have put the issue of restricting treatment high on the political agenda.

This is well illustrated by New Zealand's attempts to define core services as discussed in Chapter 4 (p. 111). Similarly, in the case of Britain, resources became tighter and health authorities were encouraged to manage their budgets by setting priorities. At the same time, rationing received considerable media and academic attention and as a result probably lost its innocence (Harrison, Moran and Wood, 2002: 14). In contrast, market-based systems like those in the USA and Singapore are unlikely to set limits on particular treatments or routes to those treatments a patient might need if they have the resources or insurance to cover the costs.

However, even in national health services the explicit exclusion of treatment is notoriously controversial among patients and not least among doctors because such measures directly constrain medical practice. In contrast, doctors (by exercising clinical freedom) have traditionally been secret accomplices in the rationing of health services (Harrison, 1998). By providing a medical rationale for the necessity or otherwise of treatment in individual cases, doctors have given legitimacy to implicit rationing. In the case of Britain, for example, the national contract states that GPs have to provide their patients with 'all necessary and appropriate personal medical services of the type usually provided by general medical practitioner' (European Observatory on Health Care Systems, 1999: 35). Nevertheless, the alliance between doctors and the state has become fragile, reflecting more assertive and demanding patients, government challenges to medical autonomy as well more general cost concerns.

The emergence and prominence of quality management in recent years has to be seen against the background of the controversies surrounding the explicit restrictions of available treatment and potentially also challenges existing mechanisms for regulating medical work (see Box 5.2.)

Quality management promises to square the circle between restricting treatment, while at the same time ensuring the quality of health care and allowing for (and even using) medical judgement (Harrison, 1998). This solution is particularly attractive because it diffuses blame for potentially unpopular decisions away from government while safeguarding the autonomy of doctors over clinical decision making. In Britain and New Zealand the prominence of quality management has coincided with a move away from purely market-based reforms. The reforms of the late 1980s and early 1990s built on the belief in the superiority of the market and business style management. In contrast, quality management redirects the attention to medical practice, although a medical practice that is expected to adhere to explicitly defined standards. Paradoxically, however, the introduction of market mechanisms has also stimulated the development of mechanisms of quality management. As Herk *et al.*

Box 5.2   Professional self-regulation of medical work

Professional self-regulation has been the traditional approach to setting and ensuring standards of medical practice, and involves licensing and (by implication) education and training. Further, self-regulation is a key indication of the 'professionalism' of doctors and is at the centre of the regulation of competitive practice in medicine (Moran and Wood, 1993).

A typical example of professional self-regulation is the General Medical Council in Britain, which is responsible for keeping a register of doctors and for regulating the education, training and professional standards of doctors. The regulatory ideology underpinning the GMC has traditionally been rather narrow and isolationist and the Council has tended to focus on protecting doctors from market competition on the one hand, and from the interference from the state on the other (Moran, 1999: 103). Similar arrangements exist in Australia, Germany and the USA. However, as recent scandals in Britain have demonstrated these arrangements are not necessarily successful at securing the quality of medical work.

In Sweden and Japan, by contrast, professional self-regulation is less prominent. The bodies regulating medical work are government agencies that include doctors, but not exclusively so. In Sweden, for example, the Medical Responsibility Board, a government agency that assesses and decides on complaints and instances of malpractice, consists of members drawn from different stakeholders in the health service, including county councils, municipalities, the unions of health professionals and the public, all appointed by the government.

(2001: 1,726) argue in the case of the Netherlands '[t]he increasing importance of health insurers as negotiating partners of the providers put[s] increasing weight on measurable quality, on quality indicators, which could be objectified and specified in contracts'.

Medical audit has been a long-standing measure of quality management. As an instrument to systematically evaluate clinical care and increase the accountability of doctors, medical audit has been promoted heavily by governments. However, as Herk *et al.* (2001: 1,721) show in their comparative study of the Netherlands and Britain, medical audit demonstrates 'the capability of the [medical] profession to maintain autonomy through re-negotiated mechanisms for self-control'. As part of this process professional controls have become more formalized and the freedom of individual doctors is circumscribed by collegial regulation through peer review.

The case of the Netherlands is indicative here. The professional organizations of doctors took the lead in developing medical audit in the late

1970s and this helped the medical profession to maintain control. Doctors are well represented on the board of trustees of the Institute for Quality Assurance in Hospitals, and while medical audit has become compulsory, doctors have remained responsible for its organization. The system of site visits as the predominant form of medical audit emerged in the late 1980s (Lombarts and Klazinga, 2001). This was a time of increasing public concerns over health care expenditure and related questions about the (economic) autonomy and accountability of hospital doctors. Here, doctors 'traded' peer-controlled quality assurance in exchange for the government not interfering with the income of specialists. External peers, under the auspices of the specialist scientific societies, conduct the site visits. Being doctor-led and owned the results of individual reviews remain confidential and the implementation of recommendations is left to the group of specialists itself.

Developments in New Zealand have been similar, although the medical audit takes a more individualized form. Doctors on general registration must work under the general oversight of a doctor who holds vocational registration in the same branch of medicine. An overseer is similar to a mentor and assists a doctor to take part in continuing education and audit. Doctors report to the Medical Council, the professional self-regulatory body, every year as part of their annual practising certificate application and each year some will be audited to ensure they are meeting requirements. This enhanced rigour of regulation, combined with the removal of the disciplinary function from the Council to a separate Tribunal, were major innovations of the Medical Practitioners Act 1995.

However, in other countries doctors have been less successful in exclusively controlling medical audit. The USA and Australia are indicative examples of this situation. The expanding role of Medicare and Medicaid in the USA has increased federal government activity through regulations and audits for hospitals that have Medicare/Medicaid patients (which means almost all of them). The states, however, remain the key players in setting and enforcing quality assurance standards for doctors, hospitals and nursing homes. Although the rigour of such programmes varies by state, as noted above, concerns over cost containment have put great emphasis on quality and efficiency. The implementation of quality programmes is in the hands of State Medical Boards, which are government agencies dominated by doctors. This means that doctors have considerable influence over quality programmes, but enjoy less autonomy compared to doctors in the Netherlands and New Zealand.

In Australia, medical acts in each state also provide the principal control over the practice of medicine and conduct of medical audit, and are administered by state medical boards that are similar to the boards in the USA. Furthermore, in the early 1990s legislative action was taken to facilitate the monitoring of doctors in specified areas by the Health Insurance Commission under the Medicare programme. Doctors suspected of excessive ordering are referred to the Medical Services Committees of Inquiry, although the test of whether a particular treatment is acceptable practice falls on local medical community standards, which vary considerably across states (Palmer and Short, 2000: 195ff.). Nevertheless this is an example of a quality programme that is clearly controlled by the payers of services rather than by doctors as the providers of services.

In some ways, clinical guidelines are the natural extension of medical audits because audits assume the existence of standards of good practice against which performance can be judged. Significantly, guidelines have become increasingly evidence-based, and '[t]he emphasis shifted from professional consensus to systematic evidence or from professional endorsement to authority derived from science' (Herk *et al.*, 2001: 1728). From the perspective of doctors, evidence-based medicine is ambivalent (Berg *et al.*, 2000). Evidence-based medicine promises to strengthen the scientific nature of medicine by reducing unwarranted variation in diagnostic and therapeutic practice. At the same time, guidelines may encourage a standardized approach to practice and constrain the leeway for professional judgement. Reflecting this ambivalence, Harrison, Moran and Wood (2002) suggest that clinical guidelines are part of a 'scientific-bureaucratic' model of medicine. Developments in Britain and Sweden illustrate the move to clinical guidelines, although initial rationales for introducing guidelines differed.

In Britain, setting, measuring and improving quality standards has been one of the priorities of the Labour government that came into office in 1997. Here, the concept of 'clinical governance' is key and NHS managers are now responsible for clinical quality, putting particular emphasis on cost-effectiveness. This builds on systems of medical technology assessment developed throughout the 1990s but, in contrast to its predecessors, the Labour government established a set of institutions that would ensure professional compliance (Harrison, Moran and Wood, 2002: 13). The National Institute for Clinical Excellence plays a central role in this and is responsible for evaluating new technologies and care guidelines with regard to their clinical and cost-effectiveness. As such, conflicts between medical and economic rationality are embedded in the Institute's work (Butler, 2002). The Institute can rule against treatment that is proven clinically effective on the basis that the costs to the NHS are disproportionate to the long-term benefits. Technically, doctors can choose not to follow NICE guidance, although this will be difficult in practice. The establishment of NICE in 1999 must be seen in conjunction with the development of the National Service Framework which sets out patterns of care for specific diseases, disabilities and patient groups, and the establishment of the Commission for Health Improvement which is responsible for monitoring and improving standards at local level (Dillon, 2001).

In Sweden, by contrast, the development of quality standards was initially underpinned by the intention to counterbalance the increasing decentralization of the health system. The debate on quality assurance was initiated in the mid-1980s by a government agency, and the National Board for Health and Welfare emerged as one of the key actors in quality management. The Board became responsible for collecting data on health outcomes and good practice and intensified its monitoring of health care personnel and health care providers. Here, guidelines on medical quality are central. For the government, quality management became a 'new means of influencing and monitoring health care' (Garpenby, 1999: 409). Significantly, and in line with the emphasis on consensus building, national agencies only provide general guidelines, leaving considerable space for doctors to develop strategies independently at the local level (Garpenby, 1997: 197). At the same time, although doctors do not have any formal representation on the relevant government agencies and consultation committees, the Medical Quality Council, a body set up by doctors, serves as a pool for recruiting individual doctors into these agencies and committees.

Medical care is at the centre of health reform, reflecting the centrality of doctors in the definition, provision and allocation of health care resources. Macro-level reforms have increasingly been complemented by micro-level reforms which affect the practice of doctors more directly. However, the picture that emerges from our countries is ambivalent. Doctors are certainly under greater pressure to account for their practice, but the turn to quality provides an opportunity for doctors to appropriate measures of control. In many ways, quality management marks the rebirth of medical practice, although under different, more closely defined terms.

Paying for medical care

How doctors are paid is not merely a technical issue; in fact, systems of remuneration are important pointers to power and are at the centre of the regulation of doctors (Moran and Wood, 1993). Here, power refers to the privilege of doctors to be rewarded according to the medical treatment they provide. Systems of remuneration can either sustain or constrain this privilege (for an overview see Jegers *et al.*, 2002). The fee-for-service system, whereby doctors are paid for the individual services rendered to patients, supports this type of medical privilege most extensively. In contrast, in the case of payment by salary there is little connection between the services rendered and the payment received by doctors. Between these two extremes is payment based on capitation, whereby doctors are paid according to the number of patients registered with their practice. Typically, hospital doctors receive a salary, whereas office-based doctors are paid on either a fee-for-service or a capitation basis. Besides systems of payment, another indication of medical power is the role of doctors in the determination of fee schedules and payment structures themselves.

As Table 5.5 illustrates, the payment of doctors is characterized by some variation and includes unexpected cases, such as salaried office-based doctors (in Sweden and in public health centres in Singapore) and hospital doctors paid on a fee-for-service basis (in Japan, the USA, the Netherlands and in private hospitals in Singapore). Significantly, however, in most cases pay is not directly related to the volume of services, and even where this is the case, there are some limitations on payments. If power refers to the privilege of doctors to be rewarded according to the medical treatment they provide, medical power is restricted.

Concerns for cost containment are likely to direct the attention to systems of remuneration, especially in countries (including Australia,

Table 5.5   *Types of payment for different types of doctor*

	Predominantly salaried	*Predominantly capitation payments*	*Predominantly fee-for-service payments*
Office-based doctors	Singapore (public) Sweden	Britain Netherlands New Zealand	Australia Germany Japan Singapore (private) USA[a]
Hospital doctors	Australia Britain Germany New Zealand Singapore (public) Sweden		Japan Netherlands Singapore (private) USA

[a] The USA is undergoing a shift due to HMO movement but is still free-for-service based.

Germany, Japan and the USA) where doctors are paid according to the volume of services provided. Germany and the USA are classical examples of the fee-for-service system and also illustrate its problems. In Germany the Uniform Value Scale (*Einheitlicher Bewertungsmasstab*) lists the services that are reimbursed by health insurance firms, together with their relative weights for reimbursement, which are measured in points. The monetary value of each point varies and depends on the total reimbursement agreed by self-administration at state level on the one hand, and the total volume of services provided by doctors on the other. This constrains the total expenditure on ambulatory care, although not necessarily the incentive to maximize the volume of services at the level of the individual practice.

Nevertheless, the fee-for-service system in Germany remains problematic from the perspective of cost containment, and has seen several changes in recent years. The number of points that can be reimbursed per patient was limited in 1997 and, since the early 1990s fee negotiations have taken place within legally set limits. In addition, doctors may be subject to utilization review, either randomly or if their levels of service provision are significantly higher than those of their colleagues. This has been accompanied by measures to change the system of payment itself including rewards for particular specialities (general practitioners in particular) and specific services (e.g., counselling rather than medical testing).

In the USA, controlling doctors' pay is even more difficult. Office-based doctors are paid through a combination of methods, reflecting the fragmentation of health care funding. Fee-for-service payments include charges, discounted fees paid by private health plans, capitation rate contracts with private plans, public programmes (such as Medicare and Medicaid), and direct patient fees. However, the growth of Health Maintenance Organizations and other managed-care schemes has resulted in changes in the methods of payment away from fee-for-service reimbursement. HMO doctors may be salaried, paid a fee for service, or a paid a capitation fee for each person on their list. However, often there are financial incentives to the doctor to reduce services to their patients. A variation of the HMO is the Preferred Provider Organization (PPO) in which a limited number of providers – doctors, hospitals, and others – agree to provide services to a specific group of people at a negotiated fee-for-service rate that is lower than the normal charge.

By contrast, in Britain, New Zealand and the Netherlands office-based doctors are paid predominantly on a capitation basis, allowing for much more direct control of doctors' remuneration. Britain is typical here, and fixed sums per patient are complemented by fixed allowances and fees for specific services such as childhood immunizations and health screenings.

Sweden is the only country where the majority of office-based doctors are public employees and paid a salary. This gives an indication of the high degree of public integration of the health system, and doctors are firmly positioned in what is a very politically controlled health system (Garpenby, 2001: 263). However, private providers of ambulatory care do exist, particularly in urban areas and the major cities. The providers are private in that their facilities are privately run, although the majority have contracts with the county councils. In 2000, a quarter of medical consultations outside hospitals took place in privately run facilities, while in 1997 some 12 per cent of general practitioners worked in private health centres and 7 per cent as private practitioners (European Observatory on Health Care Systems, 2001: 39f.).

Unlike office-based doctors, hospital doctors tend to be salaried employees. However, in many countries hospital doctors have the right to treat private patients. Private patients are an attractive source of additional income because services are often paid for on a fee-for-service basis and remuneration tends to be high. In Britain, for example, the right to practise privately was the condition on which hospital doctors agreed to become part of the NHS when it was set up in 1948. Hospital doctors were initially opposed to a tax-funded health service and instead advocated the extension of the existing health insurance system. However, hospital doctors were eventually won over by a number of concessions. Besides private practice and pay beds, this also included large increases in salaries for those receiving distinction awards. This led the then Minister of Health to remark that he had 'stuffed their [the hospital doctors'] mouths with gold' (Abel-Smith, 1984: 480 as quoted in Ham, 1999: 11). Senior hospital specialists are allowed to earn up to 10 per cent of their income from private practice, whereas no such limitation exists for those specialists on part-time contracts.

Interesting exceptions are the Netherlands and Japan, where hospital doctors are paid on a fee-for-service basis. In the Netherlands, medical specialists have traditionally been independent practitioners who have 'bought' the right to practise in a hospital and who practise in partnerships. As such, medical specialists contract directly with patients and insurance funds and are reimbursed on a fee-for-service basis separately from the hospitals. However, this changed in 2000 and now doctors submit bills directly to the hospital in which they practise rather than to the insurance funds. As a result, specialist medical services have become more firmly integrated into the hospital budget, which potentially provides a leverage for hospital managers to exercise greater control over the practice of medical specialists (Trappenburg and Groot, 2001). In Japan, hospital doctors are paid by a national fee schedule. This corresponds to the fact that many doctors work as private entrepreneurs running their own hospitals.

Table 5.6 *The involvement of doctors in systems of pay determination*[a]

	Salaries	*Capitation/Fee-for-service payments*
Set by government	Britain (with review body as intermediary) Singapore (for doctors in public health facilities)	Australia (de facto) Britain (with review body as intermediary) New Zealand (de facto)
Negotiated between Doctors and Payers of health services	Australia Germany New Zealand Sweden	Germany Japan Netherlands (government approval required)
Set by doctors		Singapore (for doctors in private health facilities)

[a] The USA has been left out as the system of pay bargaining is too fragmented.

A case on its own is Singapore, where the form of payment does not so much depend on the practice setting, but rather on whether doctors work in public or private health care facilities. Doctors in government-owned facilities receive a civil service pay scale plus a clinical supplement. Those with very heavy clinical loads may opt for an incentive based on their total billings in place of the fixed supplement. Private doctors are generally paid on a fee-for-service basis. The Singapore Medical Association publishes guidelines on fees for billing in the private sector.

The involvement of doctors in the process of determining pay is another indication of medical power. As Table 5.6 illustrates, there is some variation here. However, in the majority of cases salaries and capitation/fee-for-service payments are negotiated between doctors and the payers of health services, although there may be some restrictions (as in the Netherlands). And even where government alone decides, the decision may be based on a broad range of evidence (as in Britain) or be limited in scope (as in Singapore). Significantly, then, doctors enjoy considerable power in relation to pay determination, although they can rarely act alone.

In the case of salaries, the process of pay bargaining involves the usual pay negotiations and medical power depends on the relative strength of unions and employer organizations, together with the overall economic climate. An interesting exception is Singapore, where doctors working in public health facilities are paid on the basis of the civil service pay scale, which is set by government with little input from the medical association.

The situation is more complicated in the case of capitation and fee payments, as they are the basis for many rounds of future remuneration. Negotiations of this type require more bargaining to reach an agreement. Countries operate different kinds of bargaining systems, ranging from payments set by government and negotiated with doctors to payments set by doctors themselves. Britain provides an interesting example of the first variant. In Britain, the government determines capitation payments, fees and allowances for GPs, and salary scales for hospital specialists. However, the Minister for Health normally takes into account the recommendations of the Review Body on Doctors' and Dentists' Remuneration. The Review Body is an independent agency that is financed by government. The government also appoints the members of the Review Body, although usually with the approval of the British Medical Association, the main professional organization for doctors. The recommendations of the review body are based on demands submitted by the professional organizations and the government as well as other evidence, such as the budget plan and the evaluation of statistical material (see, e.g., Department of Health, 2003).

In contrast, in Germany, Japan and the Netherlands doctors' organizations have more direct influence and negotiate directly with insurance funds as the payers of health services. However, in some cases the negotiation process has become increasingly curtailed in recent years. In Germany, for example, the autonomy of negotiations between doctors and insurance funds has been more constrained as control over funding became more centralized (Busse and Howorth, 1999). This began with the introduction of legally fixed regional budgets for ambulatory medical care which replaced negotiated budgets after 1992. The regional budgets have now been substituted with maximum ceiling for fees per patient.

Turning to Japan, we have an example of a country where the influence of doctors on fee negotiations remains relatively unchallenged. The Japanese Medical Association (JMA) nominates all five doctors who sit on the fee-scheduling body and negotiates the fees with the Health Ministry's Health Insurance Bureau. The influence of doctors is further strengthened by the fact that '[i]n effect, those on the provider side must work through the JMA' since 'hospitals, pharmaceutical companies, and other important actors are not' directly represented on the council' (Ikegami and Campbell, 1999: 63).

The organization of doctors' interests and access to the policy process

Issues around the practice and payment of doctors often concern medical practitioners as individuals. In contrast the political organization of doctors' interests directs the attention to doctors as a group and how doctors relate to policy process. The interests of doctors can be organized in different ways, through specialist scientific societies, professional associations and trade unions. An important indicator of power is the degree of cohesion (or fragmentation): that is, to what extent as a group doctors speak with one voice, or at least with different voices complementing each other. This has become increasingly difficult as distributional struggles between different groups of doctors have intensified with pressures of cost containment. At the same time, countries offer different points of access to organized interests, reflecting the specific characteristics of the respective political and health system. The power of doctors to a great extent depends on how states are organized and also on how powerful states are.

As Figure 5.1 suggests, in the majority of countries the political organization of doctors is relatively cohesive, and one organization acts as the main representative of doctors' interests. This normally goes hand in hand with a high membership among doctors. However, as Germany, the Netherlands and the USA show, divisions between different types of doctors have led to the fragmentation of the political organization of doctors. These divisions concern the distribution of financial resources and deepen with pressures to contain costs. The relative collective strength of doctors co-exists with different types of access to the policy process, which are an indication of how the power of the state is organized.

		Access to Policy Process	
		As Outsiders Through Lobbying	As Insiders Through Corporatism
Organization of Doctors' Interests	Cohesive	Australia, Britain, Japan, New Zealand, Singapore, Sweden	
	Fragmented	USA	Germany, Netherlands

Figure 5.1 *The organization of doctors' interests and access to the policy process*

In the majority of countries, doctors have to rely on lobbying government from the outside. As Britain and Australia demonstrate, the extent of influence varies over time and the cohesion of interest organizations is only one factor in this. At the same time, lack of cohesion is not necessarily a bar to influence as the USA, Germany and the Netherlands demonstrate. The considerable influence of doctors in the USA reflects not only the economic power of the medical sectors, but also the weakness of the state in health governance. Germany and the Netherlands (although to a lesser extent) are unusual in that doctors are an integral part of health governance and as such often have privileged access to the policy process. Being insiders gives doctors considerable influence, although this may come at the price of becoming agents of cost containment.

In the majority of countries the political organization of doctors shows a considerable degree of cohesion. This reflects a number of country-specific factors, including the type of political system and the size of the country. Cohesion can be expected to be most probable in small unitary countries such as New Zealand and Singapore. New Zealand, for example, has one primary medical association that has a high level of membership among doctors. The New Zealand Medical Association (NZMA) is a voluntary organization which claims membership of about 65 per cent of New Zealand doctors. As such the Association has a broader-based membership than other national medical associations. The Association also maintains formal links with affiliates including the Royal Colleges and speciality organizations, and acts as the primary representative of the profession in dealings with the government. The New Zealand GP Association (NZGPA) is an offshoot of the NZMA and mainly represents the interests of GPs, although it has remained closely linked to the parent body (Crampton, 2001).

However, even in larger unitary countries the organization of doctors' interests can be cohesive. Britain is a case in point. The British Medical Association (BMA) is at the centre of the political organization of doctors' interests and more than 80 per cent of doctors are members of the BMA (European Observatory on Health Care Systems, 1999: 22). The BMA acts in a dual role as a professional organization and as a trade union. As a professional organization, the BMA promotes medical education and professional development, whereas as a trade union the BMA represents doctors' economic interests. This de facto monopoly puts the BMA in a strong position, but requires the BMA to cater for a diverse range of constituencies within the medical profession.

At the same time, as Sweden and Australia demonstrate, a more decentralized political system is no bar to a cohesive organisation of doctors' interests. In Sweden, more than 90 per cent of doctors are members of the Swedish Medical Association (Garpenby, 2001: 261).

The Association acts as a type of umbrella organization and the specific interests of its membership are channelled through seven professional organizations and 28 local bodies. The Swedish Medical Association co-exists with a range of scientific societies and while the Swedish Society of Medicine is the largest with over 60 per cent of doctors being members, the smaller specialist societies are the more influential actors (Garpenby, 2001: 264). The Medical Association and the Society of Medicine have different responsibilities, although in relation to some issues the two organizations compete with each other (Garpenby, 1999: 410).

In comparison to the countries discussed so far, the political organization of doctors in Germany, the Netherlands and the USA is more fragmented. The USA represents a case of fragmentation along the division between generalists and specialists, which is exacerbated by federalism and the sheer size of the profession. Although less than half of all practising doctors are members of the American Medical Association (AMA), it remains a very powerful political lobby group with significant influence in Washington, DC, and the state capitals. Interestingly, many speciality medical groups have been established which concentrate on their own interests, and at times these contradict those of the AMA. There are literally hundreds, if not thousands, of medical associations at the local, state and national level in the USA, and although the AMA is the single most influential, the voice of the medical community is considerably more diverse than in other countries.

Germany provides another, particularly interesting example as the organization of doctors' interests is divided not only between different types of doctor but also different types of organization. The *Marburger Bund* is the main professional organization and trade union for hospital doctors. The situation is more complicated with respect to office-based doctors working in ambulatory care. The vast majority of office-based doctors cannot exclusively rely on private practice and instead have to provide services under the social health insurance. However, this requires joining one of the regional associations of insurance fund doctors (*Kassenärztliche Vereinigungen*). The associations assume an intermediate position between doctors and the state (Burau, 2001). As public law bodies the associations have the statutory responsibility of ensuring the provision of ambulatory care and organizing the remuneration of doctors. At the same time, they also represent the interests of doctors when the associations negotiate contracts and fees with insurance funds. The tensions inherent in this dual role have become more prominent; intensifying distributional struggles have made it more difficult for the associations to integrate the conflicting interests of their membership (Burau, 2001). This particularly applies to generalists and specialists. The intensifying conflicts have also negatively affected the division of labour between the associations of insurance fund doctors and the two lobbying organizations for office-based doctors.

The relative cohesion of the political organization of doctors is only one measure of collective power of the medical profession. Another, complementary measure of power is the role of doctors in the policy process, and different health and political systems provide different degrees and types of access. This demonstrates how the power of doctors is tied to the power of the state. In the majority of countries, doctors' organizations have access to the policy process as outsiders, mostly through lobbying and some informal consultation.

Britain and Australia, as countries with tax-funded health services embedded in centralist and a federalist political system respectively, illustrate the ups and downs of the influence of doctors. In both countries the relationship between the medical profession and the state has traditionally been close. In Britain, for example, within the Department of Health parallel medical administrative hierarchies exist headed by the Chief Medical Officer. The Officer is directly accountable to the minister and is responsible for giving expert medical advice. However, in both countries access to the policy process has largely consisted of lobbying and informal consultation. In Britain, the fragility of this type of access became apparent in the late 1980s. Reform efforts in part were aimed at weakening the role of the profession in the governance of health care and this also affected on the influence of doctors in health policy, resulting in a widening rift between the parties. Significantly, the medical profession was practically excluded from the policy review leading up to a major reform early 1990s, and overall the insider role of doctors in government has become weaker (Harrison, 2001: 288). Similarly, in Australia, the Medical Association regressed from a comfortable corporate-style partnership to an awkward pressure group when the political struggles over national health insurance legislation erupted in 1972 (De Voe and Short, 2003). Government leaders had faced strong opposition from key players in the health arena and created fractures in the medical establishment. This resulted in a re-alignment of the power structures in the health policy.

In the USA, by contrast, the medical profession seems to have been more successful at maintaining its traditionally overwhelming influence over health policy. The medical sector is consistently ranked among the best organized and financed sectors in influencing politicians at the national and state levels (*Congressional Quarterly*, 2002). This reflects the strength of the 'health care industry', which coincides with a policy process that is typically driven by lobbying. For example, until 1964 when Medicare was initiated, the American Medical Association almost single-handedly blocked all attempts (as early as 1932) at what it labelled 'socialised medicine': that is, any form of government involvement at national level. In fact the Medicare Act passed only because Congress promised in the opening paragraph that nothing in the Act would interfere with the practice of medicine by individual doctors or professional standards.

In Germany, and to a lesser extent in the Netherlands, corporatism means that doctors are an integral part of health governance and this often gives them access to the policy process as insiders. However, as the example of Germany shows, even as insiders the influence of doctors is variable. Together with the insurance funds, doctors form a self-administration, which is responsible not only for negotiating contracts but also for implementing health care legislation. Here, the Federal Committee of Doctors and Insurance Funds is key and responsibilities include defining the benefits catalogue and guidelines that are aimed at the behaviour of office-based doctors (such as the prescription of drugs) (see European Observatory on Health Care Systems, 2000). The role of doctors in the health system is highly institutionalized and codified in the relevant Social Code Book Five. In addition, the federal structure of health governance offers doctors multiple points of access. Significantly, however, doctors are involved in a public role granted to them by the state, and are not first and foremost involved as representatives of private interests. This can lead to the kinds of conflict of interest discussed above and can also constrain the collective power of doctors. Over the last decade the federal government has expanded the scope of self-administration while at the same time circumscribing its activities; the pendulum has swung from (autonomous) negotiations towards hierarchical decisions by the state (Burau, 2001). The government has defined more precisely the substantive issues to be decided and has set deadlines by which agreement has to be reached. As such, doctors have become key agents of cost containment through self-administration precisely because the system of self-administration is adaptable and depoliticizes the implementation of potentially problematic policies (Giamo and Manow, 1999: 978).

Doctors, the state and health policy

Doctors are deeply embedded in health systems and policy as the diversity of practice settings and methods for paying doctors and the variety of initiatives of quality management demonstrate. And since the state looms large in health systems and policy, doctors inevitably have a close relationship with the state. This means two things: medical power will always be contingent, but states cannot do without doctors. Light's (1995) notion of 'countervailing powers' offers one way of understanding the close, but above all changeable relationship between doctors and the state. Here, medical power is seen to oscillate between highs and lows. Highs of medical power (dominance) produce imbalances and provoke countervailing powers originating from the state, third party payers and patients. This in turn and over time weakens medical dominance and strengthens the power of the state.

In his discussion of the Foucauldian notion of 'governmentality' Johnson (1995) goes one step further and suggests that doctors and the state are inextricably linked through the process of governing. Johnson (1995: 9) observes that '[e]xpertise, as it became increasingly institutionalized in its professional form, became part of the process of governing'. It is impossible to distinguish clearly between doctors and the state; the state depends on the independence of doctors to secure its capacity to govern, in the process of which doctors become agents of governing.

However, acknowledging independence does not mean denying changes in the relations between the doctors and the state. Over the last two decades states have become more interventionist, reflecting the need of states to assert their agency in times of concerns about costs. This has considerably changed the institutional context in which doctors work, but significantly has not necessarily reduced the power of doctors (Moran, 1999).

Chapter 6

Beyond the Hospital: Health Care in the Home

Care outside hospitals has traditionally been the poor relation of health systems. Health systems are concerned first and foremost with the provision of medical care and focus on acute illness. Doctors are the key professionals shaping the delivery of health care and hospitals are the primary location. The emphasis is on *curing* as opposed long-term *caring*. Less acute, more long-term health care is typically characterized by considerable diversity; diversity in terms of the range of services, the user groups, the localities of service provision and the professionals involved.

Care outside hospitals includes basic care to help with daily living, mobility and self-care; medical and nursing care to help with physical and mental health problems; therapy, counselling and emotional support to promote well-being; and other social, educational and leisure activities (Tester, 1996). User groups are equally diverse and reflect the support required at different stages of the life span, ranging from severally ill infants to people at the end of life. Other beneficiaries of home care include people with mental illness and handicap, physical disability, drug-related disorders, and progressive illness (Means and Smith, 1998). Care outside hospitals is also located in different settings, such as residential care and nursing homes, day hospitals and sheltered housing, as well as people's own homes. The professionals involved are equally diverse and include nurses, mental health nurses, care assistants, home helps, counsellors and physiotherapists.

The diversity of care outside hospitals reflects the diverse yet interlocking needs of people who require long-term care. Diversity makes care outside hospitals interesting, but also difficult to define, analyse and compare. At the same time, care services are often locally specific and even tailored to particular individuals and it is difficult to identify the typical, let alone to generalize. Further, although care services outside hospitals are central to the health of individuals, they can be remote from the health system. In the context of our comparative analysis of health policy we therefore need to focus on a specific aspect of care outside hospitals, and notably an aspect of care that is closely related to health systems.

149

This chapter focuses on home care for older people. Older people are one of the largest user groups of care outside hospitals and in the face of the ageing of many societies have attracted considerable attention in health policy terms. Home care for older people is also closely related to health systems, as the involvement of nurses demonstrates. Tester (1996: 76) describes home care as 'any type of care and support offered to older people in their homes, whether ordinary or specialised settings, by formal and informal carers'. Home care involves a wide range of activities, from basic, physical and mental care to counselling, support for informal carers and giving information. However, different aspects of home care have in common that the underlying disease is of secondary importance (Boom, 2001). Home care encompasses a wide range of tasks and cuts across boundaries between health and social care, and between formal and informal care. It also involves nurses (rather than doctors), as well as home helps and, most importantly, women as informal carers. Indeed, unpaid carers deliver the majority of home care; it is estimated that formal care represents only one-fifth of the total help older people receive (Jacobzone, 1999). This further contributes to the marginal position of home care in health systems. This chapter focuses on home health care: the health care aspects of home care and the services provided by home nurses. However, given the nature of home care it is important to explore the interfaces with other aspects of home care, particularly informal care, but also social care.

Although health systems continue to focus on curing acute illness, there is now a greater interest in home care and it is becoming a higher priority on the health policy agenda in many countries (Kröger, 2001). This change reflects demographic as well as cost pressures. As the number of older (and very old) people increases, both in absolute terms and as a proportion of the total population, so does the need for long-term care (for data see Chapter 1). Combined with falling birth rates, this also means a greater need for formal care, as the pool of potential informal carers becomes smaller.

Unfortunately, this increase in the need for (formal) long-term care comes at a time of intense concerns about costs and attempts to contain the public expenditure on health care as discussed in Chapter 4. However, for many observers home care promises to square the circle between demographic and cost pressures (Duff, 2001). This is based on the assumption that care in the home is much cheaper than care provided in high-tech hospitals and labour intensive nursing homes. Substituting care in the home for institutionally-based care is also said to be better for older people because home settings make it easier to combine formal with informal care arrangements. This shift in priorities also reflects the more critical attitudes towards the institutionalization of older people that emerged in the 1970s (Jenson and Jacobzone, 2000).

There is no shortage of political debate about the value of care in the home and about the appropriate balance between individual and collective responsibilities. However, it is less certain what is happening beyond the level of political rhetoric and at the level of policy. This question is interesting particularly from a comparative perspective. Home care policies are pushed by demography and costs, but are shaped by country-specific factors. Key factors include how the funding and provision of health care is organized; where health systems draw the boundary between health and social care; and cultural assumptions about appropriate divisions of labour between the state and the family.

Analysing the policies of home care is not only topical, but also offers new perspectives on health policy and systems. Home care highlights the complex interrelationships among different sectors of health care provision and between health care and other welfare services, as well as between formal and informal health care. This powerfully demonstrates the multi-faceted embeddedness of health care raised in Chapter 1. Home care, as well as public health discussed in Chapter 7 also illustrates the fact that many services now central to health are at the margins of health systems.

This chapter provides a comparative analysis of home care and home care policies for older people in our countries. A first section examines the size and importance of home care through an analysis of available figures and, as such, provides an initial overview. The next section looks more closely at the provision of home care and how the organization and the level of provision are shaped by the type of health system within which home care is embedded. Provision is closely tied to the funding of home care, which is discussed next. The relative security and generosity of funding are favourable conditions for the growth and development of home care as a distinct sector of health care provision. Another important factor is the relative strength of policies that explicitly support the substitution of institutionally-based care and informal care with formal home care (Boom, 2001).

The fourth section looks more closely at the interface between formal and informal care and the underpinning cultural expectations about the role of women in care-giving. This linkage is important because, as acknowledged by recent policy initiatives in many countries, the majority of home care continues to be provided by unpaid carers. Under the banner of a greater welfare mix, the objectives of reforms are to integrate carers more explicitly into formal care arrangements and to support carers through payments and related benefits.

The final section of this chapter compares and contrasts key trends in recent policy initiatives on home care and evaluates the extent of change. Has home care merely been redefined by acknowledging the importance of informal care and externalizing costs into the community

(Duff, 2001)? Or have there been serious attempts at substituting (formal) home care with informal and institutional care?

Home care statistics

Compared to other sectors of the health systems, international statistics on home care are scarce and almost non-existent. This paucity of data illustrates the marginal position of home care in health systems. Diverse and often non-public sources of funding, for example, make it difficult to capture in one single figure how much is spent on home care. Also, the organization of home care is often highly decentralized and this makes it more difficult to gather standardized figures across different localities, let alone different countries. Not surprisingly, the statistics discussed in this section are often incomplete and in the main are not directly about home care. Instead, the analysis looks at trends in institutionally-based care, for which more statistics are available, in order to get a sense of the degrees of de-institutionalization in different countries. However, the question as to whether de-institutionalization has been followed by the development of formal home care services remains open.

The total spending on long-term care in Table 6.1, which includes home and institutionally-based care, gives a first indication of the relative

Table 6.1   *Estimated spending on long-term care (1992–95) as a percentage of GDP*

	Total spending	Public spending
Australia	0.90	0.73
France	n/a	0.50
Germany	n/a	0.82
Italy	0.58	n/a
Japan	n/a	0.62
Netherlands	2.70	1.80
Sweden	n/a	2.70
UK	1.30	1.00
USA	1.32	0.70

n/a = not available

Source: Data from Jacobzone *et al.* (1999).

size of this sector of health care provision. The majority of countries spend very little on long-term care, around 1 per cent of GDP. The notable exceptions are the Netherlands and Sweden (for which only the figure for public spending is available), which spend 2.7 per cent of their GDP on long-term care. It is likely that the majority of expenditure goes to institutionally-based care, which is more expensive than home care.

Table 6.2   *Population aged 65 and over in different care settings as a percentage of the total population*

	In institutions	Receiving formal help at home
Australia	6.8	11.7
France	6.5	6.1
Germany	6.8	9.6
Italy	3.9	3.0
Japan	6.0	5.0
Netherlands	8.8	12.0
Sweden	8.7	11.2
UK	5.1	5.5
USA	5.7	16.0

Source: Data from Jacobzone *et al.* (1999).

The percentage of over 65-year-olds receiving formal home care in Table 6.2 offers a more direct indication of the relative size of home care services. In Australia, the Netherlands, Sweden and the USA, more than 11 per cent of older people receive formal help at home. With 16 per cent, the USA is a clear outlier. This figure, however, does not reflect generosity on the part of government, but rather the vigorous marketing of many private, long-care insurance plans. In the other countries between 9.6 per cent (in Germany) and 3 per cent (in Italy) of older people receive formal home care services. Although in all countries only a minority of older people receives formal help, the variation among countries is striking, However, this disguises the fact that many older people living in their own homes rely on informal care from female relatives. With the exception of France, Italy and Japan, in all countries the percentage of older people receiving formal home care is greater than the percentage living in institutions. This highlights the importance of

Table 6.3   *The growth of institutionalization rates of people aged 65 and over (%)*

Australia[a]	−0.35
France[b]	0.85
Netherlands[c]	−2.7
Sweden[c]	−0.96
USA[d]	−0.79

[a] Figure refers to growth between 1985 and 1996
[b] Figure refers to growth between 1990 and 1994
[c] Figure refers to growth between 1980 and 1995 among people aged between 65 and 79
[d] Figure refers to growth between 1982 and 1994

Source: Data from Jacobzone *et al.* (1999).

home care for older people; it is at home where the majority of older people live.

The growth of institutionalization rates in Table 6.3 offers a more detailed picture of how the relative importance of institutionally-based care has been changing over time. With the exception of France, growth rates are negative, ranging from −0.35 per cent in Australia to −0.96 per cent in Sweden. The Netherlands is a clear outlier with −2.7 per cent. One possible explanation is that the figure excludes the very old, who are more likely to need institutionally-based care. In most countries, then, fewer people are living in institutions. In part, this reflects policies explicitly aimed at de-institutionalization.

However, as Table 6.4 indicates, this does not necessarily mean that the number of long-term care beds has fallen. In the majority of countries for which figures are available, the number of beds per 1000 people has increased over the last two decades. In Australia and the Netherlands the increases have been moderate, whereas in France and Germany the number of long-term beds has increased 1.5 and 2-fold respectively. The UK is clearly at one extreme with an almost 9-fold increase. In short, in most countries institutionally-based care continues to be important. Here it also has to be taken into consideration that any positive effects from de-institutionalization policies may be partly offset by the increase in the number of very old people (see Chapter 1 for data on ageing: p. 3).

Irrespective of the inconclusive trends in the provision of institutionally-based care, the spending on other types of services for the elderly and disabled has increased significantly. Table 6.5 lists per capita public expenditure on day care, rehabilitation, home help services and other

Table 6.4   *Number of long-term care beds per 1,000 people*

	1978	1983	1988	1993	1998
Australia	4.1	4.7	4.4	4.2	4.3
France	n/a	0.9	1.1	1.3	1.4
Germany	1.8	1.4	3.3	3.7	n/a
Italy	0.3	0.3	0.2	0.2	0.2
Netherlands	3.1	3.3	3.4	3.5	3.7
Sweden	5.0	5.8	5.8	1.2	0.4
UK	0.5	0.5	2.8	4.3	4.4

n/a = not available

Source: Data from OECD (2001b).

services in kind. With the exception of New Zealand and the USA, in all countries public spending has increased between 1983 and 1998, ranging from 37-fold in France to 2-fold in Italy. Australia registers the largest jump in expenditures in these areas, even though Sweden continues to spend the highest per capita by far.

Table 6.5   *Per capita public expenditure on services for the elderly and disabled (US$)*

	1983[a]	1988	1993	1998[b]
Australia	17	72	115	161
France	4	109	136	148
Germany	44	62	111	166
Italy	21	33	44	42
Japan	17	24	44	73
Netherlands	72	77	98	102
New Zealand	4	4	4	1
Sweden	202	289	571	791
UK	54	76	114	116
USA	13	13	15	12

a This is the first year for which figures are available.
b The figures refer to 1997, the most recent year for which figures are available.

Source: Data from OECD (2001b).

The analysis of available statistics has given a first overview of home care in our countries. In terms of both funding and provision, home nursing is marginal in all countries, in some more so than in others. At the same time, there is no clear evidence for systematic moves away from institutionally-based care. In some countries institutionalization rates have fallen, while in many countries the number of long-term care beds has increased. Nevertheless, more public money is being spent on alternative services for older people, such as day centres and home helps. Most importantly, the analysis of the statistics highlights the need to locate home care in the different health systems it is embedded in, and this is what the remainder of the chapter will do.

Providing home health care

Home care is embedded in health systems and, as such, the provision of home care is closely related to that of health systems. However, as the poor relation, home care is often not fully integrated in the institutional fabric of health systems, thus creating distinct features in the provision of services. The degree to which this is the case is an interesting question from a comparative perspective.

The provision of home care reflects the level and security of funding discussed in the next section, but is also influenced by other factors. This includes policies explicitly aimed at substituting (formal) home care with institutionally-based care and informal care, together with cultural expectations about the role of the family in care-giving, which will be discussed in more detail later in this chapter. Substitution policies refer to a set of policies that are intended to replace institutionally-based care with care in the home and related settings. Motivations are both financial and humanitarian. Policies have focused on de-institutionalization, although any positive effects are partly off-set by the increasing number of older and very old people (Jacobzone *et al.*, 1999). Policies have focused less explicitly on developing non-institutional settings. This often results in additional demands on women as informal carers (Jenson and Jacobzone, 2000). When assessing the provision of home care, it is important to look at how services are organized and who provides these services. Again, both aspects give an indication of the degree to which home care is integrated in health systems and influences the level of service provision.

Considering the diversity of health systems, it is not surprising that the provision of home care services also shows wide variation (see Figure 6.1). Only in Britain and Sweden are home nursing services provided publicly and firmly integrated into the health system. This situation is typical of national health services, which are characterized by a

/

high degree of public integration (see Chapter 3). However, this does not necessarily guarantee a high level of service provision, and in both countries targeting and shifting responsibilities to less well integrated social care services has undermined the traditional entitlement for home nursing. The push towards a more mixed provision of services has paradoxical consequence, because the fragmentation of services not only requires more co-ordination, but also makes it more difficult (Jamieson, 1996).

		Predominant Type of Provision	
		Public	*Non-profit*
Level of provision	High	Sweden	Netherlands
	Low	Britain	Australia, Germany, Japan, New Zealand, Singapore, USA

Figure 6.1   *The provision of home health care*

The Netherlands is an unusual case, where private, non-profit providers are part of universal system of service provision, thus leading to high levels of service provision. This reflects a long-standing commitment to home care, together with service provision, which combines health and social care as well as secure funding (this last element is discussed in the following section). In all the other countries, the provision of home care is highly mixed and less well integrated into the health system, thus reflecting either a strong legacy of informal care (as in Germany, Japan and Singapore), health systems with a strong liberal elements (as in Australia and the USA) and/or weaker demographic pressures (as in New Zealand). However, with ever-present demographic and cost pressures some countries have adopted more explicit policies. In response, Japan and Germany have extended their social insurance to cover home care, whereas Australia has introduced a tax-funded home care programme.

Sweden is the paradigmatic case of a country where the level of service provision is high and where the public provision of services dominates. Home care is embedded in a national health service, which makes for strong public integration. This co-exists with a high degree of decentralization, and some even suggest that the large differences at local level make it more appropriate to talk about a multitude of 'welfare municipalities' rather than a single welfare state (Trydegård and Thorslund, 2001). Not surprisingly, the organization of services is characterized by diversity. In half of the localities, county councils have delegated the responsibility for home nursing to municipalities (National Board of Health and Welfare, 2000). This results in highly integrated service provision since municipalities also provide other long-term nursing services in institutional settings together with social care oriented home help services. In the other half of localities, county councils continue to organize home care as part of primary care services.

As the international statistics discussed in the first section indicate, Sweden has seen significant reductions in institutionalization rates and the number of long-term beds, while the percentage of older people receiving formal home help is also high. Services for older people with long-term care needs have long been well developed and the social preferences for home care, together with the need for de-institutionalization, were recognized very early. However, financial constraints combined with an emerging ideology of welfare mix have put the existing system under pressure. The number of non-public providers delivering home care for municipalities increased by 146 per cent between 1995 and 1998 (National Board of Health and Welfare, 2000). The targeting of services also disguises an overall reduction of service levels. According to a report by the National Board of Health and Welfare (2000), home-based care services have been concentrated in very old people and in older people living alone; that is, in older people who need help most. As a consequence, the number of older people receiving extensive help has increased significantly, whereas the number of older people receiving less extensive help has fallen markedly. These changes illustrate a gradual move away from universal welfare policies and contrast with earlier reforms. Here, changes in the production of welfare services (such as decentralization and provider markets) prevailed and signalled a continued commitment to tax funding, female employment and universalism (Theobald, 2003).

Recent developments in Sweden demonstrate that high public integration can facilitate but does not necessarily safeguard high levels of service provision. The case of Britain further illustrates this point, and here public provision of services has co-existed with low levels of service provision. Home nursing services are provided publicly and GP-led Primary Care Trusts are responsible for organizing the provision of services. The Primary Care Trusts are intended to commission home help services and in future this will help to better integrate the provision of home-based care services across the health and social care divide. However, the level of service provision is lower and only 5.5 per cent of older people receive formal care compared to 11.2 per cent in Sweden (see figures above). This reflects primarily lower overall spending on health care (see Chapter 3), as well as the hollowing out of entitlements to tax-funded home nursing.

Instead, over the last decade home-based health care has focused on acute care needs, while other care needs have been redefined as social care for which older people have to pay (Lewis, 2001). As a consequence, substitution policies that could have helped expand the provision of home nursing services have been weak, if not non-existent. The same applies to social care-oriented services where speedier discharge of older people from hospitals and the reduction of long-term care facilities has not been matched by comparable public funding to stimulate the development of home-based services (Gibson and Means, 2000; Glendinning, 1998).

As Sweden and Britain suggest, public provision makes for publicly integrated home care. However, as the Netherlands demonstrate, a similar degree of integration in the health system can also be achieved with a more mixed provision of services, which is dominated by non-profit providers. In the Netherlands, the provision of home care is in the hands of non-profit organizations, the regional Cross Associations. Only one organization operates in any one area and provides skilled nursing services, personal care and prevention (Tester, 1996). In the past, separate organizations existed for home nursing and home help services, but in the early 1990s the two started to merge with the aim of increasing the efficiency of service delivery (Kerkstra and Hutten, 1996). Integrated provision of services coincides with a high overall level of service provision, which is comparable to Sweden (see discussion of statistics above) and which reflects, among other things, a long-standing commitment to home care dating back to the late 1960s. Interestingly, the Netherlands has also had a higher proportion of people living in institutions than any other European country and it was only in the 1980s that policies focused more explicitly on substitution (Loo, Kahan and Okma, 1999).

The Netherlands contrast with the remaining countries, where a predominantly mixed provision of home care services coincides with low levels of integration of services in the health system as well as low levels of service provision. This reflects a range of reasons. Germany (together with Japan and Singapore) is a classical example of a country where the development of home care services has been impeded by a deeply embedded culture of informal care. The principle of subsidiarity defines home care first and foremost as the responsibility of the family. The introduction of long-term care insurance, discussed in more detail in the next section, has only partly changed this. Security of funding co-exists with basic coverage, which is cash limited and not needs-based, and there is an explicit emphasis on informal care. Fee-for-service payments also encourage the provision of services which are closely tailored to the conditions under which services are reimbursed by the insurance. As a result, services often remain highly segmented, prescribed and inflexible (Schunk, 1998: 46). Having said that, the end of the monopoly of the five main non-profit providers has led to the mushrooming of alternative, private providers. The number of providers of home care has increased from 4,300 in 1992 to 11,800 in 1999, and over 46 per cent of providers are privately owned (Cuellar and Wiener, 2000: 19). This results in greater diversity in the provision of home care, if not necessarily significant increases in the level of service provision. At the same time, the sharp separation between health and social care, acute care and medical rehabilitation, and ambulatory and hospital care continues to exist (Wasem, 1997). As Boom *et al.* (2000) suggest, policies have been concerned more generally with closing gaps in the provision of long-term care and not specifically with home care as such. Instead, the support for informal care has been strongest and most explicit.

In contrast, Australia and the USA are examples of countries where the development of home care services has been impeded by strong liberal elements in the health and welfare system. In Australia, the historically strong element of private funding and heavy role of charitable agencies in providing care for older people, combined with the provision of health care resources by the states and not the Commonwealth, resulted in highly fragmented provision of home care. However, this situation changed with a series of steps in the early 1980s culminating in the introduction of the Home and Community Care Program (HACC) in 1985, which provides secure funding for home care and encourages the states to fund more home care services.

The aims of the HACC Program are to provide a comprehensive, co-ordinated and integrated range of non-institutional care services for older people, people with a disability and their carers, and to support these people to be more independent at home (Australian Department of Health and Ageing, 2002). The goal is to enhance their quality of life and prevent their premature admission to long-term residential care. As of December, 2001, there were approximately 4,000 HACC-funded organizations, providing services to about 315,000 people at any given time, or approximately 600,000 people per year (Australian Department of Health and Ageing, 2003a). The HACC Program funds a wide range of organizations including state government services (such as community nurses in Tasmania), state statutory authorities (such as Homecare of New South Wales), local government services, church organizations (such as St Vincent de Paul), charitable bodies (such as St John Ambulance), and community organizations (such as community aid centres). According to Howe, '[t]he major outcome of the re-direction of aged-care policy in terms of service provision has been the expansion of community care and the containment of residential care' (1992: 238).

Among our countries, New Zealand is unusual in that there have not been any prominent public debates about home care, although a recent government strategic document for treatment of older people might well initiate such debate (New Zealand Ministry of Health, 2002). A possible explanation is that New Zealand has a relatively young population and has generally been well served by charitable organizations.

Funding home health care

The ways in which home care is funded are significant in two respects. Security of funding, together with the relative level of (public) funding, are important factors shaping the provision of home care services. Funding arrangements also give an indication of the extent to which home care is an integral part of a health system.

The funding of home care ranges from taxes and social insurance contributions to out-of-pocket payments (and private insurance). The first two provide secure if not necessarily sufficient funding, whereas out-of-pocket payments are a much less reliable source of funding. The funding of home care is typically highly mixed, and a substantial amount of home care is funded from private, out-of-pocket payments. The importance of non-public sources of funding is even greater if the indirect costs incurred by unpaid carers are taken into consideration. At the same time, different approaches to funding create different types of access. In countries with tax funding, patients tend to have direct access to services. In contrast, in countries with social insurance funding patients often need a medical referral to access services.

As Table 6.6 shows, countries exhibit interesting variations in relation to the funding of home care which reflect the respective health systems.

Table 6.6   *Funding home health care*[a]

Predominantly tax-based funding	*Predominantly social insurance contributions*	*Predominantly private funding*
Australia	Germany	Singapore
Britain	Netherlands	USA
New Zealand		
Sweden		

a Japan is difficult to categorize as home health care is funded by taxes and social insurance contributions to equal extents.

However, in contrast to medical care, public funding of home care often only provides basic coverage, which has to be supplemented by substantial amounts of out-of-pocket payments and/or unpaid informal care. In Britain, New Zealand and Sweden, tax funding of home nursing (and home help services in Sweden) is embedded in a health system which is universal in its orientation. This leads to generous entitlements in principle. In Australia, home care is also tax funded, but this is part of a health system with strong private elements and entitlements are means-tested.

The social insurance funding in Germany, Japan and the Netherlands makes home care an individually earned right, although individual benefits are often needs-based. Integrated funding of health and social care (as is the case in Australia, the Netherlands and Sweden) can add further security to funding arrangements. In contrast, the USA and (to a greater extent) Singapore rely extensively on private funding (Teo, Chan and Straughan, 2003). This undermines the security of funding for individuals. At the same time, entitlements to tax funded home care have also been reduced as services have been targeted to the very needy (as in Sweden) or defined as means-tested social care (as in Britain). This reflects financial pressures together with an ideological turn towards welfare mix. Nevertheless, other countries have seen the introduction of tax-funded programmes covering home care (as in Australia and the USA) and even the introduction of new additions to social insurance (as in Germany and Japan).

Britain and Sweden are typical examples of national health services in which public provision of home nursing coincides with tax funding. New Zealand is another national health service where home nursing care is tax funded, although the provision is mixed and in the hands of non-profit providers. Taxes may be combined with other, complementary sources of funding, such as out-of-pocket payments in Sweden, which add up to 10 per cent of expenditure (National Board of Health and Welfare, 2000: 6). Tax funding represents a high degree of public integration and security of funding, although the levels of funding vary between countries and over time. In Britain, for example, home nursing services are part of the National Health Service and, as such, are funded out of general taxation and are free at the point of use. Although this implies generous entitlements in principle, in practice the use of home nursing services is restricted, reflecting the tight cash limits under which the NHS operates. Over the last decade, more and more services have also been defined as social rather than health care, and as such they incur charges. Combined with targeting of services by local authorities, this also means that older people increasingly have to rely either on their own funds to pay for services or on the help of families and friends in order to stay in their own homes. Glendinning (1998a) suggests that this strategy effects a considerable reduction of citizenship rights in what used to be a universal system until the early 1980s.

An interesting, although very recent, development has occurred in Scotland, where the social right to home care was established in 2002. In addition to home nursing, patients now also have access to free personal (social) care, which covers personal assistance and hygiene, together with simple treatments. The only condition is that patients are over 65 and that their care needs have been assessed. The introduction of free home care reflects the leftist political culture in Scotland and is also an example of the emerging health care federalism in the UK. Under the 1997 devolution legislation the Scottish Parliament can pass its own laws on social issues and also raise additional taxes (Bertelsmann Foundation, 2002).

Australia is an interesting case of a country where tax funding is embedded in a health system with strong elements of private funding. Significantly, the Home and Community Care Program, which covers home nursing and home help services, was only set up in 1985 and services are means tested. The Program, an integral part of a set of changes known as the Aged Care Reform Strategy, was the result of a 1982 Commonwealth inquiry which recommended that the entire system of aged care support be overhauled and more home care services provided to enable people to stay in their own homes (Jenson and Jacobzone, 2000: 59). Nevertheless, funding for home care remains a combination of public, private, charitable and individual funding, as assets tests are used for home care support.

The HACC Program is a joint Commonwealth, State and Territory initiative and is administered by the states under different departments. Nationally, the Commonwealth government contributes approximately 60 per cent of Program funding and maintains a broad strategic policy role, while State and Territory governments provide 40 per cent and are responsible for its day-to-day management. Funding for the Program has increased over the years, for instance by 9.5 per cent between the financial years 2001 and 2003 (Australian Department of Health and Ageing, 2003a). The type of services funded by this programme combine health and social care services and include: nursing care, domestic assistance, meals and other food services, personal care, home modification and maintenance, transport, respite care, counselling, and assessment. The result of HACC has been a radical shift in balance from nursing home to hostel and home-based care. Between 1985 and 1990, for instance, while Commonwealth expenditure on nursing home care increased by 9 per cent, the corresponding increases in expenditure for home care and hostels were 95 per cent and 127 per cent, respectively (Australian Department of Health and Ageing, 2003a).

The public funding of home care has traditionally been less well established in social insurance systems. This reflects an implicit focus on the working population, together with an often strong communitarian orientation that puts self-help by individuals and communities first (see Chapter 2). Here, the principle of subsidiarity underpinning German social policy is indicative. The principle of subsidiarity says that social, political and economic activity is undertaken at the lowest appropriate level of social organization (Freeman and Clasen, 1994). This principle is the cornerstone of Catholic social teaching, which has been very influential in Germany. Subsidiarity assigns primary responsibility for welfare to the individual and to the family. As such, welfare is funded through social insurance and is provided as an earned right rather than on the basis of need. In terms of the provision of formal services, priority is given to non-government, non-profit organizations. Not surprisingly, the introduction of social insurance for home care has been a relatively recent phenomenon in Germany as well as Japan.

In 1989, faced with a fast-growing elderly population and the problem of social hospitalization, the government in Japan instituted the Gold Plan to expand services for older people. One goal of this Plan was to facilitate access to care services by challenging the assumption that home care is to be provided by family alone and by shifting resources from hospitals to social support services, such as home nursing and social care. The Plan was framed at the national level and implemented at the municipal level. Another goal was to expand significantly number of home helps, day services and in-home welfare services as described in Table 6.7. The Gold Plan mandated that non-profit organizations provide in-home welfare services to be established in all municipalities. Two criticisms of the policy were that it was not matched by government

Table 6.7   *Japan's Gold Plan strategy to promote health and welfare of the elderly*

	FY 1989	FY 1994	Goal for 2000
Home helps	31,405	59,005	100,000
Temporary stay beds	4,274	24,274	50,000
Day services centres	1,080	5,180	10,000
Home care support centres	0	2,400	10,000
Care house rooms	0	23,700	100,000

FY = Financial Year

Source: Adapted from Furuse (1996: 241).

attention to the quality of care and that it failed to adequately reimburse home health care (Kobayashi and Reich, 1993).

As a result of these shortcomings, the Gold Plan was further extended in 1997, when Japan enacted the Public Long-term Care Act, which marked a clear shift towards funding a comprehensive programme of long-term care including both health and social care. To accomplish this ambitious policy, the government created a new insurance system to cover the costs of both institutional and home-based care. The Act established a long-term care insurance based on the principle of collective solidarity. The aim of the insurance is to provide necessary health and welfare services to persons who are in need of care for bathing, excretion, or food intake, and also functional training, nurse and medical treatment (Bertelsmann Foundation, 2003). The insurance is unusual as only 50 per cent of the funding for these benefits comes from premiums for the new insurance; the other 50 per cent comes from the general budget of the central government.

In contrast, in Germany the so-called long-term care insurance is funded entirely by insurance contributions. Another distinct feature is that the insurance includes cash benefits, which older people can use to pay informal carers (Schunk, 1998). This reflects the fact that the insurance only covers basic home care, including personal care services and household help services (Wenger, 2001). At the same time, the security of the new funding arrangement contrasts with the limited levels of funding available. Not surprisingly, many older people must continue to rely on out-of-pocket payments and/or unpaid carers (Cuellar and Wiener, 2000: 17).

In comparison to Japan and Germany, the Netherlands is something of a pioneer. Home care is covered by a separate health insurance which was introduced in the late 1960s and which covers a range of exceptional medical risks. The insurance is compulsory for all employees (irrespective of income) and is supplemented by central government funds and out-of-pocket payments (Kerkstra, 1996). This represents a strong element of universalism in a health system in which almost one-fifth of the population is covered by private health insurance (see Chapter 3). The Netherlands is unusual because the insurance covers both home nursing and home help services (Bertelsmann Foundation, 1999). Integrated funding means that the scope of the insurance is relatively extensive, which in turn has led to a high level of service provision and use of formal services (Coolen and Weekers, 1998: 50).

In comparison to the countries discussed so far and even other market-based health systems such as the USA (see Box. 6.1), Singapore is an extreme case and largely relies on private funding of home care (Cheah, 2001; Teo, Chan and Straughan, 2003). As in the case of health

---

Box 6.1   Public funding of home care in the USA

In the USA, home care is also predominantly funded from private sources, either out-of-pocket and/or private insurance. As can be expected in a market-based health care system, public sources of funding are marginal, often means-tested, and highly fragmented. Until recently, reimbursement for home care services has been minimal except for the indigent. Depending on the case, Medicare and Medicaid may pay some home care costs that are related to medical care, but may not pay for informal carers. In recent years, however, Medicare has initiated programmes targeted to home care. All Medicare beneficiaries can get home nursing care if they meet certain conditions, though these conditions vary widely from one state and locale to another (see Centers for Medicare and Medicaid Services, 2003b). Medicare does not pay for 24-hour care at home, drugs, meals or home help services, and such services under Medicare are more narrowly construed as medical.

However, recently there have been a number of new programmes to provide public funding for home care, the most important of which is the Program of All Inclusive Care for the Elderly (PACE). This is an optional benefit under Medicare and Medicaid for people over 55 years of age who are frail enough to meet their state's standards for nursing home care (Centers for Medicare and Medicaid Services, 2003a). For most patients, the comprehensive service package permits them to continue living at home rather than be institutionalized. A team of doctors, nurses and other health professionals assesses participant needs, develops care plans, and delivers a mix of services integrated into a complete health care plan. The PACE organization must offer a service package that includes all Medicare and Medicaid services provided by that state as well as an additional 16 services including primary care services, social services, restorative therapies, personal care and supportive services, nutritional counselling, recreational therapy and meals. The PACE organization receives a fixed monthly payment per patient from Medicare and Medicaid. The amounts are the same during the contract year, regardless of the services an enrollee may need. Persons enrolled in PACE also may have to pay a monthly premium, depending on their eligibility for Medicare and Medicaid. PACE, however, is available only in the 14 states that have chosen to offer PACE under Medicaid.

---

care, patients are expected to pay for home care services out of their Medisave accounts or through the private or public insurance they can purchase with those accounts. The government does, however, provide financial assistance in the form of subsidies to older people who have insufficient resources for home nursing and home help services. To ensure that the subsidy goes to those who need it, an income assessment framework was introduced in 2000. The means test takes into consideration the gross income of the patient, his or her spouse and the immediate family members, the number of family members, and ownership of major assets such as private property. Subsidies are available only to Singapore citizens or permanent residents who meet the admission criteria of the care services required and are also admitted to a government-funded institution or service. The subsidy goes directly to the service providers who use it to off-set the bill for the home care fees and charges.

The interface between formal and informal care

As the analysis above suggests, home care is a complex policy field. Public funding is often not secure and hardly sufficient, and it has to be supplemented by out-of-pocket payments. Publicly funded services are also increasingly targeted at highly dependent older people and, in many instances, the entitlement to publicly funded services is being hollowed out. Furthermore, often the level of service provision is basic and involves a diverse range of providers. As a result, the emphasis on welfare mix competes with the policy goal to integrate services across different providers and the boundary between health and social care.

The analysis thus far has focused only on formal home care: that is, the care provided by paid staff with formal training/qualifications. The policy field becomes even more complex when it is realized that the majority of home care has traditionally been (and still is) provided by family and friends: that is to say, informal, unpaid carers. Tester (1996) in her comparison of community care in a number of European countries and the USA, estimates that informal carers provide 75 to 80 per cent of care. With cost containment in health care and inadequate resources to develop home care services, the burden on informal carers has actually increased in recent years. Substitution policies also mean that home care services are targeted at highly dependent older people who would otherwise require institutional care. Significantly, informal care work is women's work and the overwhelming amount of care work is still being done by women in family settings (Jenson and Jacobzone, 2000).

The importance of informal care applies to all nine countries. However, countries show interesting variations in relation to underlying cultural assumptions about the role of the family (and women in particular) in care-giving (Boom *et al.*, 2000). In those countries where family bonds and collectivist values are traditionally strong, the care-giving responsibilities of families are extensive. The reverse applies to countries where values of individual independence dominate. Here, it is more accepted that care-giving is in the hands of paid professionals, or at least that they complement informal care. These clusters of values and

		Value Orientations	
		Individual Independence	Family Responsibility
Welfare Regime	Social Democratic	Sweden	
	Conservative	Netherlands	Germany
	Liberal		Australia, Britain, New Zealand, USA

Figure 6.2   *Value orientations in informal care and welfare regimes*[a]

[a] Japan and Singapore do not easily fit into (European) types of welfare regime. However, with Germany they share an explicit emphasis on family responsibility.

cultural traditions coincide with different types of welfare regimes, as Figure 6.2 shows.

Sweden is the classic example of a social democratic welfare state regime, where equality and individual independence are the key and which is characterized by high female employment (Anttonen and Sipilä, 1996). Many responsibilities traditionally associated with families, such as care of older people and children, have been taken on by the public sector and formal care has been chosen over informal care. The overall commitment to this principle remains strong, although recent years have seen a much more explicit concern with the role of the family in care-giving. In the Netherlands, the attitude towards the role of women in care-giving is similar. However, in contrast to Sweden, the Netherlands combines comprehensive universal service provision with social insurance funding typical of conservative welfare states. This reflects the traditional 'pillarization' of Dutch society: that is, the vertical divisions in society between Catholics and Protestants, and between Socialists and Liberals (Tester, 1996).

In contrast, Britain is an example of a welfare state with increasingly strong liberal elements (Anttonen and Sipilä, 1996). The NHS is an exception to the rule that the public funding and provision of welfare is often minimal, designed as a safety net for those who cannot provide for themselves. Here, services are defined universally, but in practice are often means tested or income related. The responsibility of the individual (and the family) is central, whereas that of the state is residual. In relation to older people, it is implicitly assumed that families take on caring responsibilities. Australia has been most active in the expansion of public support for families, while New Zealand with its younger population has largely depended on private resources and charitable organizations to serve this function. Like the UK, though, New Zealand serves a residual role and provides a safety net through public subsidies to the poor. Although the US government is beginning to accept some responsibility for long-term care of the elderly, by and large it continues to be the responsibility of the family to arrange and fund this care through private insurance or personnel resources.

Germany is the archetypal example of a conservative welfare state that places great importance on the family as an organizing principle of society (Wenger, 2001). This reflects Catholic teachings on the family. However, Germany is unusual in the explicitness with which demands are made on the family. In this respect the idea of subsidiarity is key. Self-help is understood as the responsibility of individuals to help themselves. If self-help is no longer possible, it is the responsibility of the family to take over from the individual, then come voluntary organizations, and only if all else fails will the state step in. Japan and Singapore do not easily fit into (European) typologies of welfare regimes. However, together with Germany, both countries share an explicit emphasis on female caring obligations.

In Japan, direct relatives including children, grandchildren and siblings may be legally required to provide financial support to maintain their elderly relatives. Traditionally, it has been the case that elderly parents live with their eldest son's family with an arrangement for sharing resources. Moreover, this strong filial duty to care for elderly family members often falls on the daughter-in-law. Thus in some cases a woman might be caring for two sets of parents simultaneously. One of the major factors driving reform in home care in Japan is the substantial ongoing decline in the supply of in-family care-givers due to the very strong ageing process it faces (Jenson and Jacobzone, 2000). The situation is similar in Singapore, where there is also a strong filial tradition that daughters be care-givers for elderly parents. As in Japan, the Asian cultural context discussed in Chapter 2 has produced pressures in Singapore between institutionalized and home care as the population ages.

With home care on the political agenda of many health systems, there has also been a greater interest in informal care. Home care inevitably involves informal care. Home is where older people live with their spouses and partners, and home is also one of the places where older people meet with friends and family. The spatial interface of personal relationships and home care facilitates the provision of informal care. Not surprisingly, policies on home care have acknowledged the importance of informal care. From a comparative perspective, the interesting question is what this acknowledgement means in practice, and how policies define the interface between formal and informal care.

Here, a number of considerations come into play. In times of resource constraints, it seems inevitable that health systems continue to rely on informal care. Compared to formal care, this is the cheaper option, but only if the costs associated with informal care (such as lost income and pension entitlements) are ignored (Jacobszone, 1999; Jamieson, 1996). Another consideration is that the expansion of formal care might reduce the provision of informal care and even create new, additional demands for formal care (Jamieson, 1996). This can be either a desirable or an undesirable policy outcome, although studies indicate that substitution is not necessarily straightforward. For moderately disabled older people, home-based care is likely to be the best (and most efficient) option, whereas for severely disabled older people, institutional care is more appropriate (Jacobzone, 1999). If anything, this suggests that substitution needs to be tailored to the particular circumstances of individuals (see Low *et al.*, 2000). Moreover, even in countries with relatively high levels of publicly funded formal care, families continue to play a significant role as informal carers. For example, analyses of the time devoted to care of older people show that in Sweden in the mid-1980s informal care accounted for 64 per cent of total care time (OECD, 1996: 166). Nevertheless, the pool of informal carers is ultimately limited and home care cannot do without formal care (Twigg, 1996).

Policies on the informal aspects of home care pick and mix considerations about the interface between the formal and the informal in distinct ways, which are shaped by cultural assumptions about the role of the family in care-giving. At the same time, it is interesting that in recent years many countries have experienced in one way or another a more explicit integration of informal care into the (formal) health system. Twigg (1989) has developed a typology for understanding the range of relationships that exist between welfare agencies and informal carers. She distinguishes the following types: carers as resources, where carers are taken for granted; carers as co-workers, where carers are treated instrumentally to ensure the continuation of their caring activities; carers as co-clients, where agencies are concerned with the needs of carers in their own right; and superseded carers, where agencies aim to replace carers with paid formal care staff.

Looking at the interface between formal and informal care, similarities within differences are most striking. The nine countries vary significantly in terms of their expectations about the role of women in care-giving. Sweden and the Netherlands have traditionally favoured formal care, whereas Japan and Singapore, but also Germany, explicitly expect women to take on caring responsibilities. This attitude also exists, but more implicitly, in Australia, Britain, New Zealand and the USA with their liberal welfare regimes. However, despite these differences, all countries – with the exception of Singapore, New Zealand, and the USA – have started integrating informal care into the formal system of funding home care. In this regard, payments for informal carers have been vital. Payments are largely symbolic (rather than reimbursements for a service), but as such they are an important indicator of a turn towards welfare societies.

With their traditionally strong preference for formal care recent developments in Sweden and the Netherlands underline the pertinence of the emphasis on informal care and the move towards a welfare society. As Daatland (1996: 257) observes in relation to Sweden, '[t]he policy rhetoric encourages family care, voluntarism, and welfare pluralism'. For example, for the period 1999–2001, Parliament decided to allocate money to municipalities, specifically to increase support for caring relatives (National Board of Health and Welfare, 2000). Municipalities also employ carers as care assistants, although in 1999 this only applied to 2 per cent of people receiving formal care services (National Board of Health and Welfare, 2000: 86). In other cases, older people receive grants to pay informal carers for the help they receive at home.

In the Netherlands, financial support for informal carers came as part of the introduction of cash benefits for older people with care needs in 1996. The cash can be used to purchase formal home nursing and home help services or to contract and pay informal carers, with the majority of the personal budget being managed collectively by so-called Associations of Budget Holders. The implementation of the cash benefits has been piecemeal and personal budgets only account for 3 to 5 per cent of the costs of long-term care (Coolen and Weekers, 1998: 60). Also, the social democratic culture of care remains strong and only 37 per cent of older people decide to use their personal budget to pay informal carers (Coolen and Weekers, 1998: 61).

Considering the conservative orientation of its welfare regime and the explicit emphasis on family responsibility, it is not surprising that in Germany (and Japan) the introduction of the long-term care insurance also extended the commitment to unpaid informal care, and the demands made on the families of older people are now complemented by a range of support mechanisms (Schunk, 1998). Besides benefits in kind, insurance offers financial benefits which older people can use to pay their informal carers. Insurance also pays contributions to the pension and accident insurance of informal carers of older people who qualify for the long-term care insurance. In addition, insurance offers respite care as an annual benefit for older people cared for by the family (Schunk, 1998). Although the monetary value of the financial benefits is only half that of the benefits in kind, 76 per cent of older people receiving benefits from insurance prefer informal over formal home care (Cuellar and Wiener, 2000: 16). This reflects the continued strength of cultural norms about the role of the family in care-giving (Wenger, 2001).

By comparison, the emphasis on informal care has typically been more implicit in liberal welfare regimes and the explicit support of informal carers has been weaker. Significantly, in neither the USA and Singapore nor New Zealand do public payments to informal carers exist. In the first two countries, this reflects strong private elements in the provision and funding of home care. In the USA, this is exacerbated by the high degree of fragmentation in public funding. As noted earlier, in Singapore a strong emphasis on obligations of female carers plays an important role, as does the fact that individuals in effect control their own health care accounts and can use them for long-term care insurance should they so decide. In New Zealand, the relative youthfulness of the population is a possible explanation for the absence of formal support for carers.

Australia is an interesting outlier among the countries with a liberal welfare regime and has a long tradition of paying family members for home care work. The HACC program introduced in 1985 continues this tradition by shifting incentive structures towards family-provided care and providing support for respite care and other services. Two allowances exist for care-givers, the Carer Allowance and the Carer Payment (Australia Department of Health and Ageing, 2002). The Carer Allowance is a non-means or asset-tested and non-taxable payment of small (25 per cent of average weekly full-time earnings) cash benefits to family members who support a person who requires continuous nursing care at home and who would otherwise be eligible for admission to a nursing home. The second, the Care Payment allowance, is a means-tested, non-contributory income support payable to those who are unable to maintain paid employment because they have full-time responsibilities for the daily care of a highly dependent person. The level of benefit is the same as a retirement pension, similar in level to unemployment benefit, which is quite low.

Policy trends and developments

Home care is full of contradictions. Home care is varied and diverse, yet it is a basic health need across countries. Home care is hardly visible in international statistics, yet it is central to the health of an increasing number of people. Home care funding and provision is often fragmented, yet home care is high on the health policy agenda of many countries. These are some of the salient contradictions in home care. The interesting question is what, if anything, recent policy trends and developments have changed.

The provision of home care services is diverse, traditionally so in countries such as Australia, New Zealand and the USA and more recently in Britain and Sweden, reflecting a political emphasis on a mixed economy of welfare and competition. Diversity means a greater number and wider range of providers. This requires greater co-ordination, but at the same time makes co-ordination (and ultimately the integration into the health system) more difficult. Problems of co-ordination can be exacerbated by a sharp divide between different types of care (e.g., health and social care in Britain), the absence of national legislation (as in the case of the USA) or highly decentralized governance structures (as in the case of Sweden). Also, diversity of provision does not necessarily translate into adequate levels of provision, as all countries demonstrate. This gives credence to the more general tenet that in times of cost containment, diversity of provision often coincides with a targeting of services to those in greatest need (as in the case of Britain and Sweden) or to those without any other means (as in the case of Australia, and social care in Britain and New Zealand).

At the same time, the funding of home care remains insecure and continues to rely to a large extent on private funding and unpaid informal care. Only in Singapore and the USA does the insecurity of funding arise from the effective absence of public funding schemes. All other countries have schemes funded from either taxes or social insurance contributions, but which are restricted because of needs and/or means testing or because the scheme only provides basic coverage (as in the case of the long-term care insurance in Germany). Notwithstanding the continued insecurity of funding and the limits on funding, over the last two decades three countries have seen the wholesale introduction of new schemes. In Germany and Japan this took the form of the extension of social insurance and in Australia it took the form of a tax-funded programme. Even in the USA, some states participating in the publicly funded Medicare and Medicaid PACE programme include a home care component.

However, regardless of the policy trends in the provision and funding of services, home care remains overwhelmingly informal: it is women's work. In comparison to formal home care, informal women's work continues to be cheap and readily available. Irrespective of differences among health systems and cultural attitudes towards the role of women, the majority of countries acknowledge the centrality of informal care. This takes different forms, ranging from the gender-blindness of liberal welfare traditions (such as in the USA) and gender-specific expectations in male-dominated, collectivist societies (such as in Japan and Singapore), to the ideology of the welfare society (such as in Britain and Sweden), the revival of subsidiarity (in Germany), and symbolic payments to carers (as in Australia, Germany, Japan and the Netherlands). However, what has changed is that the marginality of home care has come more sharply into focus.

Chapter 7

Public Health

Chapter 5 demonstrated the wide range of settings and activities needed for the delivery of modern medical care. Chapter 6 extended this need to integrate health care with non-health arenas by demonstrating that with home care it is not possible to separate health care from social care. The health of the client is as dependent on personal care as it is on medical care, in many cases perhaps more so. Even this more comprehensive picture of health care, however, has been criticized for minimizing what according to some observers are its most critical dimensions, health promotion and disease prevention. These two elements together are often defined as public health. Due to the expansive and rather amorphous nature of public health, this chapter is more an overview of the policy areas facing our countries rather than a comparative analysis, as in the previous chapters. Examples from our countries, however, are used throughout the discussion.

Simply put, public health is medicine concerned with the community as a whole. Although public health can be defined in many ways, common denotations of the term include health promotion, disease prevention, primary care, community health and population health. Public health encompasses a wide range of activities including the protection of the health of the population, the assessment of the health needs of specific populations, and the provision of care for individual patients within the context of the culture and health needs of their specific population.

Generally, public health activities focus on communities or populations rather than individuals, although De Ferranti (1985: 67) makes a useful distinction between patient-related and non-patient-related preventive care. Patient-related approaches are generally defined as primary care, take place in a clinical setting, and include immunization, health education between patients and GPs, and cancer or cholesterol screening programmes. Non-patient-related preventive approaches include such disparate activities as improved sanitation and water systems, promotion of health and hygiene, provision of adequate housing, control of pests, food safety, and the monitoring of disease patterns (epidemiology). Specific public health strategies, then, run the gamut from quarantining individuals with highly communicable diseases deemed to be threats to the public health, to regulating the workplace for health and safety, to reducing unemployment and economic disparities, to reducing greenhouse emissions and depletion of the ozone layer.

Although still a part of health care, primary care services to well patients (such as pregnant women and infants), general physical examinations, immunization programmes, and health promotion activities have received consistently smaller shares of the health care budgets. In the USA, for instance, less than 1 per cent of the health care budget is spent on public health. Despite the AIDS epidemic and increased problems with substance abuse, violence and teenage pregnancy, public health strategies as a proportion of the health care budget fell by 25 per cent between 1981 and 1993. For example, while $3,007 was spent per person on medical care in the USA in 1992, only $34 was spent on prevention (US Public Health Service, 1995). Furthermore, in recent years governments struggling with large deficits have preferred to sacrifice the personnel and services of their public health agencies rather than cut medical care to individual patients (Sultz and Young, 1999: 353). In other countries, moves towards efficiency and cost containment have exacerbated the withdrawal of support from public health activities.

Despite a recent shift in many countries back towards a more public health oriented strategy, there is evidence that even the most attentive countries would be well served to put a significantly larger proportion of their health care budgets into public health efforts (Blank, 1997: 87ff.). Mounting evidence suggests that the most significant improvements in health have come from public health measures, not curative medicine, even though the latter efforts are the most dramatic and therefore the most easily funded (Fries *et al.*, 1993). For instance, it is estimated that while 99 per cent of health spending in the USA goes on medical treatment, this spending prevents only 10 per cent of early deaths. In contrast, population-wide, public health approaches have the potential to help prevent some 70 per cent of early deaths through measures targeted at the social, environmental and behavioural factors that contribute to those deaths (Sultz and Young, 1999: 352). The point is not to undermine medical care, but rather to restore a proper balance between patient-centred and population-centred health care.

The case of Severe Acute Respiratory Syndrome

Although public health is often viewed as a distant and esoteric field involving only statistical people, the spread of Severe Acute Respiratory Syndrome (SARS) in 2003 highlights the importance of public health and the fact that, because infectious diseases do not respect borders, international co-operation is essential. Although the epidemic apparently dissipated after several months, during that time it caused much concern and economic problems across populations. SARS began in China but was quickly spread around the world by travellers. While researchers found evidence of the virus in the civet cat which is eaten as a delicacy by some Chinese (Ross, 2003), most SARS victims contracted it after being in close contact with an infected person, often in hospital. Although the number of persons killed by SARS was small by disease standards, it demonstrated how vulnerable to the rapid spread of communicable diseases we are in an age of air travel and concentrated health care facilities where, ironically, many of the victims had been infected. Moreover, threats of biological terrorism and the emergence of even more virulent strains of viruses clearly require more proactive attention to public health and increased funding.

China's early handling of the disease, in particular, has been seen by many observers as reprehensible. When the first SARS cases appeared in southern China in March, Beijing denied it and tried to suppress the news, thus allowing the disease to be spread beyond its borders by unsuspecting victims. In May, 2003, Henen Province in central China punished 800 health workers for failing to perform their duties to protect the public health ('Central China's . . .', 2003). One of the key lessons resulting from China's delay in reporting the outbreak and the disease's rapid spread around the world, according to Alfred Lam Ping Yan, deputy director of health in Hong Kong, is that 'We need stronger public health systems and more co-ordinated ways to handle emerging infections. It's not a problem of an individual city or country. This is a global problem' (cited in Manning, 2003).

To contain the spread of a contagious illness, public health authorities rely on many strategies including isolation and quarantine (Centers for Disease Control, 2003). The two strategies differ in that isolation applies to people who are known to have an illness and quarantine applies to those who have been exposed to an illness but who may or may not become infected. Isolation of people who have a specific illness separates them from healthy people and restricts their movement to stop the spread of that illness. Isolation allows for the focused delivery of specialized health care to people who are ill and protects healthy people from getting sick. People in isolation may be cared for in their homes, in hospitals, or at designated health care facilities. In most cases, isolation is voluntary; however, governments have the authority to compel isolation of sick people to protect the public.

Quarantine, in contrast, applies to people who have been exposed and may or may not be infected but are not yet ill. Separating exposed people and restricting their movements is intended to stop the spread of that illness and quarantine has proved most effective in protecting the public from disease. Although governments generally have wide authority to declare and enforce quarantine within their borders, often it is a difficult call politically because of its severe human rights and economic impact. In the USA, for instance, the Centers for Disease Control and Prevention (CDC), through their Division of Global Migration and Quarantine, are empowered to detain, medically examine, or conditionally release individuals suspected of carrying certain communicable diseases. This authority derives from the Public Health Service Act (42 USC 264), but to date, while the CDC has recommended isolation of individuals with SARS, it has not compelled quarantine or isolation of these individuals.

As might have been predicted given its strong community-centred culture (see p. 48), Singapore instituted an aggressive home-quarantine system in response to SARS. Whereas health officials in Toronto, Canada, simply asked citizens suspected of SARS exposure to self-quarantine, Singapore took more extreme steps to enforce quarantine, including the use of video cameras and electronic bracelets to monitor the movements of those suspected of incubating the disease. It also passed a bill requiring quarantine-breakers to be fined up to $5,000 without being charged in court. The Health Minister also warned that the government might name and shame quarantine-breakers. Although criticized by some Westerners, Singapore's tough approach was supported by the WHO (Greenlee, 2003). In the end, SARS was controlled (at least for the time being) in all countries but only after they adopted more rigorous public health policies. WHO credited old-fashioned quarantines with breaking the back of the outbreak (Wong, 2003).

Framing a public health policy

Despite general agreement that it is more humane and cost-effective to avoid a condition of ill health in the first place than to have to treat it later, modern health systems continue to emphasize curative approaches. In part this is because the medical community has an intrinsic interest in curative medicine and, as illustrated in Chapter 5, it is a dominant force in all systems. In addition, prevention deals with statistical, future lives while curative medicine deals with identifiable patients who need help now. When a patient is facing imminent death, the individual, his or her family, and society as a whole are willing to pay heavily for any innovation that offers even a small promise of postponing death. In contrast, we are less likely to demand preventive innovations that will save many more lives in the distant future, because while health promotion/preventive programmes also ultimately help individuals, it is difficult to identify who they might be. Curative medicine, on the other hand, relates to specific patients in a 'direct, immediate and documentable way' (Baird,

1993: 347). Not surprisingly, a report by the US Institute of Medicine (1985) found a poor public image of public health and a complete lack of knowledge and appreciation for the mission and content of public health on the part of the public.

In spite of the considerable evidence that the most significant advances in the health of populations have come from outside medicine – particularly through improved sanitation, housing, nutrition and education – many groups including physicians, hospital employees and the health care industry, have strong interests in maintaining or increasing funding for treatment. In combination with potential patients (remember, virtually any one of us is a potential patient) and a public strongly influenced by optimistic media coverage, these groups have aggrandized curative medicine. Moreover, human-interest stories and favourable media coverage naturally follow technological breakthroughs in treatment, although not public health efforts. Television dramas exalt those who save individual lives (e.g., trauma teams and surgeons), but not the public health nurses or epidemiologists. Together, these forces can provide formidable obstacles against a reallocation of scarce resources from curative medicine to public health strategies. However, if the goal of the health care system is to improve the health of the population, public health programmes, particularly those that effect changes to healthier lifestyles, are critical.

Many observers have argued that a reallocation towards disease prevention and health promotion would not only enhance health but also save money. For instance, for Cundiff and McCarthy it is 'essential that preventive medicine be emphasised if costs are to be contained while overall quality of care is improved' (1994: 11). Likewise, for Mueller, the 'three goals of health policy – cost containment, quality, and access – can all be well served by policies related to promoting health' (1993: 152). Richmond and Fein (1995: 71) agree that efforts towards prevention and promotion have 'borne much fruit' and that we are on the threshold of being able to do even better. A modest increase, they argue, would yield significant benefits.

Other observers, however, are more sceptical of the savings from preventive strategies. In fact, a growing array of studies on programmes for hypertension screening, reducing high blood cholesterol by either diet or drugs, major screening tests for cancer, and routine mammography tests demonstrate that the net costs per year of life saved are exceedingly high. A review of available data by the US Office of Technology Assessment reported that of all the preventive services it evaluated, only three were potentially cost saving (childhood immunizations, pre-natal care for poor women, and several neonatal tests for congenital disorders). Similarly, screening for high blood pressure generally costs more than treating heart attack and stroke victims (Leutwyler, 1995: 124).

The low per unit cost of some population screening procedures may obscure their true cost, which is the cost of achieving the desired outcome for the few who will benefit. Even though the cost of a single procedure might be reasonable, if the condition is rare, a large number of such procedures might be necessary to identify and prevent one case.

The fact that prevention does not always save money should not detract from the need to rebalance health care systems towards disease prevention and health promotion. The investment in better health in itself is a worthwhile goal even when the costs are high. The rationale behind spending more on public health, then, is the intrinsic value we place on the health it confers on the population, not its monetary savings. Commitment to public health is a measure of concern for the future. Any investment in preventive/promotion programmes shifts benefits from present patients to statistical persons, who will enjoy healthier lives in the future because of these investments. Prevention can also compress morbidity by extending a person's healthy years and thereby reducing the individual and social burden of illness. By postponing the time at which we become victims of a chronic disease, prevention allows people to live healthier and more active lives, even though it might not necessarily extend their life span.

There is one other caveat regarding preventive/promotion strategies that must be raised here. Prevention programmes aimed at today's diseases must focus on changing lifestyles, though many of the ties between lifestyle and health remain speculative. More importantly, even where evidence of danger is strong, such as alcohol and drug abuse, there is considerable debate over how effective preventive measures might be. To effect these changes requires investment of considerable resources both to fund research on behaviour modification and to carry out the preventive programmes. It also requires extensive investment in research to better understand the linkages between social factors and personal factors. Despite these problems, health promotion must be a central element of health care reform and all efforts should be made to educate, encourage and motivate essential behavioural changes.

Although modern medicine is by no means ineffective, Western cultures have overestimated its effectiveness and underestimated its limitations (Palmer and Short, 2000: 52). Therefore, 'reform of the medical delivery system and improvements in access to medical care alone will make possible only limited gains in health, the remaining gains require community-level interventions that public health provides' (US Public Health Service, 1995: 6). Later in the chapter, we raise the question of whether it might not be an even more effective health care strategy to reduce health budgets and put the money saved into social and educational areas. The trade-off is that while this is more likely to improve the health of the population, it does so at the expense of individual patients.

There are now strong pressures in many countries to shift priority back towards primary care/prevention/health promotion activities. Ageing populations and the resulting changes in disease structures are also leading to alterations that favour shifts towards chronic care facilities and less expensive nursing home care as opposed to more costly hospital care. These moves are politically difficult because they are often justified on the grounds of cost-effectiveness and because they threaten the medical establishment. Furthermore, they give the appearance of sacrificing the lives of a vulnerable group of identifiable patients for a more amorphous aggregate population. Also, because of the unpredictable nature of disease, few members of the public are able to distance themselves from the plight of these persons and their need for immediate support.

Public health responsibility and funding

While it can be argued that public health is woefully underfunded compared to curative medicine, all our countries have extensive public health programmes although many of the efforts have been poorly co-ordinated and administered (Institute of Medicine, 1985). As with other areas of health care, each of these countries brings with it a particular orientation for organizing public health services. While Singapore, for instance, has a highly centralized and active public health policy, in most of our countries at least the non-medical aspects of public health are locally administered programmes. In most countries, the major responsibility for public health falls on states, municipalities or other subnational units, although in recent years some governments, such as Australia's, have tried to provide central co-ordination and increased funding to the localities in order to strengthen public health programmes.

Next to Singapore, New Zealand has the most centralized framework for public health, with responsibility vested in the Ministry of Health, but even here many public health activities are carried out through local programmes or, in the case of health, District Health Boards. The National Health Committee is an autonomous committee appointed by and reporting directly to the Minister of Health which evolved from its earlier form as the Core Services Committee in 1996 when its brief was expanded to include advice on public health. Section 14 of the Public Health and Disability Act 2000 commissioned the Public Health Advisory Committee as a sub-committee of the National Health Committee (New Zealand Ministry of Health, 2003). Its role is to provide independent advice on public health issues, including factors influencing the health of people and communities, the promotion of public health, and the monitoring of public health. The Committee's mandate includes giving advice on measures that would deliver the greatest benefit to the health of the population and to groups of the population that are at risk of disadvantage. It has done extensive work on the social, cultural and economic determinants of health.

In Britain, central government, health authorities and GPs share responsibility for public health (Baggott, 2000). Within central government, public health falls under the remit of the Department of Health, although only since 1997 has there been a separate ministry devoted to public health. The minister has a broad portfolio, which covers several departments and includes policies such as on tobacco and food safety. The Chief Medical Officer has a more narrow focus and specifically provides medical advice to the Department of Health. The health authorities for their part are responsible for pursuing public health strategies within the framework set by the Department of Health. Each health authority has a department of public health that, until recently, had to be headed by medically qualified director. This highlights the traditionally strong medical orientation of public health in Britain (Evans, in press). Since the introduction of the purchaser–provider split in the early 1990s, departments of public health have also played an important role in providing assessments of local health needs, which have informed the purchasing decisions of health authorities. GPs have traditionally focused on the demands of individual patients, but have increasingly been integrated in public health initiatives. The 1990 contract includes financial incentives for GPs to achieve immunization and disease screening targets. This has been complemented by performance-related payments for health promotion and chronic disease programmes. The role of GPs in public health is certain to increase further with the introduction of Primary Care Trusts as the new commissioning bodies, taking over many responsibilities from health authorities.

In contrast to Britain, responsibility for public health in Germany has always been more decentralized, reflecting its federal structure. As in Australia and the USA, public health has traditionally been the remit of the states and included activities ranging from prevention/monitoring of communicable diseases, environmental health, counselling, health education and promotion as well as physical examinations of school children (European Observatory on Health Care Systems, 2000). The range of services covered varies from state to state, as does the structure of the local public health offices responsible for the delivery of services. However, since the 1970s an increasing number of public health activities have become part of social health insurance and responsibility has shifted from the public health offices to office-based doctors. This particularly applies to health promotion and disease prevention measures, such as screening for cancer, regular check-ups for young children and preventive dental care. The provision of public health services has become more standardized as a result because doctors are legally obliged to deliver public services as part of the benefits catalogue of the health insurance. However, the focus of office-based doctors on individual patients, together with the fact that many practise single-handedly, potentially undermines the public orientation of measures of health promotion and disease prevention. Significantly, immunization rates are relatively low by international comparison (European Observatory on Health Care Systems, 2000: 60). Unfortunately, the role of local public health offices is now mainly supervisory, focusing on controlling food safety and drinking water and compiling health statistics (Greiner and Schulenburg, 1997).

Sweden resembles Germany in that the responsibility for public health is decentralized and rests with county councils and municipalities as service providers, again reflecting the federalist structure of health care governance in Sweden. Preventive and population-based measures more specifically are integrated into the delivery of primary care services (European Observatory on Health Care Systems, 2001). Health centres employ school nurses to provide health education to children, and doctors provide one-to-one health education on eating and alcohol consumption, run well-women clinics and immunize children. Complementing this at the national level is the National Institute for Public Health, which is responsible for national programmes of health promotion and disease prevention, focusing on issues such as alcohol, drugs and accidents. As in other areas of health care provision, the National Board of Health and Welfare is responsible for supervising and monitoring what is happening at the level of county councils and municipalities. Here, the Board is supported by the work of a specialist centre for epidemiology which analyses the health status and social situation of the population, together with morbidity hazards (Håkansson and Nordling, 1997).

Compared to Sweden, the responsibility for public health is even more decentralized in the Netherlands. Following the 1989 Public Prevention Act, some core responsibilities for public health services, including health monitoring and dealing with contagious diseases, have been delegated to local authorities. The activities of local public health agencies are only loosely prescribed, but typically focus on the young, elderly, minority groups and include health promotion and education, vaccination and public health research projects (Maarse, 1997). The considerable autonomy at local level has resulted in substantial diversity in the delivery of public health services (Okma, 2001). In response to concerns about inequalities in access to public health services, a Commission was established and in 1998 recommended that local authorities present an annual review of their public health activities. It also recommended that the Ministry of Health define a basic set of services which all local authorities must provide. Furthermore, the activities of the local authorities are to be overseen by the Inspectorate of Health, which is responsible for monitoring the quality of health services and health protection measures.

As in the Netherlands and Sweden, a large share of the responsibility for public health services in Japan falls on the local governments and to a lesser extent the prefectures. Each of the 3,200 or so municipalities has a division responsible for health and the employment of public health nurses (Nakahara, 1997: 123). Also, in addition to basic environmental services such as water supply and waste disposal, under the Community Health Law of 1994 the primary local governments administer community health programmes including maternal and child care, immunization, nutrition guidance, health education, health screening, and health examinations for those over 40.

If the organization of public health is so decentralized in these countries, it is bound to be even more so in the federal systems of the USA and Australia. As discussed earlier (p. 33), the USA is a federal system with responsibility for many functions falling on the sub-national units. Moreover, the US Constitution explicitly gives to the states the authority to protect the health of their residents. Each of the 50 states has its own public health agency or department. In addition, there are 3,066 counties in the USA, ranging in area from 67 to 227,559 square kilometres and in population from 140 in Loving County, Texas, to 9.2 million people in Los Angeles County, California, and each one has public health responsibilities. Furthermore, there are tens of thousands of cities, towns and other municipalities, all of which have some public health activities, many quite extensive like that of San Francisco which is typical of a large city health department (see Box.7.1). At the federal level, the Centers for Disease Control and Prevention have prime responsibility for monitoring and policy making in disease prevention, but they depend on compliance from the state and local agencies to implement their guidelines.

Although Australia is a federal system like the USA and Germany, and although public health traditionally has been the province of the states and territories, in recent years there have been some efforts to provide increased national co-ordination. The Population Health Division of the Commonwealth has responsibility to help Australians stay healthy and live longer by helping them avoid illness and injury. Funding for public health activities in Australia is diverse and comprises contributions from states and territories, local government, non-government organizations and in some cases private industry (Australia Department of Health and Ageing, 2002). The distribution of this

> ## Box 7.1   San Francisco Department of Public Health
>
> The Division of Population Health and Prevention focuses on disease prevention and health promotion. Policy units include:
>
> **Community Health and Safety Branch:** Performs prevention, control and surveillance of communicable diseases including HIV/AIDS, sexually-transmitted diseases, tuberculosis and others. Enforces public health policies and regulations including environmental health, occupational safety and health, and emergency medical services. Monitors the health status of the population through epidemiology and research.
>
> **Community Health Promotion and Prevention Branch:** Responsible for promoting health and preventing disease and injury in the population. Programmes include health education, HIV prevention, women's health, tobacco control, refugee health services, and childhood environmental health promotion.
>
> **Community Health Services Branch:** Purchases and monitors approximately $200 million for health services, including mental health, substance abuse, AIDS, medical care financed through the state tobacco tax and maternal/child/adolescent health services. (San Francisco Department of Health, 2003)

Commonwealth funding among the states and territories is based on a resource allocation formula that takes account of a range of factors including population, mortality rates, the extent of remoteness and other elements that affect the cost of delivering services. This formula has been developed to reflect key determinants of health and well-being in communities. The Commonwealth invests in population health activity through Public Health Outcome Funding Agreements (PHOFAs), direct grants to states/territories, and direct grants to community organizations, as well as through supporting population health activity undertaken by GPs and their divisions.

Health promotion

The health promotion efforts have taken different intensity, form and focus in our countries and to some extent their approaches and commitment reflects the general health goals predominant in each. In countries such as Germany, New Zealand and Sweden, where the prevailing culture is more communitarian and egalitarian, health promotion strategies have focused on social factors, while in more individualistic countries such as Singapore and the USA the focus has tended to be on individual factors. Another variation is the extent to which health promotion is directed towards the population at large or at specific groups such as smokers, pregnant women or children. Moreover, some countries have tended to target promotion policies at specific diseases or issues while others have taken considerably broader approaches. In all cases, the health promotion strategies reflect the organizational variation in public health activities in general, with some countries displaying rigorous national programmes and others leaving it to various sub-units.

Although health promotion is but one aspect of public health, it has received more attention recently as the links between individual behaviour and health have been elucidated. Even those countries that lacked well established health promotion policies have realized that promoting healthy lifestyles is not only an effective way of improving the health of their populations, but also a crucial strategy for reining in burgeoning health care costs. In other words, health promotion is viewed as a key factor in cost containment. Not surprisingly, then countries across the full range of health systems have produced initiatives for health promotion and disease prevention. A sample of highlights and orientations of these disparate programmes is presented here, moving from those that have focused more on social factors to those that have focused on individual factors.

As a prime example of an egalitarian country, it is not surprising that New Zealand has taken a broad health promotion approach that emphasizes social factors. In 2002 the New Zealand Ministry of Health launched the *Achieving Health for All People* document which is due for completion in 2003. The purpose of this document is to provide the public health sector with a framework for a broad health promotion action for the New Zealand Health Strategy. The Health Strategy supports the role of public health and emphasizes the importance of taking a population health approach to the improvement of health and the reduction of inequalities. A key theme of this initiative is that 'public health action is not the responsibility of public health services alone, or even of health services as a whole. It is about the organised efforts of society' (New Zealand Ministry of Health, 2003).

Likewise, Japan launched its broadly based First National Movement for Health Promotion in 1978 and the second wave in 1988. A major measure taken in the first movement was the creation of Municipal Health Centres (MHCs) in every municipality to co-ordinate health promotional activities. The second wave was dubbed 'Active 80 Health Plan' because its purpose was to promote a prolonged life span of 80 years. After more than 20 years since its inception, these health promotional activities are beginning to bear fruit as reflected in the third wave of the national health promotion movement, 'Healthy Japan 21'. The period covered is between the years 2000 and 2010 with a defined set of goals in health promotion. In this wave, emphasis is placed in the prolongation of the 'healthy life span' which means a life span without disability. This emphasis reflects the problem of a considerable number of elderly with disability in the face of the world's longest life span.

In Germany, the fragmented structure of public health and its increasing medicalization over past decades have tended to mitigate against a national strategy for health promotion. At federal level, responsibility for health promotion falls under the remit of the Ministry of Health, although the Federal Centre for Health Education is responsible for initiating and co-ordinating national health promotion campaigns. Significantly, however, the work of the Federal Centre has focused on a number of selected campaigns. Long-term campaigns include AIDS, drugs and sex education, whereas more recent campaigns have been concerned with encouraging organ and blood donation (Bundeszentrale für gesundheitliche Aufklärung, 2003).

As in other European countries, Dutch patients have access to a wide range of health services and the availability of publicly mandated insurance schemes makes this access practically universal. This is complemented by programmes for vaccinations, screening for cancers and pre- and post-natal screening, many of which have expanded over recent years. Recent policy initiatives have focused more specifically on promoting healthy lifestyles, reducing alcohol and tobacco consumption and targeting new diseases such as HIV/AIDS, as well as health problems related to socio-economic status (Okma, 2001). A recent National Contract for Public Health (2001) also stresses the need for local and national levels as well as different sectors of health care provision, to co-operate.

By international comparison, people in Sweden enjoy good health and life expectancy is one of the highest, as is the number of older people. However, there have been concerns about health inequalities among certain social groups and, in 1991, a national strategy for public health was published (Whitehead, 1998). The strategy emphasized the importance of co-operation between different levels and coincided with the setting-up of the National Institute of Public Health, which is responsible for national programmes. In 2000, this was complemented by the publication of national goals in public health, which again highlighted the need to reduce health gaps between different social groups (Ministry of Health and Social Affairs, 2001). Structural determinants of health, such as education and unemployment, also play an increasingly important role in health promotion activities by municipalities. Nevertheless, health promotion in Sweden continues to be primarily concentrated on disease prevention (European Observatory on Health Care Systems, 2001).

Britain, too, has seen many initiatives in health promotion, but the White Paper, *The Health of the Nation*, in 1992 provided the first national strategy for England (Baggott, 2000). The White Paper identified priorities for health promotion and also set specific targets in relation to heart disease, strokes, cancers, mental illness, sexual health and accidents. The underlying view was that individual behaviour is the key factor responsible for poor health. This strong individualist orientation is not surprising considering the New Right orientation of the government at the time. The emphasis has changed somewhat since the Labour government came into power in 1997. The new strategy, encapsulated in the 1999 White Paper, *Saving Lives: Our Healthier Nation*, combines health promotion focused on the individual with an acknowledgement that social factors such as poverty also cause poor health. There is now a greater focus on improving the health of disadvantaged people and narrowing health gaps using health improvement programmes and designated health action zones. A central feature of these new initiatives is that they rely on collaboration with a wide range of actors, from central government and health authorities to local government and voluntary organizations, and even private businesses.

Like the UK, the USA has a very individualist orientation in its recent health promotion initiatives. In 1980, the US Public Health Service (PHS) in response to a 1979 Surgeon General's Report, *Healthy People*, presented a ten-year strategy for pursuing goals and measuring progress in health promotion and disease prevention. In 2002, the PHS released its new plan, *Healthy People 2010: A Systematic Approach to Health Improvement*. According to the Report:

> Healthy People 2010 seeks to increase life expectancy and quality of life over the next 10 years by helping individuals gain the knowledge, motivation, and opportunities they need to make informed decisions about their health. At the same time, Healthy People 2010 encourages local and State leaders to develop community wide and state wide efforts that promote healthy behaviors, create healthy environments, and increase access to high-quality health care. Because individual and community health are virtually inseparable, both the individual and the community need to do their parts to increase life expectancy and improve quality of life. (p. 5)

As is clear in this quotation, this document, rather than being simply a directive from the central government's public health agency, is a set of goals set before the states, localities and individuals where the real action will take place. The emphasis on the responsibility of the individual is also obvious.

Similarly, this heavy emphasis on individual responsibility in health care is reflected in the ambitious health promotion activities of

Singapore. In 1992, Prime Minister Goh Chok Tong launched the National Healthy Lifestyle Programme designed to educate Singaporeans about the importance of leading a healthy lifestyle and to encourage them to participate in regular exercise, eat healthily, avoid smoking and manage stress. The Programme takes an integrated approach that includes creating a supportive social and physical environment to encourage individuals to practise healthy behaviour. Between its inception in 1992 and 2001, the percentage of Singaporeans aged 18 to 69 years who exercised regularly increased from 17 to 20 per cent and those smoking dropped from 18 to 14 per cent (Singapore Ministry of Health, 2002). However, because the diet of Singaporeans has not improved and is still linked to high blood cholesterol and high blood pressure, the 2002 National Healthy Lifestyle Campaign focused on the promotion of healthier food choices. The key message was to reduce salt intake to prevent high blood pressure and strokes: 'Fight Stroke. Take Less Salt' (Singapore Ministry of Health, 2002b).

Health promotion, then, is an arena of increasing attention by many governments. This trend would represent going full circle back to the roots of health care if not for the fact that the resources being put into health promotion remain but a small fraction of what is put into curative, acute care. Also, as noted earlier, because health is so tied to lifestyle choice, the success or failure of these health promotion initiatives is heavily dependent on our capacity to alter individual behaviour. Increasingly, public health will come up against the notion of the right to live one's preferred life free from government constraint. One area where this conflict over health is replaced by yet another antagonism is in the occupational health arena where the conflict more often pits health and safety concerns against the economic interests of employers or countries in a competitive global marketplace.

Occupational health

Occupational health encompasses a broad range of health and safety concerns within an economic context. In other words, occupational health is often viewed as being inversely related to profit, at least in the short run: to improve workplace health and safety costs money. On the other hand, there is considerable evidence that even seemingly safe workplaces present unacceptable risks for some workers. In addition to direct hazards in the workplace, toxic hazards may be released into the environment or transported home on the clothing of contaminated workers. Still, the full magnitude of occupational harm might be obscured because many diseases are misdiagnosed or incorrectly attributed to other causes. Moreover, the long latency period between exposure and the onset of symptoms also helps mask occupational diseases: for instance, the latency period for asbestos-related lung cancer can be 25 years or more (Baker and Landrigan, 1993: 72).

These data demonstrate the need to focus more attention on occupational health if our goal is to maximize the health of the population. Health promotion in the workplace, likewise, can be expanded in order to preclude or reduce the health risks and educate workers concerning early signs of illnesses that may be linked to their specific jobs. Occupation health represents an area where preventive programmes and anticipatory health policy are warranted but often avoided due to opposition on economic grounds. However, while workplaces can never be risk-free, the more that is known about possible hazards in each workplace setting, the better able we are to minimize their impact. This area again illustrates differences among our countries regarding their willingness to use regulatory policies and to enforce them. As a result, some countries such as Germany and Japan have invested substantial resources in occupational health areas and built effective regulatory frameworks, while other countries have been less active and successful.

Germany has been something of a pioneer in the area of occupational health. As part of the legislation creating the different branches of the social insurance, the Accident Insurance System was set up in 1884. This form of insurance has been characterized by considerable continuity and has changed little over the last 120 years (Standard Committee of the Hospitals of the European Union, 2003). The scheme provides compensation for an industrial accident or an occupational disease in the form of rehabilitation and payment of benefits (such as a pension). Accident prevention is also covered by the scheme. The insurance is funded by contributions from member companies and is run by professional associations. The professional associations are statutory accident insurance companies and are organized on the basis of industrial sectors. Accident Insurance is complemented by industry-wide occupational safety organizations, the Technical Inspectorates and the Public Factory Inspectorates.

Like Germany, Japan has a long history of occupational safety and health policies that can be traced back to the Factory Act in 1911 and that have consistently been expanded since that time. Since then, the increasing number of work-related accidents and chronic work-related diseases (such as pneumoconiosis among mine workers) has prompted a series of laws on occupational health and safety. In 1955, special acts for silicosis and traumatic spinal injuries were enacted to promote such measures. In 1972, the Occupational Safety and Health Act (OSHA), among other things, created a medical speciality in occupational health. Under the Administrative Structure of Occupational Safety and Health of OSHA, employers who employ 1,000 or more workers must employ an industrial doctor on a full time basis. Industrial doctors are responsible for the health maintenance of all workers and must conduct an on-site inspection of the working conditions to make sure they are safe and healthy. Although not legally binding, industrial doctors make recommendations to employers and managers regarding safety and health maintenance of the workers. All employers, regardless of industry, are required to conduct health check-ups once a year. For workers working under special conditions, additional examinations are included in the regular health check-ups.

As compared to Japan, occupational health in the USA is more recent and more fragmented. Moreover, the US Occupational Safety and Health Administration has been controversial because of its complicated and very bureaucratic rules on safety covering over 100 million workers and 6.5 million employers. Established by the Occupational Safety and Health Act of 1970, the mission of the Administration is to save lives, prevent injuries, and protect the health of America's workers. The Occupational Safety and Health Administration and its state partners have approximately 2,100 inspectors, plus complaint investigators, standards writers, and other technical and support personnel spread over more than 200 offices throughout the USA. This staff establishes protective standards, enforces those standards, and offers employers and employees technical assistance and consultation programmes. Despite its far-ranging scope, the Scheme does not cover mine safety, transportation safety, and most public employees. Although it is heavily involved with workplace health, it is located in the Department of Labor and has virtually no communication with the Public Health Service even when dealing with the same health problem.

Occupational health in Britain is situated at the opposite end of the regulatory spectrum from Germany, Japan and the USA. In Britain there are no statutory regulations for employers to provide occupational health services and occupational health is also excluded from the NHS. Instead, with the 1974 Health and Safety at Work Act, Britain adopted a quasi self-regulatory approach. 'As a result only a minority of the British workforce have access to Occupational Health, with some employers providing in-house Services, and others making use of Service providers under contract' (Society of Occupational Medicine, 2003).

Singapore recently initiated a comprehensive policy emphasis on occupational health. In 2000, the Tripartite Committee on Workplace Health Promotion (TriCom) issued its recommendations on how to expand and improve workplace health promotion programmes. Responsibility for implementing these recommendations falls on the Workplace Health Promotion Programme (WHPP) which, in turn, is directed by the Intersectoral Management Committee on Workplace

Health Promotion composed of representatives of the unions, employers and the government. The goal of the WHPP is to develop a healthy workforce so as to contribute to Singapore's productivity and prosperity for a better quality of life. A specific objective is to cover at least 50 per cent of the private sector workforce with a workplace health promotion programme by the year 2005. The primary focus of the WHPP is to encourage employers to engage in workplace health promotion and to provide technical assistance to those wanting to strengthen existing programmes to demonstrate tangible health outcomes (Singapore Ministry of Health, 2003).

Other dimensions of public health

So far this chapter has examined the structures and funding sources of public health efforts in our countries, health promotion strategies and activities, and occupational health and safety policy. It should be clear that many of these programme areas are leading us far away from health care as medicine into the realm of health education and even labour policy. The discussion that follows demonstrates that this can easily be extended even further afield into employment, education, housing, anti-crime and environmental science policy. Although we do not have time here for a full comparative analysis of each of these areas, we briefly discuss the main health issues in each. Some areas that we are not able to discuss here but which are closely tied to the sections below on homelessness and violence are drug and alcohol abuse and mental illness. Each of these factors exacerbates all other public health problems and together they represent a major public health crisis largely ignored by the predominant medical model that now drives health care.

Tobacco and alcohol policy

In Chapter 4 (p. 115) it was noted that a significant proportion of health care costs in all countries is linked to individual behaviour. Predominant among these behaviours is smoking and alcohol abuse. Cumulatively, tobacco, alcohol and illicit drugs 'prematurely kill about 7 million people world wide each year and the number is rising' (Reuters, 2003). All of the countries examined here have instituted public health measures designed to reduce the incidence of smoking, including high taxes, restrictions on where people are allowed to smoke, bans on certain types of advertising, and regulations for sales and distribution (see www5.who.int/tobacco/ for specific country regulations).

Although systematic comparative estimates on the costs of smoking and alcohol abuse are not available, tobacco especially causes a significant number of deaths, and smokers generally consume more health care resources than non-smokers. In the USA, for example, it is estimated that 19 per cent of all premature deaths (about 400,000 annually) are caused by tobacco use (McGinnis and Foege, 1993). Given that the USA has mid-range rates of smoking (see Table 7.1), death rates from smoking in other countries can be assumed to be similar, if not higher. Similarly, the cost of alcohol-related problems alone in the USA was estimated by the National Institutes of Health to be $148 billion in 1992 (National Institutes of Health, 1998).

Table 7.1   *Smoking rates, men and women (%), ranked by*
women

	% women who smoke	% men who smoke
Netherlands	29	36
France	27	40
Italy	26	38
UK	26	28
Sweden	24	22
USA	23	28
Germany	21	37
Australia	21	29
Japan	15	59
Singapore	<3	32

Source: Data from WHO (1996).

Table 7.1 illustrates that smoking rates vary significantly across our countries, especially among women. In Singapore, high prices and strict regulations have cut overall smoking rates, but obviously the extremely low rate for women is cultural since male smoking is near the average for these countries. Similarly, Japan's low rates for women are cultural because, comparatively speaking, Japan has relatively relaxed regulations and by far the highest rate of male smoking.

However, evidence suggests that laws can make a difference and that public health and education programmes can reduce smoking rates to a degree (WHO, 2003). Some countries have significantly reduced the consumption of tobacco and the harm it causes. Data from ten European countries where advanced tobacco control policies have been implemented for some time, including France, Italy, Sweden and the UK, show a decrease in the number of tobacco-related deaths in recent years (WHO, 2003). The most effective control measures include high prices on tobacco products, total bans on advertising, support for cessation treatment and policies requiring the creation of smoke-free environments.

According to WHO (2003), most countries could strengthen controls in these areas and others. For example, less than 25 per cent of countries in the European Region earmark any tobacco tax revenues for control measures and health promotion, and only five countries allocate more than 1 per cent. New European Union directives and the Framework Convention on Tobacco Control are being negotiated with the aim to counter the industry's ability to undermine national controls (WHO, 2003).

The European report on tobacco control policy shows that, while smoking rates stabilized at 30 per cent for the region as a whole (38 per cent for men and 23 per cent for women) over the last five years, increases in population meant that the number of smokers rose (WHO, 2003). Most countries show a gap in smoking rates between the lowest and highest socio-economic groups. In some countries, the poorest smoke three times more than the richest. This report further found that smoking rates among young people across Europe are converging, eliminating former differences according to gender and geography. The report shows that, although several countries reported reductions in adult smoking, none showed significant reductions in smoking by young people. In addition, the gender gap has become less significant among teenagers: in 12 countries girls smoked as much as, or more than, boys (WHO, 2003).

Like smoking, alcohol causes severe health problems, and there is 'sufficient evidence to indicate that alcohol is a significant threat to world health' (WHO, 2001). In fact, alcohol contributes far more years of life lost to death or disability than tobacco and illegal drugs combined (WHO, 2001). To date, most of the countries have not been as rigorous in their attempts to reduce alcohol consumption as they have tobacco, but instead have focused on reducing drinking and driving and other alcohol-related behaviours. Table 7.2 illustrates the range of consumption represented by our countries. Not surprisingly wine-producing countries in Europe have traditionally had the highest rates, but trends indicate that the UK rates are closing the gap (Institute of Alcohol Studies, 2002). Sweden, due to high prices, and Singapore, due to high prices, strict regulations and its emphasis on personal responsibility for health, display the lowest consumption rates.

The most common form of alcohol regulation is the setting of a minimum age for purchase or consumption. Studies have found that such restrictions are effective in reducing motor vehicle crash fatalities even with relatively low levels of enforcement (Wagenaar and Wolfson, 1995). At present, Australia, the Netherlands and the UK have set the

Table 7.2   *Alcohol consumption, per capita in litres,*
1996 and 2000

Country	1996	2000
France	11.1	10.5
Germany	9.8	10.5
Italy	8.2	7.5
Netherlands	8.0	8.2
UK	7.6	8.4
Australia	7.5	7.8
New Zealand	6.8	7.4
USA	6.6	6.7
Japan	6.6	6.5
Sweden	4.9	4.7
Singapore	1.6	1.5

Source: Data from *World Drink Trends* (2002).

legal drinking age at 18; Japan, New Zealand and Sweden at 20; the US states generally at 21; and France, Italy and Germany at 16 for beer and wine and 18 for distilled spirits (WHO, 2002). Key to the effectiveness of such preventive efforts is enforcement, which varies considerably both across and within countries.

Other alcohol control policies include prohibition, monopolies over production and/or sale, licensing, warning labels, restrictions on advertising and promotion, education and taxation. Also central to any comprehensive health strategy for alcohol is the provision of adequate treatment facilities for alcohol dependence. According to the WHO, very few countries have 'systematically evaluated various forms of treatment and the resources allocated for treatment are often very scarce, if existent. Globally, access to affordable and effective treatment is still largely inadequate' (WHO, 2001: 13). No attempt is made here to summarize the specific control policies, but it is important to reiterate that across our countries, with the possible exception of Singapore, public health measures remain inadequately funded, thus undermining their effectiveness to combat the types of problems raised by tobacco and alcohol.

Homelessness and inadequate housing

One public health factor which is virtually ignored by the medical model but which takes on significance in the more inclusive social model, is housing. Lack of housing obviously puts people, particularly children, at serious health risk. While the homeless suffer from the same acute and chronic illnesses as those in the general population, they do so at much higher rates (Box 7.2). 'Because the homeless have little or no access to adequate bathing and hygienic facilities, survive on the streets or in unsafe and generally unsanitary shelters, smoke and drink to excess, and suffer from inadequate diets, their physical health is compromised' (Institute of Medicine, 1993: 210). As a result upper respiratory tract infections, trauma and skin ailments are commonplace. High levels of alcohol abuse, drug abuse and mental illness complicate the picture.

Although the health impact of a lack of housing is most severe, poor or inadequate housing can also lead to poor health. Poor housing is linked to a wide array of physical and mental health problems as described in Box 7.2. Sub-standard housing is related to house fires and increased accidents. Furthermore, damp and cold living conditions are

---

Box 7.2   Homelessness, poor housing and health in Britain

The poor health of homeless people is made worse by inadequate access to health services, as two reports on the health of 'rough sleepers' in the UK suggest. A report by the housing charity Crisis highlights the fact that homeless people are often denied the right to register with a GP (Carvel, 2002). Instead, homeless people have to rely on overstretched casualty departments in hospitals when their health problem has become an emergency. Medical treatment can also be rendered useless when homeless people are discharged back on to the streets without any adequate support. This is echoed by a government report, which states that the health needs of homeless people are not met in a systematic and effective way (Ward, 2002). For example, only one-third of health improvement plans of Primary Care Trusts mention homeless people.

One need not be homeless to suffer adverse health effects, however. A report by the London School of Hygiene and Tropical Medicine (1999) lists the many health aspects on which housing has an impact, ranging from excess winter morbidity because of inadequate home heating, respiratory problems because of damp and mould to noise disturbance because of poor sound insulation. However, it is difficult to quantify the amount of ill health caused by poor housing because many health effects are qualitative in nature and concern poor quality of life and social isolation. Housing-related health problems are particularly acute in London, where the housing stock is comparatively old and often of poor quality. London also has some of the most deprived populations in the UK and a high proportion of residents from ethnic minorities.

associated with respiratory ailments, while improperly ventilated housing is linked to heat-related health problems. In combination with overall poverty, unemployment, poor education, and violence and crime, inadequate housing remains a health hazard for many citizens. These factors share in common their isolation from the medical model. Although medical care is beneficial for many individuals affected by these health-threatening factors, 'medical care cannot compensate for economic deprivation, social disorganisation, personal alienation, and low levels of education and social integration' (Mechanic, 1994: 3). In the end, solutions to these problems lie fully outside the medical community. Unfortunately, as argued by Kassler (1994: 166), health care reformers have focused so much on medical care that they have ignored those factors that ultimately make the biggest difference in people's health.

Violence and health

As nurses and doctors in any accident and emergency unit can confirm, violence is a major health problem that accounts for a large part of their time and a huge economic outlay. Importantly, all violence is fully preventable. Often, violence is tied to alcohol and drug abuse. Moreover, although not the sole domain of any social class or race, rates of violent behaviour are considerably higher among the poor. Furthermore, there appears to be a trend in many countries that the perpetrators of crime are becoming younger and younger.

In 1998, over 30,000 people died from gunshot wounds in the USA, making it the second most frequent cause of death for persons aged 15–34 and the highest among black youth (Federal Bureau of Investigation, 2000). Moreover, for every fatality it is estimated that there are seven non-fatal injuries that require hospitalization or outpatient treatment. The average estimated cost for each fatality is $938,500 (Miller and Cohen, 1997). For those with spinal injury, the lifetime costs can be many times that figure. The total cost of health care and lost production from firearm-related injury alone is put in excess of $100 billion per year in the USA (Cook and Ludwig, 2000). Because the population with firearm-related injury tends to be disproportionately poor, a large proportion of the cost is borne by the public, not private insurance. Futhermore, such injuries are skewed by race with blacks highly over-represented. If the rest of the population were being killed at the same rate as young African–American males, over 460,000 people would die that way each year (Kizer *et al.*, 1995). Reduction of firearm-related injuries, however, is difficult in an environment where the number of firearms is proliferating. Although long seen as a problem largely confined to the USA, or at least primarily a US problem, increasingly violence has become a major health risk in many countries. According to government figures in the UK, for instance, the number of offences involving firearms increased by nearly 10 per cent in 2001. In the same year, the number of gun attacks investigated by London's Metropolitan Police rose by more than a third ('Gun Crime Survival Rates Rising', 2002).

Firearm-related injuries are just one manifestation of the health impact of violence. Incidence of reported family-related violence continues to rise in the forms of child abuse, spousal abuse and elder abuse. Often overlooked by medical professionals, battering is a major factor in illness and injury among women. According to the US-based National Organisation for Women:

> Women who are battered have more than twice the health care needs and costs than those who are never battered. Approximately 17 per cent of pregnant women report having been battered, and the results include miscarriages, stillbirths and a two to four times greater likelihood of bearing a low birth weight baby. Abused women are disproportionately represented among the homeless and suicide victims. (National Organisation for Women, 2003)

The actual health impact is no doubt significantly higher than the health care costs because battered women often do not receive care since their access to the health care system is often controlled and blocked by their abusers. In addition to this structural barrier, financial and cultural barriers to health care deny battered women, children and elders access to needed care and thus a full accounting of the problem. Data on battering in most countries are sketchy and unreliable, but there is growing evidence to suggest it is not a uniquely American phenomenon and that it has significant health ramifications across countries.

Environmental change and health

Global environmental change is ultimately a matter of health. However, while the health effects of environmental change have received considerable press, serious policy attention has been more subdued, in part because they are viewed as trans-national problems. Training and research on environmental health issues remains a low priority in general medical education and health research budgets in environmental health are less than a fraction of 1 per cent of total health care spending. In the last decade, for instance, the US National Institute of Environmental Health Sciences ranked last in funding of the 23 institutes in the National Institutes of Health. Medical students in the USA on average receive only six hours of education on environmental and occupational health over their four years of medical school and virtually no exposure to the impact of global issues such as population growth, climate change and ozone depletion on human health (Chivian, 1994: 36). For all practical purposes, then, the medical profession as a whole is not well positioned to fully appreciate health within a global environment perspective despite increasing evidence of substantial health effects.

Although local and national environmental health hazards have always been endemic (see Quah and Boon, 2003), concern has recently been raised over new global threats. For instance, global climate change resulting from the accumulation of greenhouse gases is likely to have a significant impact on the health of the population. If global warming trends are accurate, the increase in the number of days with temperatures over 100°F (38°C) will produce a sharp rise in heat-related mortality from heat strokes, heart attacks and cerebral strokes, especially among the very young, the elderly, and those with chronic respiratory diseases (as evidenced by events in France in the summer of 2003 where an estimated 15,000 died from the heat). Moreover, global warming and changing patterns of rainfall could result in the spread of infectious diseases as insects carrying the agents move into areas that until now have been too cold for their survival. Although the full health impact of global climate change and as yet unanticipated outcomes is unlikely in the near future, evidence suggests that commitment is needed now to avert these threats and prevent major health problems (Epstein, 2000; US Environmental Protection Agency, 2002).

Similarly, depletion of the ozone layer poses severe health risks that appear to be emerging already. Higher levels of ultraviolet B radiation (UVB) reaching the surface of the earth can damage DNA and proteins and kill cells in all living organisms. There is evidence that heightened exposure of humans to UVB leads to an increase in all forms of skin cancer (Garvin and Eyles, 2001). Most at risk are Australia and New Zealand, although the incidence of malignant melanomas, with mortality rates of 25 per cent, have increased faster than any other cancer even in Scotland where the incidence of melanoma for men tripled between 1980 and 2000 (British United President Association, 2002). In the USA, over 1 million Americans are diagnosed with skin cancer, making it the most common cancer. The American Cancer Society estimates that 7,600 people die each year from fully preventable malignant melanomas in the USA, many of them young (Doneny, 2003).

In terms of numbers, cataracts represent an even wider health threat caused by UVB radiation. Because UVB exposure can be reduced by 90 per cent though a combination of the use of plastic lens glasses and a hat, this is one area where relatively straightforward strategies could easily be integrated in health promotion programmes such as that of Singapore to avert considerable health problems and costs.

In addition to the health threats of long-term environmental changes, more immediate and localized conditions can have considerable adverse health consequences for exposed populations. Despite efforts to reduce their impact, air and water pollution levels remain high in many locales and continue to put large numbers of persons at risk. Respiratory problems in urban areas caused or aggravated by air pollution are also likely to be exacerbated by global warming and population concentration (Epstein, 2000). Drinking water systems are not only threatened by industrial and waste disposal contamination, but also by the methods used for disinfecting them due to the toxic effects of the disinfectants and their by-products. The imminent breakdown of old and deteriorating water and sewage systems in some of the larger urban centres of many countries represents a growing health concern that requires urgent attention. Unfortunately, infrastructure funding in many countries has decreased as medical care consumes larger shares of state and local budgets.

All this is not to say that there have been no efforts to deal with environmental health problems. At the international level, a number of initiatives have arisen from the 1984 WHO's 'Health for All' strategy. Its definition of health as physical, mental and social well-being directed attention to the importance of the environment for promoting health. In 1989, the Member States of the WHO's European region agreed on a 'European Charter on Environment and Health', which recognizes the right to an environment conducive to health and the right to relevant information. In 1994, this was followed by an 'Environmental Action Plan for Europe' prepared by the WHO. The Plan calls for management instruments in the area of environmental protection where this is relevant to health. The participating Member States committed themselves to implementing the Plan through 'National Action Plans on Environment and Health' (WHO Regional Office for Europe, 2003c). The WHO set up the European Environment and Health Committee to support the implementation of the Action Plan (WHO Regional Office for Europe, 2003a). The Committee meets twice a year and comprises health and environment ministries and intergovernmental organizations, as well as civil society organizations. The work of the Committee is complemented by the WHO Programme on Global Change and Health, which is concerned with assessing and monitoring the health impact of global environmental changes (WHO Regional Office for Europe, 2003b).

Among our countries, Sweden has considered environmental health an important issue and has had a pioneering role in environmental policies (European Observatory on Health Care Systems, 2001). In Sweden, the municipalities are responsible for a wide range of areas of environmental health, including disease prevention, food quality, water management and chemical control. Municipalities are also experimenting with new forms of environmental auditing and accounting as well as with new environmental tariffs to improve environmental protection and food security. Further, municipalities in Sweden have been at the forefront of implementing the UN's local agenda 21, a participatory process aimed at sustainable development, which includes health issues (Eckerberg, Fordberg and Wickenberg, 1998).

Social and economic determinants of health

There is substantial evidence that health status is highly correlated with socio-economic status (Kawachi, Kennedy and Wilkinson, 1999; Marmot and Wilkinson, 1999). If a primary goal of health policy is to improve the health status of the population, it is essential to focus on economic and social determinants of health. A workable model of health requires a shift away from the dominance of the medical care system towards this more inclusive model of health. 'Social problems are resolved primarily through non-medical means, signifying a shift away from the current practice of defining and treating them as medical illnesses' (Hurowitz, 1993: 132). Although there is variation in health status across nations (see Table 7.3: p. 205), often the variation among groups within a particular nation is even higher. Because this variation cannot be attributed to differences in the health system of the country, other factors must be important. Key factors are social and economic, which in turn might be reflected in differences in health by race, religion or ethnic background. Lower social class, as measured by income, education or other socio-economic status (SES) indicators, is related to higher death rates overall and higher rates of most diseases that are the most common causes of death. Moreover, social class differences in mortality and morbidity continue to widen (Nuthall, 1992: 15).

Health status disparities linked to SES are probably the result of a complicated mix of factors suggested by three distinct theories. The first, *natural and social selection*, contends that one of the key determinants of social class is health status. This theory assumes that those with poor health, high-risk behaviour and social pathologies naturally concentrate in the lower social class. If good health is indeed necessary in order to pursue life goals and affords one the opportunity to succeed in meeting them, it should not be surprising to find that persons in poor health would tend to attain lower SES. Although this might explain the disparity at the margins, however, it is not generally seen as a major explanation.

A second theory, the *structuralist*, attributes class differences in health to structural factors such as the production and consumption of wealth. Lower SES persons generally exist in less healthy environments, both at home and work. For example, a recent study concluded that there is 'widespread evidence that the poor in the US, UK, and perhaps other countries at well, face a disproportionate burden of environmental risks' (Huggins, 2002). They face more exposure to air pollution, poor water, ambient noise, sub-standard housing, and overcrowding. In contrast, higher SES persons enjoy healthier homes, safer appliances and vehicles, and less hazardous jobs.

The third theory, a *cultural and behavioural* one, sees disparities in health among social classes as the result of differences in behaviour. Often the culture of the lower classes leads to engagement in multiple high-risk behaviour that, in turn, leads to poor health. Smoking, alcohol and drug abuse, violence, sedentary lifestyles, obesity, poor diet, and other unhealthy behaviours are disproportionately present in lower SES groupings. Many observers have concluded that this last theory is the most explanatory, but most conclude that it must be accompanied by the structuralist theory because the behaviour occurs within this broader social context. As noted by Mechanic, SES is 'perhaps the single most important influence on health outcomes, in part through its direct influence, but more importantly, through the many indirect effects it has on factors that directly shape health outcomes' (1994: 149). These indirect factors are most apparent when one examines the several components of SES: income and education.

Income has been found to be a critical variable in determining health status at two levels. At a cross-national level, research consistently shows that the distribution of income has more to do with the health of the population than does the level of medical spending. The best health results are achieved in those societies that minimize the gap between the rich and the poor. Wilkinson (1997) suggests that healthy, egalitarian societies are more socially cohesive, they have a stronger community life, and they suffer fewer of the corrosive effects of inequality. He also found that approximately two-thirds of the variation in mortality rates within developed nations is related to the distribution of income in the population. This includes the UK where, despite universal access to health care, mortality rates among the working-class population increased as income distribution widened in the 1980s (Wilkinson, 1992: 167). In contrast, Japan has the most equal income distribution and the highest life expectancy despite relatively low levels of health care spending (Kawachi, Kennedy and Wilkinson, 1999).

At the individual level as well, low income is consistently related to ill health. Low-income families are more likely to assess their health status as 'poor'. Low-income persons are significantly more likely to have preventable hospitalizations than high-income persons with one study finding that the lowest income group was four times as likely to be hospitalized as the highest-income group (Angell, 1993: 126). The most likely explanation of these disparities is to be found in some combination of the theories discussed above, but its implication for health policy is significant. The impact of any efforts to constrain health care costs will hit most severely those groups which are not only most likely to need the care but also least likely to have other options. Despite greater need, larger proportions of the poor have difficulty in gaining access to health services that might avert poor health.

Not surprisingly, given its close association with income, education is also significantly related to health status. Persons with less education have more frequent short-stay hospitalizations, they have a higher prevalence of chronic conditions and are significantly more limited in activity due to such conditions, and they have significantly lower self-assessment of their health. One study found that of all indicators, education had the strongest and most consistent relationship with health and was the single most consistent predictor of good health (Winkleby *et al.*, 1992).

Health status, then, is intimately related to various measures of SES, particularly education and income (Marmot and Wilkinson, 1999). These differences are critical in understanding the social and cultural context of health and require considerably more research on how these factors operate. The interactive model of health care attributes poor health outcomes to a broad range of social factors that are bound up in the SES construct. Although SES might have a direct impact on health, it is more likely that it operates indirectly through other factors. In addition to inequitable access to primary care, health promotion and disease prevention efforts, other critical factors include unemployment, violence, breakdown of family support structures and inadequate housing.

Unemployment can influence health by reducing income level and standard of living. Moreover, the importance of work to one's well-being, over and above the financial aspects, is well-documented (Hummelgaard, Baadsgaard and Nielsen, 1998; Turner, 1995). The unemployed have lower self-esteem and experience significant psychological stress which is linked to higher levels of both subjectively and objectively assessed levels of physical and mental ill-health. Heightened unemployment rates are associated with heightened death rates. A recent study concluded that 'increases in the unemployment rates in European Union countries are related to deteriorated health as measured by elevated mortality rates over the following 10 to 15 years' (Brenner, 2001). Interestingly, the relationship was strongest in the UK, Sweden, Germany and Finland. Suicide and deliberate self-harm are more prevalent among the unemployed, as are smoking and alcohol and drug abuse, particularly among the unemployable youth. At the community level, death rates have been found to increase during times of economic depression and joblessness, and to decrease during times of economic growth (Barwick, 1992). Although the full dynamics are unclear, the assumption that employment is crucial to both mental and physical health is supported by a broad array of studies. Reduction of unemployment has significant health benefits for the population as well as the individual.

The family has traditionally played an important role in integrating health-promoting routines into the daily lives of the members. It has also served as an important facilitator of self-esteem and a social setting that provides critical contributions to psychological and physical development. While reality has often fallen short of this ideal, the decline first of the extended family and more recently the nuclear family has had adverse effects on health. Studies consistently find that marriage is associated with lower levels of mortality, better overall health status and healthier behaviour patterns (Stanton, 2003). A study from the Netherlands, for instance, concludes that married people have the lowest morbidity rate, while the divorced show the highest (Joung *et al.*, 1994). Another study from the University of Warwick in the UK found that even when the effects of smoking, drinking and other unhealthy activities were factored in, married men had a 9 per cent lower risk of dying as compared to unmarried men (BBC News, 2002). Although the reasons for this are unclear, a likely factor is the 'social support' of having a wife or husband nearby. Another explanation is that both single men and women tend to have a less healthy lifestyle including sleep, diet and work habits, and to be more prone to loneliness and depression. Family relationships, however, in whatever form do appear to encourage good health practices and provide strong social links that reduce the likelihood of ill health.

Public health: putting medicine in context

While there is no doubt that medical care can be decisive in individual cases, there is substantial evidence to demonstrate that it is but a relatively minor determinant of the health of populations. If the goal of health care is to improve the health of populations, then the medical model must be reassessed. Almost three decades ago, Ivan Illich (1976) vehemently criticized modern medicine as a nemesis and a cause, not a cure, of illness. Although Illich's criticisms of medicine are unduly harsh, he raises many legitimate questions and forces us to place medicine in a social context. There is strong support, for instance, for his conclusion that major improvements in health derive from changes in the way in which people are able to live, thus suggesting the need to replace the medical model with one based in subjective reality. Too much medicine is not good for health! Not only does it divert resources from more useful endeavours, but it also produces ill health and disrupts traditional social and cultural institutions and values that are central to good health in the broader sense. Medical misadventure alone contributes to many deaths each year, over 100,000 in the USA alone (Kohn, Corrigan and Donaldson, 1999; Starfield, 2000).

Health, therefore, must be put into perspective along with a wide array of elements of an enjoyable life including art, entertainment, music and work, as well as family and social interaction. To place health above everything else risks underestimating the contribution of these many other factors to the fulfilment of our goals and the enhancement of the human condition. According to Lamm (1993:17), we cannot live by health alone, but must invest in education, infrastructure, and other essential components. Although health is important, it is not all-important. It makes little sense to invest disproportionate amounts of societal resources into health at the expense of those things that make life worth living. It appears that while Western nations accept the notion that health is but one aspect of well-being at the personal level, as societies we expect the health care systems to resolve many problems that at their core are not medical ones.

This nearly exclusive focus on medical care is flawed not only because it tends to emphasize only one dimension of health (see p. 54) but also because it elevates health as a primary goal instead of as a means to broader life goals. Implicit in the conventional health care model is the assumption that improved health status is achieved primarily by higher expenditures on medical care. Although the health status of individuals is influenced by medical care and it has the potential to improve quality of life or save the lives of some persons, there is little correlation between how much money is spent on doctors and hospitals and how healthy a society is. As illustrated in Table 7.3, countries that expend the highest amounts on health do not score higher on health outcomes and, in fact, often do less well. Any relationship between medical care and health, even in its narrow physical sense, is minimal compared to other determinants of health status such as heredity, personal behaviour, and the physical and social environment. The impact of medical care is further limited because many health conditions are self-limiting, some are incurable, and for many others there is little or no effective treatment. The cases where health care is effective and significantly affects health outcomes 'comprise only a small proportion of total medical care – too small to make a discernible impact on the statistics in populations' (Fuchs, 1994: 109).

Figure 7.1 further casts doubt on the assumption that more spending on health care is the answer. It shows that the near-exponential increase in spending in the USA over the last decades has not been accompanied

Table 7.3   *Total health care expenditure, life expectancy at birth and infant mortality, 1998 (ranked by % GDP)*

	Total health care expenditure (as percentage of GDP)	Life expectancy at birth (in years)	Infant mortality (in deaths per 1,000 live births)
USA	12.9	76.7	7.2
Germany	10.3	77.5	4.7
France	9.4	78.4	4.6
Netherlands	8.7	78.0	5.2
Australia	8.6	78.7	5.0
Italy	8.2	79.0	5.3
New Zealand	8.1	77.8	6.4
Sweden	7.9	79.4	3.5
Japan	7.4	80.6	3.6
UK	6.8	77.3	5.7
Singapore	2.9	80.1	3.6

Sources: Data from OECD (2001b) and Singapore Ministry of Health (2001).

by a corresponding decrease in mortality rates. The major decrease in mortality rates actually occurred early in the twentieth century as a result of broad public health measures, and has only moderated despite huge increases in spending on medical care. Although gross mortality rates may not be the optimal measure of health status, the vast discrepancies here raise critical concerns. Expending additional resources on medical care is unlikely to pay dividends in terms of health outcomes for the population.

Moreover, in those cases where health gains have been presumed to be the result of medical intervention, data indicate that medical technology has, in fact, not played the major role. For instance, it has been estimated that at least two-thirds of the reduction in mortality rates during the 1970s and 98 per cent of the modest mortality rate improvement in the 1980s was tied to the reduction in death from cardiovascular disease (Drake, 1994: 133). Under the medical model, the reduction in deaths from cardiovascular disease is assumed to be the result of impressive innovations in treatment, especially coronary by-pass surgery and angioplasty. However, evidence suggests that most, if not all, of this drop is attributable to lifestyle changes reflected in the decline in smoking, increase in exercise, and decreases in saturated fat consumption. 'Only a small part, if any, can be attributed to medical

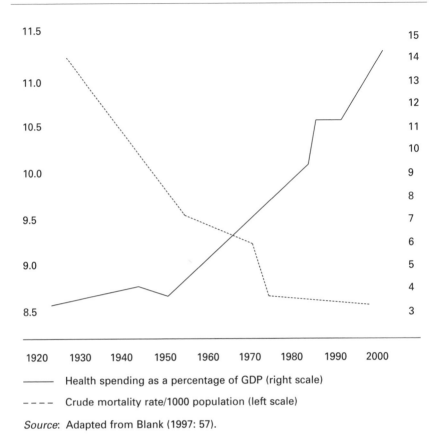

Figure 7.1   *Mortality rates and percentage of GDP spent on health
care in the USA, 1900–2000*

technology' (Cundiff and McCarthy, 1994: 18). Similarly, Bunker, Frazier and Mosteller conclude that 'current data provide no evidence that medical care has reduced mortality when all cancers are added together' (1994: 233).

These findings regarding the inadequacy of explaining health status by health care have significant implications for any efforts to restructure the health care system. If a system really wants to achieve the goal of maximizing the health of its population, resources would better be directed towards alleviating poverty, reducing crime, changing lifestyles and so forth. A healthy person does not need medical care. 'Good health often does not require access to medical care and is largely dependent on the condition of society' (Hurowitz, 1993: 130).

On these grounds, recent efforts to reform health care systems may be misguided because no amount of restructuring health care along the lines proposed by the reformers will have a major impact on the health of their populations. Reforms for universal access, improved quality of care, and cost containment might improve the medical care system, but they cannot be expected to improve substantially the health of the population. As a result, 'there is little evidence . . . to suggest that providing universal coverage or changing the delivery system will have significant favorable effects on health, either in the aggregate or for particular socio-economic groups' (Fuchs, 1994: 109). Chapter 8 will attempt to integrate this theme with the many others running through this book.

Understanding Health Policy Comparatively

In analysing health policy in a comparative context, the preceding chapters have covered a wide range of topics including the historical and cultural trajectories of health policy; systems of funding, providing and governing health care; policies of allocating health resources; health care in the home; and the diverse policies that constitute public health. As in any cross-country comparison, a tension emerges between similarities and differences, between common policy trends, such as the ubiquity of rationing, and policy divergence, such as welfare mix in the provision of hospital services. Chapter 1 suggests that typologies of health systems help to make sense of health policies across countries, pointing to those similarities and differences that are theoretically significant.

Subsequent chapters used a typology based on government involvement in the funding and provision of health care. This typology helped to identify and order some of the basic characteristics of health systems and policies. As such, the typology was particularly strong at offering an overview of the health systems and policies in different countries. However, as Chapter 3 demonstrates, a significant number of our countries do not easily fit into the typology and the public control of the funding and provision of health care does not coincide in the way predicted by the typology. This underlines the point made in Chapter 1 (p. 23), that typologies are first and foremost heuristic tools that help to order complexity, not precise descriptors of reality. Nevertheless, the fewer the cases that fit the framework underpinning the typology, the weaker the heuristic value of the typology. Furthermore, the typology of government involvement in the funding and provision of health care tends to be less useful when it comes to the analysis of more specific health policy issues. As Chapters 4 to 7 demonstrate, such a comparison requires additional typologies such as typologies of rationing, paying doctors, or value orientations in relation to home care.

In part, the two sets of limitations discussed may be specific to the typology used, but they raise the more general question about the use of typologies to order material about health systems and policies from different countries. The next three sections discuss some limitations of typologies and point to the embeddedness of health policies in country-specific contexts and the importance of differences, the convergence of health policies and the predominance of similarities, and the complexities of health policies. The last point refers to the fact that policies often vary between functionally distinct aspects of health care and are broader than health systems themselves.

Policy embeddedness and the importance of differences

One reason why health policies do not easily fit into typologies is that health policies are embedded in contexts that are often highly specific to individual countries. This makes first and foremost for differences, especially as country-specific contexts are also highly complex. As Chapter 2 highlights, the contexts in which health policies are embedded encompass a wide range of aspects, and include demographic factors, biomedical technology, social values and cultural factors, as well as the legal and political systems, social structures, the mass media and public expectations. In the extreme, policy embeddedness suggests that the differences between countries are too significant and too numerous for typologies (and maybe even comparisons) to work. In its more moderate usage, embeddedness suggests that more often than not health policies follow country-specific trajectories.

Moran (1999, 2000), for example, highlights the political embeddedness of health care and introduces the notion of health care states. Health care and states penetrate each other to such an extent that it is impossible to understand one without the other. Health care is about more than systems of funding and providing services and instead involves the state in a big way. This makes health care an arena for the struggle over the distribution of scarce political and economic resources, a process shaped by market economies and democratic politics. Embeddedness also underpins Wilsford's (1994) notion of path dependency, which highlights the importance of structural forces. Past policies become so institutionalized and historically embedded that they closely shape emerging health policies. Health policies tend to be incremental and build on what is already there.

The analysis in the previous chapters contains many examples of how country-specific contexts shape health policies and how differences between countries are often particularly pertinent. In the Netherlands, for example, the health system is unusual in that it combines social insurance with strong universalist elements. Health policies combine considerable diversity of sources of funding, including private insurance for acute medical risks for those earning above a certain ceiling, with compulsory membership in the case of insurance for exceptional medical risks. This reflects the historical legacy of a society segmented into different groupings and the gradual weakening of this legacy. And this also helps to explain why the Netherlands with its social insurance system has been a pioneer in home care policies, while the social insurance orientation has been one of the factors holding back policy developments in Germany.

In Singapore, country-specific factors have shaped health policy in such a way that the health system is almost in a category of its own. Health care funding combines high individual responsibility and limited, familial risk pooling with strong government control of funding. Health care is funded by individual savings accounts, which are compulsory. Government also caps contribution rates, while out-of-pocket payments are high. As such Singapore defies the dictum that private funding is unlikely to lead to public control. Government control extends to hospitals, most of which are publicly owned, although ambulatory care is firmly in private hands. The strength of government control reflects not only the spatial concentration of political power typical of city-states, but also a strongly centralized approach to health policy. Government education programmes are aimed at lowering the demand for health care and also emphasize the importance of primary health care and prevention over hospital care. Not surprisingly, public health policies are strong, and the government heavily subsidizes health promotion and disease prevention programmes, emphasizing the responsibility of the individual to look after her own health.

Differences even lurk behind health policies that look similar at first sight. An interesting example is the public contract model, which is predominant in the countries we looked at. Here, Jacobs (1998) suggests that similarities in policy instrument choice mask differences in policy contents and goals. The public contract model is a typical feature of social insurance systems and a more recent innovation in national health services. However, beyond this point similarities often end. In Germany, the contracting function lies with insurance funds, which are non-public, statutory bodies and which are embedded in a complex system of self-administration. This is typical of the decentralized health governance in Germany. In Britain and New Zealand, by contrast, contracting responsibilities are in the hands of public bodies, the health authorities/Primary Care Trusts and Regional Health Authorities respectively, which are 'creatures of statute'. This results in public integration, which is enhanced by the fact that health policy is embedded in two centralized, unitary political systems. Not surprisingly, the responsibilities of these bodies go beyond contracting and also include service planning. The same applies to the county councils in Sweden, although they are democratically elected and accountable bodies. This reflects a long tradition of decentralized health governance.

Policy convergence and the predominance of similarities

As the examples above suggest, country-specific contexts in form of historical legacies, cultural orientations or political systems are a prominent and salient force shaping health policies and lead to both embeddedness and difference. This is one possible explanation why health policies do not easily fit typologies. Another, potentially contradictory explanation is the predominance of similarities, which is often associated with policy convergence.

As Chapter 1 suggests, health policies in many industrialized countries are confronted with similar problems arising from ageing populations, rapid advances in medical technology, and expanded public expectations and demands. Similar problems could suggest similar solutions, and under these circumstances health policies are likely to converge. This is supported by the fact that ultimately there are only a limited number of policy instruments available to address a certain policy problem, thus suggesting that function rather than politics informed by historical legacy or culture shapes health policies. As Gibson and Means (2000) argue in their analysis of restructuring long-term institutional care in Australia and Britain, policy levers are limited and there are simply relatively few 'good ideas' around to solve a specific problem.

This kind of policy convergence is also encouraged by the fact that health systems are not as different from each other as typologies suggest. Health systems all fulfil similar types of function: they are concerned with raising public funds to pay for medical care and organizing the delivery of this type of care. The differences between countries are variations on this basic principle. Not surprisingly, as Chapter 4 suggests, equity/access, quality and cost containment are the common goals of health policies across vastly different health systems and countries: it is only the relative importance which individual countries attach to each goal that differs.

Policy convergence is also related to processes of policy learning and transfer across different countries (Stone, 1999). Such processes reflect not only common problems and functional similarities that occur in the broad context of globalization (and European integration), but also the explicit efforts by governments supported by international organizations such as the OECD, WHO and the EU to foster a transfer of policies. Here, the initiatives of the WHO in relation to environmental health (as discussed in Chapter 7, p. 199) and the setting up of the European Observatory on Health Care Systems are indicative examples. As such, international organizations help to prepare the ground for what Harrison, Moran and Wood (2002) in their study of evidence-based medicine refer to as 'ideational convergence'. This suggests convergence in relation to the framing of policy problems and the intellectual underpinnings of policy solutions.

The comparative analysis in the previous chapters points to many examples of health policy convergence. Home care is a prominent example of a policy that has been pushed by ageing as a trend common to many countries. A key feature of policies has been the move to integrate home care into the regular health system by supporting informal carers. The ubiquity of this trend is striking considering the variation in cultural attitudes towards families and the responsibilities of women as carers. It points to a common shift in the goals of health policies from equity and quality to cost containment, which is underpinned by the salience of male dominance and the functional focus of health systems on acute, medical care. Considering this overall marginality, the differences in degree are less significant.

Policies on rationing and priority are another pertinent example of health policy convergence. The predominance of public funding means that health care resources are naturally limited, making priority setting and rationing inevitable. The shift of health policy goals towards cost containment and efficiency, together with the pressures identified above, have further intensified the management of scarcity. This is reflected in the ubiquity of co-payments and medical technology assessment, for example. Although there are differences in the forms co-payments take, there are ultimately only a certain number of ways in which co-payments are raised. Co-payments can take the form of charges as a flat rate per unit service, some proportion of the fee, or some combination of the two. Countries vary in the form and extent of co-payments, but in all countries co-payments are a key measure of demand-side cost containment putting a symbolic price on the use of health services. Similarly, while the mechanisms and scope vary, in all countries medical technology assessment is an important measure to ration health care resources. Over recent years many countries have seen the strengthening of medical technology assessment, even in countries where the medical model is strong (as in Germany) and where the restrictions on the availability of health care resources are seen as problematic (as in the USA). Medical technology assessment is an attractive policy instrument because it promises to square the circle between rationing, ensuring quality and using medical judgement.

The complexities of health policy

Health policy is shaped by contradictory forces. Health policy is embedded in country-specific contexts that lead to differences. At the same time, health policy is subject to pressures that apply across countries and result in similarities. Not surprisingly, many countries do not fit easily into the categorizations provided by the typologies introduced in Chapter 1.

The ordering of health policies across countries is also made difficult by the fact that health policies are highly complex. This echoes Freeman's (2000: 7) observation that health systems are actually not very systematic. The complex emergence of health systems often defies the order and complexity implied by modelling, and typologies may be looking for order where there is little. Complexity manifests itself in two ways. In functional terms, health policies are highly differentiated. As the previous chapters have demonstrated, health policy encompasses a wide and diverse range of issues, from micro-issues such as ensuring the quality of medical practice and supporting informal women carers of older people, to macro-issues such as national campaigns to encourage healthy living and global budgets to contain health care expenditure. Typologies claim to focus on those functions that are theoretically significant. However, there are additional functions that are not captured in a typology based on funding and provision, such as allocation of health care resources. The typologies also focus on macro-institutional characteristics but, as the examples above indicate there are many different aspects to funding and providing health care, and in the same country a variety of approaches can exist side by side.

The complexity of health policy also manifests itself in the fact that policies concerned with health care go well beyond health systems. Health systems are typically associated with all those activities directed at the funding, provision and governance of medical care. However, as the cases of home care and public health demonstrate, many health-related services that are central to the well-being of individuals, communities and populations at large are not medically-based. Instead, they are located on the interface with social care, environmental services and health and safety in the workplace, as well as economic, educational and family policies, and even day-to-day care provided by women.

The comparative analysis in the previous chapters contains many examples of the complexities of health policy. The funding and provision of health care illustrates the functional complexities of health policy. In five out of the nine countries we looked at, the degrees of public control of funding and provision are distinct rather than congruent as the dominant typologies of health systems suggest. New Zealand, for example, combines public provision of hospital care, typical of national health services, with strong private components in the funding of health care, characteristic of social insurance systems. In contrast, Japan combines high public control of funding, typical of national health services, with private provision of services, characteristic of market-based health systems.

It is also significant that, with its implicit focus on the distinction between public and private, the typology of government involvement in health care primarily applies to the provision of hospital care. However, ambulatory care is central to health policy. For patients, ambulatory care often provides the first point of contact with the health service and, as such, ambulatory care also has an important function in the allocation of health care resources. This gap points to another weakness of the typology, which tends to focus on how health resources are raised rather than how they are allocated. Scarcity of resources is a salient feature of health care and has again come into the spotlight with the concern for cost containment. Scarcity puts the allocation of health care resources at the centre of health policy.

Home care and public health exemplify the other key aspect of the complexity of health policy. Home care is a central aspect of health care for many older people, yet it is at the margins of what tends to be understood as health policy. Few older people receive home nursing care and, even when they do, it only accounts for a small share of their home care. Instead, home care predominantly means unpaid (informal) care by women and often also includes social care, such as help with domestic tasks. This reflects not only the inadequacy of existing home nursing services, but also the fact many of the health care needs of older people are probably not medically related. Analysing home care as an integral aspect of health policy requires embracing the real-life complexities of health policy. The same applies to public health. As discussed in Chapter 7 (p. 204), the relationship between medical care and health is minimal compared to other determinants of health status, such as heredity, personal behaviour, and the physical and social environment. For example, social and economic determinants of health suggest that education, employment and tax policies are the key to health policy.

Identifying 'best practices' and cross-national learning

Policy embeddedness, convergence and complexity all help to account for why health policies across countries do not easily fit into typologies of health systems. Typologies are meant to be neutral tools that help to order the complexity generated by cross-country comparison. Nevertheless typologies often reflect health policies at a certain point in time and are based on specific geographical points of refer⟨ Typologies are historically and culturally contingent and reflect ... context of specific analyses and address specific debates. A particular historical moment easily becomes represented as the 'natural state', as if the label could tell the true nature of the state in question (Henriksson, Wrede and Burau, 2002). And this is the tension comparative studies of health policy come up against. Health policies across countries are at the same time too different and too susceptible to similar pressures (as well as change more generally) and too complex to be ordered in a satisfactory way by typologies.

However, irrespective of the complexity of the process of comparing health policies across different countries, comparison remains an attractive strategy for social enquiry. Cross-country comparison is not only interesting but also provides a basis for identifying the variety of policy options that exist in health policy. As such, comparison holds the implicit promise of learning from other countries and their policy successes and failures. Health policy learning occurs naturally as information about other countries has become more readily available as part of the process of globalization. Policy learning is also explicitly encouraged by international organizations such as the OECD and the WHO, as they disseminate information about health systems and reforms in different countries. To policy makers, cross-country comparison and the opportunity to identify which health policy/system works 'best' is attractive for several reasons. Looking at other countries offers a virtual 'test' of different policy options and as such promises 'evidence-based' policy making, policy innovation and above all, policy success (Stone, 1999).

The basic logic underpinning cross-country learning suggests two things: that it is relatively straightforward to identify what is 'best', and that it is relatively straightforward to transfer what is 'best' from one country to another. However, the complexity of health systems and policies in different countries emerging from the analysis in the previous chapters suggests otherwise. There are many definitions of what are 'best' health policies/systems, and transferring best practices across countries is difficult because health policies are deeply embedded in country-specific contexts.

Health policy making is a complex process. Chapter 4 identifies quality, equity/access and cost containment/efficiency as the central goals of health policy. The three goals represent different and potentially competing ideas about what is the 'best' health policy/system. This makes learning from other countries a value-laden exercise, which is further complicated by the fact that different actors in health care have different ideas of what is 'best'. Thus, what is the 'best' health policy/system also depends on whom you ask.

		Actors in Health Care			
		Users	Payers	Providers	The State
Goals of Health Policy	Quality	X		X	X
	Equity/Access	X		X	
	Cost Containment/ Efficiency		X		X

Figure 8.1   *The goal orientation of actors in health care*

As Figure 8.1 suggests, there are four sets of actors in health care: users, payers (including both third-party payers and the public), and the state. Significantly, the different actors in health care often support different goals of health policy and as such have different ideas about what the 'best' health system or policy is. Payers are primarily concerned with cost containment and efficiency, whereas for providers quality of health care is the key. In contrast, the goal orientation of the public is ambivalent; as patients the public puts quality and access/equality first, whereas as payers the public has a predominant interest in cost containment/efficiency. Importantly, the different actors in health care may also have different ideas about the same goal. For users of health care, quality means a well-funded health system that allows for patient choice and fast access to the medical technology. This definition of quality is shared by providers of health care, who also emphasize the importance of autonomy in the provision of health care services. In contrast, states are more likely to highlight the public health aspects of quality.

The discussion above suggests that health systems/policies are 'best' in relation to specific goals, and that the importance attached to the individual goals (and ideas about what is 'best') varies between different actors in health care. Figure 8.2 offers an overview of the 'best' health systems in relation to the goals of quality, equity/access, and cost containment/efficiency for our countries. It also includes several definitions (or indicators) of each health policy goal. Considering the complexity of health care this overview uses selected indicators and examples and does not claim to be comprehensive.

Quality of health care is often measured in terms of the financial resources spent on health care. Based on the measure of the percentage of GDP spent on health care, the USA, Germany and France are the 'best' health systems. Other measures of quality relate to the technical and human resources of health systems such as the speed of access to

Quality
Defined as . . .

Level of health care spending (percentage of GDP)	*Highest*: USA, Germany and France *Lowest*: Singapore, Britain, Japan
Speed of access to medical technology	*Fast*: USA, Germany *Slow*: Britain, Netherlands
Number of doctors (per 1,000 inhabitants)	*Highest*: Italy, Germany and Sweden *Lowest*: Singapore, Britain and Japan
Extent of patient choice	*High*: Singapore, USA *Medium*: Germany and Sweden *Low*: Australia, Britain, Netherlands, New Zealand
Commitment to public health	*High*: Singapore, Sweden *Low*: Germany, USA

Access/Equity
Defined as . . .

Public funding of health care (percentage of total expenditure)	*Highest*: Sweden, Britain, Japan *Lowest*: Singapore, USA, Italy
Coverage of population	*High*: Britain (universality), Japan (social solidarity) *Low*: USA

Cost Containment/Efficiency
Defined as . . .

Control of costs	*High (direct budget control)*: Britain, Japan, New Zealand, Sweden *Medium (contractual control)*: Germany, Netherlands *Low (decentralized, market-oriented systems)*: Australia, USA
Supply-side rationing	*High in national health services*: Britain, New Zealand and Sweden *Low in market-based health systems*: Singapore, USA

Figure 8.2 *Identifying 'best' health systems*

medical technology and the number of doctors, respectively. Subsidiary policy goals are patient choice and commitment to public health. The assumption is that the more money spent, the better the technical and human resources of health systems. Countries such as Germany and Britain support this assumption, although the relationship between different indicators of quality is more complex than this. For example, while the health system in Singapore ranks very low in terms of the level of health care spending and the number of doctors, quality in terms of the extent of patient choice and commitment to public health is high. Other cases highlight the tradeoffs between different indicators of quality. Germany, for example, does very well on all indicators except commitment to public health, suggesting that quality is primarily defined as high-tech medical care.

The share of health care expenditure coming from public sources is an important indicator of equity/access in health systems. Public funding in the form of taxes or social insurance contributions is underpinned by the principles of universality and social solidarity, respectively, and as such makes for universal or near universal (and in principle equitable) access to health care. On this count, Sweden, Britain and Japan are the three 'best' health systems, whereas the USA is one of the worst. Here, low coverage means that a significant proportion of the population is excluded from what is otherwise a very 'high quality' health care system.

Such tradeoffs also exist between the policy goals of cost containment/efficiency and quality. The extent of control of costs is an important indicator of cost containment/efficiency and here the 'best' health systems are characterized by extensive cost control. Direct budget control, such as in Britain, Japan, New Zealand and Sweden, allows for greatest cost control, followed by contractual control as it exists in Germany and the Netherlands. Cost control is weakest in decentralized, market-oriented systems such as Australia and the USA. Health systems with extensive cost controls also make greater use of supply-side rationing. However, this comes at the price of quality in terms of level of health care spending (such as in Japan), speed of access to medical technology (such as in Britain) and the extent of patient choice (such as in New Zealand). Not surprisingly, the 2000 World Health Report by the WHO ranked Britain eighteenth in terms of responsiveness to patients (Laurance and Norton, 2000). The inverse is also true. In the USA and Germany, high quality in terms of level of health care spending and fast access to medical technology come at the price of low to medium control of costs.

Identifying the 'best' health system/policy is a highly complex process that depends on what is defined as 'best': that is, which policy goal is considered to be most important. In an ideal world, all three goals would be equally important. However, as health care resources are ultimately limited, the different policy goals in effect compete with each other. The emphasis put on individual goals and definitions of what is the 'best' health policy/system varies over time as well as between countries. This reflects historical trajectories and the health systems in individual countries together with the balance of power among the different actors in health care.

As such, the lessons policy makers want to learn from other countries also vary among individual health systems. Lesson learning is not necessarily a politically neutral process, but the value of policy lessons lies precisely in their power to bias policy choice (Stone, 1999: 73). Lesson learning is politically motivated and selective and is used to substantiate already made policy choices. Here, Britain is an indicative example. In response to the perceived funding crisis of the British NHS in the late 1980s, the government looked towards the USA and its models of managed care. The strong market orientation of the US health system resonated with the neo-liberal outlook of the Conservative government of the time. The focus on the organization of health services also helped to avoid the politically sensitive issue of making changes to the way in which the NHS is funded.

Moreover, there are only certain lessons policy makers in individual countries can learn, and this points to the limits of transferring 'best practices'. As Chapter 2 emphasizes, health policies are embedded in highly specific historical, cultural and political contexts, and any policy success is ultimately tied to a specific place and point in time. Irrespective of political will, not all policies work everywhere. Successful lesson learning is as much about the substance of policies as it is about the circumstances in which policies succeed (Klein, 1997). For instance, the New Zealand government's attempts to introduce user part charges for hospital care in the early 1990s were inspired by a series of reports by US-based health care consultants, but they failed. The policy engendered strong opposition not only from the public but also from the health care professions, which forced the government to withdraw the policy. A possible explanation is that the success of this policy was predicated on a health system that puts great emphasis individual responsibility (as in the USA) rather than public responsibility (as in New Zealand).

The complexity and contingency of identifying 'best practices' and cross-country learning in health policy does not mean that it cannot or should not be done. Instead, cross-country learning requires sensitivity, notably in two respects. Cross-country learning requires sensitivity towards the different and potentially competing ideas about what are the 'best' health policies/systems. There is no single, universally applicable definition of what is 'best', but rather there are as many definitions as there are goals of health policy. Some health systems are particularly successful in relation to cost containment/efficiency, whereas others score highly on quality as measured in terms of levels of spending and access to medical technology. Importantly, there are tradeoffs between different goals of health policy, and health systems are unlikely to be 'best' in respect to all policy goals. Which health policies are considered 'best' and worthy of lesson learning is ultimately a political decision. Nevertheless, cross-country learning also requires sensitivity towards the specific contexts under which policies succeed.

Contribution to the comparative study of health policy

In many respects the analysis presented in this book has covered familiar ground. Analyses of health systems, doctors and health reform are central topics in the comparative study of health policy. What, then, does the analysis presented in this book contribute to the debate? The contribution of the present analysis lies in the range of countries and policy issues covered. The breadth of the analysis results in a relatively comprehensive map, in which specific health policies in individual countries can be located. As such, the analysis offers a basis for more in-depth analyses of a wide range of more specific cases which vary in terms of both countries and policy issues.

The map is based on an analysis that covers a diverse range of countries; from the pioneers of publicly funded health systems (such as Germany and Sweden) to health systems that put individual responsibility first (such as Singapore and the USA) and hybrids (such as Australia); from health systems embedded in Western capitalist democracies to health systems embedded in Asian political systems; from large health systems such as America's which covers well over 275 million people to small health systems such as New Zealand's which covers only 4 million people. The map is also based on an analysis that covers a diverse range of health policy issues including basic issues such as the funding and provision of health care, health policy issues that are high on the political agenda such as issues relating to the allocation of health care resources, and health policy issues that are located on the margins of the health systems such as home care and public health.

By offering a comprehensive map in which specific health policies in individual countries can be located, the analysis presented in this book also contributes to the comparative study of health policy in another way. The map offers one way of moving away from one-dimensional typologies of health systems. Adopting a map means moving away from the notion that health policies across countries are either different or similar and that health policies will either continue to be embedded in country-specific contexts or will be submerged by convergence. Over time, health policies across countries will be both different and similar in differing degrees and in different respects. Adopting a map also means embracing complexity, exploring differences in health policy within the same country, and analysing the interfaces with other, related policies. In short, using a map acknowledges the existence of similarities within differences and differences within similarities, and acknowledges that health policy includes more than health systems. Although this more complex and dynamic view of health policy might lack the comfort that comes with one-dimensional typologies, the analysis in the earlier chapters demonstrates that it better reflects the real world of health care.

Guide to Further Reading

1 Comparative health policy: an introduction

There are many useful books on comparative health systems and health policy for readers to explore for more information. Raffel (1997), DeVoe (2001) and Ham (1997a and c) specifically look at health reform in an international context. Saltman, Figueras and Sakellarides (1998) examine critical challenges for health care reform in Europe. Freeman (2000) offers a good overview of the politics of health in Europe as do Lee, Buse and Fustukian (2002). Coulter and Ham (2000) specifically discuss the global challenge of rationing and Ham and Robert (2003) place it in the international context. Green and Thorogood (1998) analyse health policies across nations. Ranade (1998) offers a valuable comparative analysis of the role of markets and Schwartz (1997) compares seven countries in Europe and North America as regards budgets and management. For a look at how health care in developing countries differs from the countries analysed here see Green (1999) and Mills *et al.* (2001).

2 Political, historical and cultural contexts

There are many valuable resources on the context of health care for these countries. The websites in the appendix are most useful for current data as well as contextual information. For Australia, the key books are Duckett (2000) and Palmer and Short (2000). A most useful contextual book on New Zealand health care is Davis and Dew (2000), while Blank (1994) and Gauld (2001) provide good overviews of the health care system. There are numerous books on US society as it relates to health policy including an excellent historical perspective in Raffel and Raffel (1994). Also valuable are *Healthy People 2010* (US Department of Health and Human Services, 2000) and Blank (1997) who focuses on the unique US value context. An excellent source on Japanese culture and health care is Ohnuki-Tierney (1984). More recent compendiums on Japan health policy include Campbell and Ikegami (1998) and E. Feldman (2000). Ham (2001) provides a useful article on values and health policy in Singapore and the work of Quah (2003) is most helpful in understanding the Singapore system. Klein (2001) provides a detailed analysis of the politics of the British NHS since it was set up, while Twaddle (1999) focuses on policies of health reform in Sweden.

3 Funding, provision and governance

Suggestions for further reading on the funding, provision and governance of health care must necessarily be highly selective. The edited collections by Altenstetter and Björkman (1997), Ham (1997a), Mossialos and Le Grand (1999) and Ranade (1998) contain chapters on our European countries, focusing on health policy from the perspective of reform. In contrast, the reports by the European Observatory offer detailed overviews of the health systems in Britain (1999), Germany (2000) and Sweden (2001). For the Netherlands see Okma (2001). Davis and Ashton (2001) have edited a focused account of New Zealand health reforms, and a good general work on Australia is Palmer and Short (2000). Among the myriad of books on health policy in the USA, are R. Feldman (2000) and Aaron (1996). The publication on affordable health care published by the Singapore Ministry of Health (1993) is invaluable in explaining its unique system. For good summaries of the Japanese health care system, see Ikegami and Campbell (1999), Imai (2002) and especially the Japanese Ministry of Health (2000).

4 Setting priorities and allocating resources

General books on rationing medicine include Blank (1988) and Ubel (2001). Coulter and Ham (2000) and Ham and Robert (2003) provide very useful comparative analyses of rationing and argue it is a global issue, whereas Ham (1997) specifically focuses on priority setting. Ranade's (1998) comparative analysis of health care markets is a good introduction to the topic. Ikegami and Campbell (1996) provide an important analysis of cost containment in Japan, and Campbell and Ikegami (1998) extend this analysis to priority setting. More technical books on health allocation techniques include Drummond *et al.*, (1997) and, especially, McKie *et al.* (1998). R. Busse (1999) and Perleth *et al.* (1999) specifically focus on issues of rationing and the regulation of medical technology assessment in Germany, whereas Locock (2000) deals with rationing in Britain.

5 The medical profession

Johnson (1995) and Light (1995) provide useful introductions to the conceptual issues around doctors and health policy, as do Moran and Woods (1993) and Moran (1999) in their comparative analysis of Britain, Germany and the USA. The edited collection by Bovens, t'Hart and Peters (2001) contains chapters on recent medical reform in our European countries. Harrison (1998, 2001, *et al.* 2002) has written widely about doctors in Britain, whereas Garpenby (1997, 1999, 2001) has focused on Sweden. Yoshikawa, Bhattacharya and Vogt (1996) provide good coverage of the medical profession in Japan. A good introduction to the medical professions in the USA is provided by Badasch

(1993), while Birenbaum (2002) looks at the impact of managed care on US doctors.

6   Beyond the hospital: health care in the home

There are a number of works that offer introductions to key issues and concepts of comparing home care; these include Alber (1995), Anttonen and Sipilä (1996), OECD (1996) and Tester (1999). Few works focus specifically on home care. However, Glenndinning (1998a), Hutten and Kerkstra (1996) and Tester (1996) include useful overviews of our European countries, whereas Duff (2001) and Jacobzone (1999) adopt a broader international perspective. Here, Jenson and Jacobzone (2000) specifically focus on payments of informal carers. More specific country perspectives include the works by Gibson and Means (2000) on Britain and Australia, Wenger (2001) and Cuellar and Wiener (2000) on Germany, Means and Smith (1998) on Britain and the National Board for Health and Welfare (2000) on Sweden. Watson and Mears (1999) on women and care of the elderly is a good look at the social issues surrounding home care in Australia. The encyclopaedia of home care for the elderly by Romaine-Davis, Boundas and Lenihan (1995) is a valuable sourcebook for the USA.

7   Public health

Since public health comprises such a broad range of areas, many of which fall outside the scope of health care, the resources here are expansive. Among the best recent general works on public health per se are Turnock (2001), Henderson, Coreil and Bryant (2001), and Garrett (2000). Beauchamp and Steinbock (1999) offer valuable insights on the ethical aspects of public health, while Mackenzie (1998) presents a 'holistic' approach to public health policy. One of the best general books on health promotion is DiClemente, Crosby andKegler (2002). More specific country perspectives on public health include books on Europe by Holland and Mossialos (1999), the USA by Milio (2000) and Calman (1998), Australia by Leeder (1999) and Hancock (1999), Britain by Baggot (2000) and Japan by Okamoto (2001). Recent books on environmental and global health include Nadakavukaren (2000) and the massive edited collections of Merson, Black and Mills (2001) and Koop, Pearson and Schwartz (2002). Marmot and Wilkinson (1999) offer a contemporary review of the social determinants of health and Witherick (2002) a short but useful look at the relationship of health and welfare. Finally, Wilkinson (1997) and Kawachi, Kennedy and Wilkinson (1999) delve more deeply into the relationship between inequality and poor health.

Appendix: Websites

In the light of the growing importance of the Internet for transferring health policy information, below is a selection of health-related websites for our countries and for key international health organizations. Where possible, we have included English language sites but often the sites include an English option. This list of websites is also available online at www.palgrave.com/politics/blank where it will be updated periodically.

Australia

Bureau of Statistics: www.abs.gov.au
Commonwealth Government: www.fed.gov.au
Department of Health and Ageing: www.health.gov.au
Department of Health and Community Care: www.health.act.gov.au
Health Communication Network: www.hcn.net.au
Health Insurance Commission: www.hic.gov.au
Institute of Health and Welfare: www.aihw.gov.au
Public Health Association of Australia: www.pha.org.au

Germany

Expert Panel for the Concerted Action in Health Care (*Sachverständigen Rat für die Konzertierte Aktion im Gesundheitswesen*): www.svr-gesundheit.de
Federal Association of Insurance Fund Doctors (*Kassenärzliche Bundesvereinigung*): www.kbv.de
Federal Association of Welfare Organizations (*Bundesarbeitsgemeinschaft der Freien Wohlfahrtspflege*): www.bagfw.de
Federal Centre for Health Education (*Bundeszentrale für Gesundheitliche Aufklärung*): www.bzga.de
Federal Chamber of Doctors (*Bundesärztekammer*): www.bundesaerztekammer.de
Federal Ministry for Health (*Bundesministerium für Gesundheit und Soziale Sicherung*): www.bmgesundheit.de
German Hospital Assocation (*Deutsche Krankenhaus Gesellschaft*): www.dkgev.de

Japan

Ministry of Health and Welfare: www.mhlw.go.jp/english

225

The Netherlands

Association of Dutch Municipalities (*Vereniging van Nederlandse Gemeenten*): www.vng.nl
Association of Municipal Health Services (*Vereniging vor GGD'en*): www.ggd.nl
Central Agency for Health Care Tariffs (*College Tarieven Gezondheidszorg*): www.ctgzorg.nl
Ministry for Health, Welfare and Sport (*Ministerie van Volksgezondheid, Welzijn en Sport*): www.minvws.nl
National Statistics Bureau (*Centraal Bureau voor de Statistiek*): www.cbs.nl
Royal Dutch Medical Association (*Koninklijke Nederlansche Maatschappij tot bevordering der Geneeskunst*): www.knmg.nl

New Zealand

Maori Health Policy: www.nzgg.org.nz/maori_health.cfm
Ministry of Health: www.moh.govt.nz
New Zealand Health Information System: www.nzhis.govt.nz
New Zealand Health Network: www.nzhealth.net.nz
New Zealand Health Technology Clearinghouse: nzhta.chmeds.ac.nz

Singapore

Department of Health: www.moh.gov.sg
Health Sciences Authority: www.hsa.gov.sg
National Centre for Policy Analysis: www.ncpa.org

Sweden

Medical Responsibility Board (*Hälso- och sjukvårdens ansvarsnämnd*): www.hsan.se
Ministry for Health and Social Affairs (*Social Departementet*): www.social.regeringen.se
National Board of Health and Welfare (*Socialstyrelsen*): www.sos.se
National Institute for Public Health (*Statens Folkhälsoinstitutet*): www.fhi.se
Swedish Association of Local Authorities (*Svenka Kommunförbundet*): www.svekom.se
Swedish Federation of County Councils (*Landstingsförbundet*): www.lf.se
Swedish Medical Association (*Läkarförbundet*): http://www.slf.se/default.aspn

UK

British Medical Association: www.bma.org.uk
Commission for Health Improvement: www.chi.nhs.uk
Department of Health: www.doh.gov.uk
General Medical Council: http://www.gmc-uk/.org
The King's Fund: www.kingsfund.org.uk
Her Majesty's Stationery Office: www.hmso.gov.uk
National Institute for Clinical Excellence: www.nice.org.uk
NHS Confederation: www.nhsconfed.org

USA

Agency for Healthcare Research and Quality: www.ahcpr.gov
American Hospital Association: www.aha.org
Center for Disease Control: www.cdc.gov
Center for Medicare and Medicaid Services: www.medicare.gov
Department of Health and Human Services: www.hhs.gov
Department of Veterans Affairs: www.va.gov
Health Resources and Services Administration: www.hrsa.gov
Health Services/Technology Assessment: www.nlm.nih.gov
National Center for Health Statistics: www.cdc.gov/nchs
National Institutes of Health: www.nih.gov

International organizations

European Observatory on Health Care Systems: www.euro.who.int/
    observatory/toppage
Organisation for Economic Development and Co-operation: www.oecd.org
World Health Organization: www.who.org
World Health Organization, Regional Office for Europe: www.who.dk

Bibliography

Aaron, Henry J., (ed.) (1996). *The Problem That Won't Go Away: Reforming U.S. Health Care Financing*. Washington, DC: The Brookings Institution.

Abel-Smith, Brian (1984). *Cost Containment in Health Care: The Experience of 12 European Countries 1977–83*. Luxembourg: Commission of European Countries.

Abrams, Jim (2002). 'Divided Congress Puts off Many Issues Until after the Election', Associated Press, 17 October.

Alber, Jens (1995). 'A Framework for the Comparative Study of Social Services', *Journal of European Social Policy*, 5 (2): 131–49.

Altenstetter, Christa (1997). 'Health Policy-making in Germany: Stability and Dynamics', in Christa Altenstetter and James Warner Björkam, (eds), *Health Policy Reform, National Variations and Globalization*. London: Macmillan.

—— and James Warner Björkam, (eds), (1997). *Health Policy Reform, National Variations and Globalization*. London: Macmillan.

American Hospital Association (2002). 'Fast Facts on U.S. Hospitals from Hospital Statistics', www.aha.org

Andersen, Ronald, Björn Smedby and Denny Vågerö (2001). 'Cost Containment, Solidarity and Cautious Experimentation: Swedish Dilemmas', *Social Science and Medicine*, 52 (8): 1,195–204.

Anderson, Gerard F. and Jean-Pierre Poullier (1999). 'Health Spending, Access, and Outcomes: Trends in Industrialized Countries', *Health Affairs*, 18 (3): 178–91.

Anell, Anders and Patrick Svarvar (1999). 'Health Care Reforms and Cost Containment in Sweden', in Elias Mossialos and Julian Le Grand, (eds), *Health Care and Cost Containment in the European Union*. Aldershot: Ashgate.

Angell, Marcia (1993). 'Privilege and Health – What is the Connection?', *New England Journal of Medicine*, 329, (2): 126–7.

Anttonen, Anneli, and Jorma Sipilä (1996). 'European Social Care Services: Is it Possible to Identify Models?', *Journal of European Social Policy*, 6 (2): 87–100.

Appleby, John (1992). *Financing Health Care in the 1990s*. Buckingham: Open University Press.

Australian Bureau of Statistics (1999). *Disability, Ageing, and Carers, 1998*. Canberra: Australian Bureau of Statistics.

Australian Department of Health and Ageing (2000). 'Public Health Outcome Funding Agreements', www.health.gov.au/pubhlth/about/phofa/phofa.htm.

—— (2001). 'Population Health', www.health.gov.au/pubhlth/about/whatis.htm.

—— (2002). *A Summary of the National Program Guidelines for the Home and Community Care Program 2002*. Canberra: Commonwealth of Australia.

—— (2003a). 'Home and Community Care', www.health.gov.au/acc/hacc/index.htm.

—— (2003b). 'The National Public Health Partnership', www.health.gov.au/pubhlth/about/nphp.htm.

—— (2003c). 'Public Health Education and Research Programme', www.health.gov.au/pubhlth/about/pherp.htm.

Australian Medical Association (2003). 'About the AMA', http://domono.ama.com.au.

Australian Medical Association Queensland (2003). 'About Us', www.amaq.com.au/main.htm.

Australian National Health and Medical Research Council (1990). *Discussion Paper on Ethics and Resources Allocation in Health Care.* Canberra: Australian Government Publishing Service.

Babcock, Lyndon, and Anthony Belotti (1994). 'Defining and Measuring Health over Life', in George Tolley, Donald Kenkel and Robert Fabian (eds), *Valuing Health for Policy: An Economic Approach.* Chicago: University of Chicago Press.

Badasch, Shirley A. (1993). *Introduction to Health Occupations.* New York: Regents/Prentice Hall.

Baggott, Rob (1998). *Health and Health Care in Britain*, 2nd rev. edn. London: Macmillan.

—— (2000). *Public Health. Policy and Politics.* Basingstoke: Palgrave Macmillan.

Baird, Patricia (1993). *Proceed with Care: Final Report of the Royal Commission on New Reproductive Technologies.* Ottawa: Minister of Government Services Canada.

Baker, Dean B. and Philip J. Landrigan (1993). 'Occupational Exposures and Human Health', in Eric Chivian *et al.*, (eds), *Critical Condition: Human Health and the Environment.* Cambridge: MIT Press.

Barr, Michael D. (2001). 'Medical Savings Accounts in Singapore: A Critical Inquiry', *Journal of Health Politics, Policy and Law*, 26 (4): 709–26.

Barwick, H. (1992). *The Impact of Economic and Social Factors on Health.* Wellington: Public Health Association of New Zealand.

Batty, David (2001). 'The GMC in Crisis', *The Guardian*, 29 May.

—— (2002). 'Flagship Free Care Policy Hit by Delays', *The Guardian*, 17 January.

BBC News (2002). 'Being Single Worse Than Smoking', www.news.bbc.co.uk/1/hi/health/2195609.stm.

Beauchamp, Dan E. and Bonnie Steinbock (eds) (1999). *New Ethics for Public Health.* New York: Oxford University Press.

Bennett, Colin J. (1991). 'What is Policy Convergence and What Causes It?', *British Journal of Political Science*, 21 (2): 215–33.

Bensoussan, A. and S. P. Myers (1996). *Towards a Safer Choice: The Practice of Traditional Chinese Medicine in Australia.* Sydney: University of Western Sydney Press.

Berg, Marc, Klasien Horstman, Saskia Plass and Michelle van Heusden (2000). 'Guidelines, Professionals and the Production of Objectivity: Standardisation and the Professionalism of Insurance Medicine', *Sociology of Health and Illness*, 22 (6): 765–91.

Berk, Mark L. and Alan C. Monheit (1992). 'The Concentration of Health Expenditures: An Update', *Health Affairs*, 11 (5): 145–9.

Bertelsmann Foundation (1999). *International Reform Monitor. Social Policy, Labour Market Policy, Industrial Relations*. Issue 1/1999. Gütersloh: Bertelsmann Foundation. www.reformmonitor.org.

Bertelsmann Foundation (2002). *Free Long Term Nursing and Social Care in Scotland, in Contrast to the UK as a Whole*. Gütersloh: Bertelsmann Foundation. http://www.reformmonitor.org/index.php3?mode=reform.

Bertelsmann Foundation (2003). *International Reform Monitor, Social Policy, Labour Market Policy and Industrial Relations*. Issue 3/2003. Gütersloh: Bertelsmann Foundation. www.reformmonitor.org.

Birenbaum, Arnold (2002). *Wounded Profession: American Medicine Enters the Age of Managed Care*. Westport, CT: Praeger Press.

Birrell, Bob (2002). 'A Bitter Pill for Rural Australia', www.monash.edu.au/pubs/montage/Montage_97-02/pill.htm.

Björkman, James Warner and Kieke G. H. Okma (1997). 'Restructuring Health Care Systems in the Netherlands: The Institutional Heritage of Dutch Health Policy Reforms', in Christa Altenstetter and James Warner Björkman (eds), *Health Policy Reform, National Variations and Globalization*. London: Macmillan.

Blank, Robert H. (1988). *Rationing Medicine*. New York: Columbia University Press.

——— (1994). *New Zealand Health Policy: A Comparative Study*. Auckland: Oxford University Press.

——— (1997). *The Price of Life: The Future of American Health Care*. New York: Columbia University Press.

——— (2001). 'Agenda Setting and the Policy Context', in Peter Davis and Toni Ashton (eds), *Health and Public Policy in New Zealand*. Auckland: Oxford University Press.

Blendon, Robert J., R. Leitman, R. Morrison and K. Donelan (1990) 'Satisfaction with Health Systems in Ten Nations', *Health Affairs*, 9 (2): 188–9.

Blendon, Robert J., Minah Kim and John M. Benson (2001). 'The Public versus the World Health Organization on Health System Performance', *Health Affairs*, 20 (3): 10–20.

Boom, Hannerieke, Fred Stevens and Hans Philipsen (2000). 'Cross-cultural Comparison in the Institutionalisation and Professionalisation of Home Care in Six European Countries', paper presented at the Interim Conference of the ISA Research Committee on Sociology of Professional Groups, Lisbon, 13–15 September.

Boom, Hannerieke (2001). 'Dilemmas and Difficulties in Home Nursing: Theoretical Perspectives', paper presented at the Fifth Conference of the European Sociological Association, Helsinki, 28 August–1 September.

Boseley, Sarah (2000). 'Peers Say NHS Could Embrace Alternative Therapies', *The Guardian*, 29 November.

——— (2001a). 'Alzheimer's Patient in NHS "lottery"', *The Guardian*, 29 May.

——— (2001b). 'Organ Horror Report Outcry', *The Guardian*, 30 January.

Bovens, Mark, Paul t'Hart and B. Guy Peters (eds) (2001). *Success and Failure in Public Governance. A Comparative Analysis*. Cheltenham: Edward Elgar.

Brenner, M. Harvey (2001). 'Unemployment, Employment Policy and the Public Health', paper presented at European Commission Expert Meeting on Unemployment and Health in Europe, Berlin, 6–7 July.

British United Provident Association (2002). 'Skin Cancer on the Rise', www.bupa.co.uk/health_information/html/health_news/250602skin.htm.

Broadbent, Jeffery P. (2000). 'Social Capital and Labor Politics in Japan: Cooperation or Cooptation?', *Policy Sciences*, 33 (3/4): 307–21.

Brown, Malcolm C. and Peter Crampton (1997). 'New Zealand Policy Strategies Concerning the Funding of General Practitioner Care', *Health Policy*, 41 (2): 87–104.

Bundeszentrale für gesundheitliche Aufklärung (2003). *Informations- und Komunikationsaufgaben der BzgA*, www.bzga.de.

Bunker, John P., Howard S. Frazier and Frederick Mosteller (1994). 'Improving Health: Measuring Effects of Medical Care', *The Milbank Quarterly*, 72 (2): 225–55.

Burau, Viola (2001). 'Medical Reform in Germany: The 1993 Health Care Legislation as an Impromptu Success', in Mark Bovens, Paul t'Hart and B. Guy Peters (eds), *Success and Failure in Public Governance. A Comparative Analysis*. Cheltenham: Edward Elgar.

——, Lea Henriksson and Sirpa Wrede (forthcoming). 'Comparing Professional Groups in Health Care: Towards a Context Sensitive Analysis', *Knowledge, Work and Society*.

Busse, Carolyn (1998). 'Study Shows Foreign-Trained Doctors Can Ease Rural Physician Shortage', Carolina News Service, no. 850 (13 November).

Busse, Reinhard (1999). 'Priority-setting and Rationing in German Health Care', *Health Policy*, 50: 71–90.

—— and Chris Howorth (1999). 'Cost Containment in Germany: Twenty Years Experience', in Elias Mossialos and Julian Le Grand (eds), *Health Care and Cost Containment in the European Union*. Aldershot: Ashgate.

Butler, Patrick (2002). 'How Nice Works', *The Guardian*, 22 March.

Califano, Joseph A. Jr. (1992). 'Rationing Health Care: The Unnecessary Solution', *University of Pennsylvania Law Review*, 140 (5): 1,525–38.

Callahan, Daniel (1987). *Setting Limits: Medical Goals in an Aging Society*. New York: Simon and Schuster.

Callahan, Daniel (1990). *What Kind of Life? The Limits of Medical Progress*. New York: Simon & Schuster.

—— (1998). *False Hopes: Why America's Quest for Perfect Health is a Recipe for Failure*. New York: Simon & Schuster.

Calman, Kenneth C. (1998). *Potential for Health*. Oxford: Oxford University Press.

Campbell, John, C. and Naoki Ikegami (1998). *The Art of Balance in Health Policy: Maintaining Japan's Low-Cost, Egalitarian System*. Cambridge: Cambridge University Press.

Carter, Helen (2002). 'Death Recording System "Left Shipman Free to Kill" ', *The Guardian*, 8 October.

Carvel, John (2002a). 'Britons Say Non to C'est la Vie Philosophy', *The Guardian*, 16 October.

—— (2002b). 'Homeless Suffer for Want of a GP', *The Guardian*, 9 December.

Casciani, Dominic (2002). 'Asylum Seeker Health Crisis in London', BBC News, 12 November. http://news.bbc.co.uk/1/hi/2453263.stm.

Centers for Disease Control (2003). 'Severe Acute Respiratory Syndrome', www.cdc.gov/ncidod/sars/quarantineqa.htm.

Centers for Medicare and Medicaid Services (2003a). 'Alternatives to Nursing Home Care', www.medicare.gov/Nursing/Alternatives/Other.asp.

—— (2003b). *Medicare and Home Health Care*. Washington, DC: Government Printing Office.

'Central China's Henen Province Punishes 800 Officials and Others over SARS' (2003). Yahoo News, 24 May. www.story.news.yahoo.com...fp/health_sars_china_punish_030524083117.htm.

Chan, Angelique (2002). *Singapore's Changing Age Structure and the Policy Implications for Financial Security, Employment, Living Arrangements and Health Care*. Singapore: Asian MetaCentre for Population and Sustainable Development Analysis.

Cheah, Jason (2001). 'Chronic Disease Management: A Singapore Perspective', *British Medical Journal*, 323 (7): 990–3.

Chernichovsky, Dov (1995). 'Health System Reforms in Industrialized Democracies: An Emerging Paradigm', *The Milbank Quarterly*, 73 (3): 339–56.

Chivian, Eric (1994). 'The Ultimate Preventive Medicine', *Technology Review* (Nov./Dec.): 34–40.

Churchill, Larry R. (1994). *Self-Interest and Universal Health Care*. Cambridge, MA: Harvard University Press.

Commonwealth Fund (2000). *The Elderly's Experiences with Health Care in Five Nations*. New York: The Commonwealth Fund.

Cook, Philip J. and Jens Ludwig (2000). *Gun Violence: The Real Costs*. New York: Oxford University Press.

Coolen, Jan, and Sylvia Weekers (1998). 'Long-term Care in the Netherlands: Public Funding and Private Provision within a Universalistic Welfare State', in Caroline Glenndinning (ed.), *Rights and Realities. Comparing New Developments in Long-term Care for Older People*. Bristol: Policy Press.

Coulter, Angela and Chris Ham (eds) (2000). *The Global Challenge of Health Care Rationing*. Buckingham: Open University Press.

Cowan, Edith (2001). 'Financing to Foster Community Health Care: A Comparative Analysis of Singapore, North America, and Australia', *Current Sociology*, 49 (3): 135–54.

Crampton, Peter (2001). 'Policies for General Practice', in Peter Davis and Toni Ashton (eds), *Health and Public Policy in New Zealand*. Auckland: Oxford University Press.

Cromwell, David A., Rosalie Viney and John Halsall (1998). 'Linking Measures of Health Gain to Explicit Priority Setting by an Area Health Service in Australia', *Social Science and Medicine*, 47 (12): 2,067–74.

Cuellar, Alison Evans and Joshua M. Wiener (2000). 'Can Social Insurance for Long-term Care Work? The Experience of Germany', *Health Affairs*, 19 (3): 8–25.

Culyer, A. J. (1990). 'Cost Containment in Europe', in OECD (ed.), *Health Systems in Transition: The Search for Efficiency*. Paris: OECD.

Culyer, A. J., J. E. Brazier and O. O'Donnell (1988). *Organising Health Service Provision: Drawing on Experience*. London: Institute of Health Services Management.

Cumming, Jacqueline, and Claudia D. Scott (1998). 'The Role of Outputs and Outcomes in Purchaser Accountability: Reflecting on New Zealand Experiences', *Health Policy*, 46(1): 53–68.

Cundiff, David and Mary Ellen McCarthy (1994). *The Right Medicine: How to Make Health Care Reform Work Today*. Totowa, NJ: Humana Press.

Daatland, Svein Olav (1996). 'Adapting the "Scandinavian Model" of Care for Elderly People', in OECD (ed.), *Caring for Frail Elderly People. Policies in Evolution*. Social Policy Studies no. 19. Paris: OECD.

Danzon, Patricia M. (1985). 'Testimony before the Committee on Labor and Human Resources, U.S. Senate', *Duke Law Magazine*, 3 (1): 11–5.

David, Ronald (1993). 'The Demand Side of the Health Care Crisis', *Harvard Magazine* (March/April): 30–2.

Davis, Peter and Toni Ashton (eds) (2001). *Health and Public Policy in New Zealand*. Auckland: Oxford University Press.

—— and Kevin Dew (eds) (2000). *Health and Society in Aotearoa New Zealand*. Auckland: Oxford University Press.

De Ferranti, David (1985). *Paying for Health Services in Developing Countries: An Overview*. Washington, DC: World Bank Staff Working Paper 721.

Department of Health (2003) *Review Body on Doctors' and Dentists' Remuneration. Review for 2003. Written Evidence from the Health Department for Great Britain*. London: Department of Health.

De Voe, Jennifer E. (2001). *The Politics of Health Care Reform: A Comparative Study of National Health Insurance in Britain and Australia*. Kensington, NSW: School of Health Services Management.

—— and Stephanie D. Short (2003). 'A Shift in the Historical Trajectory of Medical Dominance: The Case of Medibank and the Australian Doctors Lobby', *Social Science and Medicine*, 57(3): 343–53.

DiClemente, Ralph J., Richard A. Crosby and Michelle C. Kegler (2002). *Emerging Theories in Health Promotion Practice and Research: Strategies for Improving Public Health*. San Francisco: Jossey-Bass.

Dillon, Andrew (2001). 'NICE Idea. The UK National Institute for Clinical Excellence', *Eurohealth*, 7 (1): 32–4.

Döhler, Marian (1989). 'Physicians' Professional Autonomy in the Welfare State: Endangered or Preserved', in Giorgio Freddi and James Warner Björkman (eds), *Controlling Medical Professions. The Comparative Politics of Health Governance*. London: Sage.

Doneny, Kathleen (2003). 'Skin Cancer: More than 1 Million New Cases in U.S. This Year', *HealthScoutNews*, 26 May.

Drake, David F. (1994). *Reforming the Health Care Market*. Washington, DC: Georgetown University Press.

Drummond, Michael F. (1993). 'Health Technology Policy and Health Services Research', in Michael. F. Drummond and Alan Maynard (eds), *Purchasing and Providing Cost-Effective Health Care*. London: Churchill Livingstone.

Drummond, Michael F., Bernie J. O'Brien, Greg L. Stoddart and George T. W. Torrance (1997). *Methods for the Economic Evaluation of Health Care Programmes*. Oxford: Oxford University Press.

Duckett, S. J. (2000). *The Australian Health Care System*. Melbourne: Oxford University Press.

Duff, John (2001). 'Financing to Foster Community Health Care: A Comparative Analysis of Singapore, Europe, North America, and Australia', *Current Sociology*, 49 (3): 135–54.

Dunne, Ray (2002). 'Analysis: GPs and Asylum Seekers', BBC News, 7 November, http://news.bbc.co.uk/1/hi/health/2414887.stm.

Durie, Mason (1994). *Whaiora: Maori Health Development*. Auckland: Oxford University Press.

Eckerberg, Katarina, Björn Fordberg and Per Wickenberg (1998). 'Sweden: Setting the Pace with Pioneers Municipalities and Schools', in William M. Lafferty and Katarina Eckerberg (eds), *From the Earth Summit to Local Agenda 21*. London: Earthscan.

Eddy, David M. (1991). 'What Care is "Essential"? What Services are "Basic"?', *Journal of the American Medical Association*, 265 (6): 782–8.

Elston, Mary Ann (1991). 'The Politics of Professional Power: Medicine in a Changing Health Service', in Jonathan Gabe, Michael Calnan and Michael Bury (eds), *The Sociology of the Health Service*, London: Routledge.

Epstein, Paul R. (2000). 'Is Global Warming Harmful to Health?', *Scientific American*, 20 August.

European Observatory on Health Care Systems (1999). *Health Care Systems in Transition: United Kingdom*. Copenhagen: European Observatory on Health Care Systems.

—— (2000). *Health Care Systems in Transition: Germany*. Copenhagen: European Observatory on Health Care Systems.

—— (2001). *Health Care Systems in Transition: Sweden*. Copenhagen: European Observatory on Health Care Systems.

Eurostat (1999). ' "Profound Consequences" as EU Grows Older', *News Release* no. 75/99, 29 July.

Evans, David (in press). ' "Taking Public Health out of the Ghetto": The Policy and Practice of Multi-disciplinary Public Health in the United Kingdom', *Social Science and Medicine*.

Evans, Robert G. and Morris L. Barer (1990). 'The American Predicament', in OECD (ed.), *Health Systems in Transition: The Search for Efficiency*. Paris: OECD.

Evers, Adalbert and Ivan Svetlik (eds) (1993). *Balancing Pluralism. New Welfare Mixes in Care for the Elderly*. Aldershot: Avebury.

Fattore, Giovanni (1999). 'Cost Containment and Health Care Reforms in the British NHS', in Elias Mossialos and Julian Le Grand (eds), *Health Care and Cost Containment in the European Union*. Aldershot: Ashgate.

Federal Bureau of Investigation (2000). *Crime in the United States*. Washington, DC: Government Printing Office.

Feldman, Eric A. (2000). *The Ritual of Rights in Japan: Law, Society, and Health Policy*. Cambridge: Cambridge University Press.

Feldman, Roger D. (ed.) (2000). *American Health Care: Government, Market Processes, and the Public Trust.* New Brunswick: Transaction Books.

Figueras, J. and Richard B. Saltman (1997). *European Health Care Reform: Analysis of Current Strategies.* Geneva: WHO.

Fine, Michael D. (1999). 'Coordinating Health, Extended Care, and Community Support Services: Reforming Aged Care in Australia', *Journal of Ageing and Social Policy,* 11 (1): 67–90.

Finlayson, Mary (2001). 'Policy Implementation and Modification', in Peter Davis and Toni Ashton (eds), H*ealth and Public Policy in New Zealand.* Auckland: Oxford University Press.

Foster, David (2001). 'Frequent Flyer Racks up Big Bill', *Detroit News,* 10 October.

Franck, Matthew J. (1996). *Against the Imperial Judiciary. The Supreme Court vs. the Sovereignty of the People.* Lawrence: University of Kansas Press.

Freeman, Richard (1998). 'Competition in Context: The Politics of Health Care Reform in Europe', *International Journal of Quality in Health Care,* 10 (5): 395–401.

—— (2000). *The Politics of Health in Europe.* Manchester: Manchester University Press.

Freeman, Richard, and Jochen Clasen (1994). 'The German Social State: An Introduction', in Jochen Clasen and Richard Freeman (eds), *Social Policy in Germany.* Hemel Hempstead: Harvester Wheatsheaf.

Freidson, Elliot (1994). *Professionalism Reborn. Theory, Prophecy and Policy.* Cambridge: Polity.

Fries, James F., C. Everett Koop, Carson E. Beadle, P.P. Cooper, M.J. England, R.F. Greaves, J.J. Sokolov and D. Wright (1993). 'Reducing Health Care Costs by Reducing the Need and Demand for Medical Services', *The New England Journal of Medicine,* 329 (5): 321–5.

Fuchs, Victor R. (1994). 'The Clinton Plan: A Researcher Examines Reform', *Health Affairs,* 13(2): 102–14.

Fuller, Benjamin F. (1994). *American Health Care: Rebirth or Suicide?* Springfield, IL: Thomas.

Furuse, Tohru (1996). 'Changing the Balance of Care: Japan', in OECD (ed.), *Caring for Frail Elderly People.* Paris: OECD.

Garpenby, Peter (1992). 'The Transformation of the Swedish Health Care System, or the Hasty Rejection of the Rational Planning Model', *Journal of European Social Policy,* 2 (1): 17–31.

—— (1997). 'Implementing Quality Programmes in Three Swedish County Councils: The Views of Politicians, Managers and Doctors', *Health Policy,* 39(2): 195–206.

—— (1999). 'Resource Dependency, Doctors and the State: Quality Control in Sweden', *Social Science and Medicine,* 49: 405–24.

—— (2001) 'Making Health Policy in Sweden: The Rise and Fall of the 1994 Family Doctor Scheme', in Mark Bovens, Paul t'Hart and B. Guy Peters (eds), *Success and Failure in Public Governance. A Comparative Analysis.* Cheltenham: Edward Elgar.

Garrett, Laurie (2000). *Betrayal of Trust: The Collapse of Global Public Health.* New York: Hyperion.

Garvin, Theresa and John Eyles (2001). 'Public Health Responses for Skin Cancer Prevention: The Policy Framing of Sun Safety in Australia, Canada and England', *Social Science and Medicine*, 53 (9): 1,175–89.

Gauld, Robin (2001). *Revolving Doors: New Zealand's Health Reforms.* Wellington: Institute of Policy Studies and Health Services Research Centre.

Giamo, Susan and Philip Manow (1999). 'Adapting the Welfare State: The Case of Health Care Reform in Britain, Germany, and the United States', *Comparative Political Studies*, 32 (8): 967–1,000.

Gibson, Diane and Robin Means (2000). 'Policy Convergence: Restructuring Long-term Care in Australia and the UK', *Policy and Politics*, 29 (1): 43–58.

Glenndinning, Caroline (1998a). 'Health and Social Care Services for Frail Older People in the UK: Changing Responsibilities and New Developments', in Caroline Glenndinning (ed.), *Rights and Realities. Comparing New Developments in Long-term Care for Older People.* Bristol: Policy Press.

—— (ed.) (1998b). *Rights and Realities. Comparing New Developments in Long-term Care for Older People.* Bristol: Policy Press.

Green, Andrew (1999). *An Introduction to Health Planning in Developing Countries.* Oxford: Oxford University Press.

Green, Judith and Nicki Thorogood (1998). *Analysing Health Policy: A Sociological Approach.* London: Longman.

Greenlee, Gina (2003). 'Singapore is Right to Get Tough'. www.ctnow.com/news/opinion/op_ed.

Greiner, Wolfgang and J.-Matthias Graf von der Schulenburg (1997). 'Germany', in Marshall W. Raffel (ed.), *Health Care and Reform in Industrialized Countries.* University Park, PA: Pennsylvania State University Press.

'Gun Crime Survival Rates Rising' (2002). BBC News, 8 November, http://news.bbc.co.uk/1/hi/health/2419705.stm.

Håkansson, Stefan and Sara Nordling (1997). 'Sweden', in Marshall W. Raffel (ed.), *Health Care and Reform in Industrialized Countries.* University Park, PA: Pennsylvania State University Press.

Hall, Jane (1999). 'Incremental Change in the Australian Health Care System', *Health Affairs*, 18 (3): 95–113.

Ham, Chris (ed.) (1997a). *Health Care Reform: Learning from International Experience.* Buckingham: Open University Press.

—— (1997b). 'Priority Setting in Health Care: Learning from International Experience', *Health Policy*, 42(1): 49–66.

—— (1997c). 'The United Kingdom', in Christopher Ham (ed.), *Health Care Reform: Learning from International Experience.* Buckingham: Open University Press.

—— (1999). *Health Policy in Britain*, 4th rev. edn. London: Macmillan.

—— (2001). 'Values and Health Policy: The Case of Singapore', *Journal of Health Politics, Policy and Law*, 26 (4): 739–45.

—— and Glenn Robert (eds), (2003). *Reasonable Rationing: International Experience of Priority Setting in Health Care.* Buckingham: Open University Press.

Hamilton, Clive (2001). 'Putting Doctors where They are Needed', *The Australia Institute*, 27 (June).

Hancock, Linda (ed.) (1999). *Health Policy in the Market State*. St Leonard's, NSW: Allen & Unwin.

Harrison, Stephen (1998). 'The Politics of Evidence-based Medicine in the United Kingdom', *Policy and Politics*, 26 (1): 15–31.

—— (2001). 'Reforming the Medical Profession in the United Kingdom, 1989–97: Structural Interests in Health Care', in Mark Bovens, Paul t'Hart and B. Guy Peters (eds), *Success and Failure in Public Governance. A Comparative Analysis*. Cheltenham: Edward Elgar.

—— and Christopher Pollitt (1994). *Controlling Health Professionals. The Future of Work and Organization in the NHS*. Buckingham: Open University.

—— , Michael Moran and Bruce Wood (2002). 'Policy Emergence and Policy Convergence: The Case of "Scientific-bureaucratic Medicine" in the United States and United Kingdom', *British Journal of Politics and International Relations*, 4 (1): 1–24.

Harrop, Martin (1992). 'Introduction', in Martin Harrop (ed.), *Power and Policy in Liberal Democracies*. Cambridge: Cambridge University Press.

Havighurst, Clark C. (2000). 'Freedom of Contract: The Unexplored Path to Health Care Reform', in Roger D. Feldman (ed.), *American Health Care*. New Brunswick: Transaction, 145–67.

HCFA (Health Care Financing Administration) (2000). *Highlights: National Health Expenditures, 2000*. Washington, DC: HFCA.

Henderson, J. Neil, Jeannine Coreil and Carol Bryant (2001). *Social and Behavioral Foundations of Public Health*. London: Sage.

Henriksson, Lea, Sirpa Wrede and Viola Burau (2002). 'Comparing How Occupational Boundaries are Governed: Reflections on Home Nursing in Finland and Germany', paper presented at World Congress of Sociology, Brisbane, 7–13 July.

Herk, R. van, N.S. Klazinga, R.M.J. Schepers and A.F. Casparie (2001). 'Medical Audit: Threat or Opportunity. A Comparative Study of Medical Audit among Medical Specialists in General Hospitals in the Netherlands and England, 1970–1999', *Social Science and Medicine*, 53(12): 1,721–32.

Heywood, Andrew (1997). *Politics*. London: Macmillan.

Holland, Walter and Elias Mossialos (eds) (1999). *Public Health Policies in the European Union*. Aldershot: Ashgate.

Howe, A. L. (1992). 'Participating in Policy Making: The Case of Aged Care', in H. Gardner (ed.), *Health Policy: Development, Implementation and Evaluation in Australia*. Melbourne: Churchill Livingstone.

Howlett, Michael and M. Ramesh (1995). *Studying Public Policy: Policy Cycles and Policy Subsystems*. Toronto: Oxford University Press.

Huggins, Charnicia E. (2002). 'Poor Face Multitude of Environmental Health Threats', Reuters, 17 October.

Hummelgaard, Hans, Mikkel Baadsgaard and Jorgen Bloesdahl Nielsen (1998). *Unemployment and Marginalisation in Danish Municipalities*. Copenhagen: Institute of Local Government Studies.

Hurowitz, James C. (1993). 'Toward a Social Policy for Health', *New England Journal of Medicine*, 329 (2): 130–3.

Hurst, Jeremy and Jean-Pierre Poullier (1993). 'Paths to Health Reform', *OECD Observer*, 179: 4–7.

Hutten, Jack B. F. and Ada Kerkstra (eds) (1996). *Home Care in Europe: Country-specific Guide to its Organization and Financing.* Aldershot: Ashgate.

Iglehart, John K. (1999). 'The American Health Care System: Medicaid'. *New England Journal of Medicine* 340(5): 393–5.

Ikegami, Naoki (1992). 'Japan: Maintaining Equity through Regulated Fees', *Journal of Health Politics, Policy and Law,* 17 (4): 689–713.

—— and John C. Campbell (eds) (1996). *Containing Health Care Costs in Japan.* Ann Arbor, MI: University of Michigan Press.

—— and John C. Campbell (1999). 'Health Care Reform in Japan: The Virtues of Muddling Through', *Health Affairs,* 18 (3): 56–75.

—— Shunya Ikeda and Hiroki Kawai (1998). 'Why Medical Care Costs in Japan Have Increased Despite Declining Prices for Pharmaceuticals', *Pharmacoeconomics,* 14 (1): 97.

Iliffe, Steve and James Munro (2000). 'New Labour and Britain's National Health Service: An Overview of Current Reforms', *International Journal of Health Services,* 30 (2): 309–34.

Illich, Ivan (1976). *Limits to Medicine: Medical Nemesis: The Expropriation of Health.* Harmondsworth: Penguin Books.

Imai, Yutaka (2002). 'Health Care Reform in Japan', Economics Working Papers no. 321. Paris: OECD.

Immergut, Ellen M. (1992). *Health Politics: Interests and Institutions in Western Europe.* Cambridge: Cambridge University Press.

Institute of Alcohol Studies (2002). 'Alcohol Consumption and Harm in the UK and EU', www.ias.org.uk/factsheets/default.htm.

Institute of Medicine (1985). *Assessing Medical Technologies.* Washington, DC: National Academy Press.

—— (1993). *Access to Health Care in America.* Washington, DC: National Academy Press.

INSWorld (2002). 'Medical Malpractice Costs Skyrocket.' www.insworld.com/web/broker/assurex_global/archive/ebmay02.asp.

Jacobs, Alan (1998). 'Seeing Difference: Market Health Reform in Europe', *Journal of Health Politics, Policy and Law,* 23 (1): 1–33.

Jacobzone, Stephane (1999). *Ageing and Care for Frail Elderly Persons: An Overview of International Perspectives.* Labour Market and Social Policy Occasional Papers no. 38. Paris: OECD.

—— , E. Cambois, E. Chaplain and J. M. Robine (1999). *The Health of Older Persons in OECD Countries: Is it Improving Fast Enough to Compensate for Population Ageing?* Labour Market and Social Policy Occasional Paper no. 37. Paris: OECD.

Jamieson, Anne (1996). 'Issues in Home Care Services', in OECD (ed.), *Caring for Frail Elderly People. Policies in Evolution.* Social Policy Studies no. 19. Paris: OECD.

Japanese Ministry of Health (2000). 'Establishing a Reliable and Stable Medical System', White Paper: *Annual Report on Health and Welfare.* Tokyo: Ministry of Health.

Jegers, Marc, Katrien Kesteloot, Diana De Graeve and Willem Gilles (2002). 'A Typology for Provider Payment Systems in Health Care', *Health Policy,* 60, 255–73.

Jennett, B. (1986). *High Technology Medicine: Benefits and Burdens*. London: Oxford University Press.

Jensen, Gail A. (2000). 'Making Room for Medical Savings Accounts in the U.S. Health Care System', in Roger D. Feldman (ed.), *American Health Care*. New Brunswick, NJ: Transaction.

Jenson, Jane and Stephane Jacobzone (2000). *Care Allowances for the Frail Elderly and Their Impact on Women Care-givers*. Labour Market and Social Policy Occasional Papers no. 41. Paris: OECD.

Joeng, H. S. and J. Hurst (2001). *An Assessment of the Performance of the Japanese Health Care System*. Labour Market and Social Policy Occasional Papers no. 56. Paris: OECD.

Johnson, Malcolm and L. Cullen (2000). 'Solidarity Put to the Test. Health and Social Care in the UK', *International Journal of Social Welfare*, 9(4): 228–37.

Johnson, Terry (1995). 'Governmentality and the Institutionalization of Expertise', in Terry Johnson, Gerry Larkin, and Mike Saks (eds), *Health Professions and the State in Europe*. London: Routledge.

Jones, Peter (1992). 'Evaluation', in Martin Hallop (ed.), *Power and Policy in Liberal Democracies*. Cambridge: Cambridge University Press, pp. 241–62.

Joung, I. M., H. van der Mheen, K. Stranks, F. W. van Poppel and J. P. Mackenbach (1994). 'Differences in Self-Reported Morbidity by Marital Status and Living Arrangement', *International Journal of Epidemiology*, 23: 91–7.

Kalisch, D., T. Aman and L. Buchele (1998). *Social and Health Policies in OECD Countries: A Survey of Current Programmes and Recent Developments*. Paris: OECD.

Kassler, Jeanne (1994). *Bitter Medicine: Greed and Chaos in American Health Care*. New York: Birch Lane Press.

Kawachi, Ichiro, Bruce P. Kennedy and Richard G. Wilkinson (eds), (1999). *The Society and Population Health Reader: Income Inequality and Health*. New York: New Press.

Kenner, Dan (2001). 'The Role of Traditional Herbal Medicine in Modern Japan', *Acupuncture Today*, August.

Kerkstra, Ada (1996). 'Home Care in the Netherlands', in Jack B. F. Hutten and Ada Kerkstra (eds), *Home Care in Europe: Country-specific Guide to its Organization and Financing*. Aldershot: Ashgate.

—— and Jack B. F. Hutten (1996). 'A Cross-national Comparison of Home Care in Europe', in Jack B. F. Hutten and Ada Kerkstra (eds), *Home Care in Europe: Country-specific Guide to its Organization and Financing*. Aldershot: Ashgate.

Kizer, K. W., M. J. Vassar, R. L. Harry and K. D. Layton (1995). 'Hospitalization Charges, Costs, and Income for Firearm-Related Injuries at a University Trauma Center', *Journal of the American Medical Association*, 273 (22): 1,768–73.

Klein, Rudolf (1997). 'Learning from Others: Shall the Last Be the First?', *Journal of Health Politics, Policy and Law*, 22 (5): 1,267–78.

—— (2001). *The New Politics of the NHS*, 4th edn. Harlow: Prentice Hall.

Kobayashi, Yasuki and Michael R. Reich (1993). 'Health Care Financing for the Elderly in Japan', *Social Science and Medicine*, 37 (3): 343–53.

Kohn, L., J. Corrigan and M. Donaldson (eds), (1999). *To Err is Human: Building a Safer Health System*. Washington, DC: National Academy Press.

Koop, C. Everett, Clarence Pearson and M. Roy Schwartz (eds) (2002). *Critical Issues in Global Health*. San Francisco: Jossey-Bass.

Kröger, Teppo (2001). *Comparative Research on Social Care. The State of the Art*. Brussels: European Commission.

Lamm, Richard D. (1993). 'Intergenerational Equity in an Age of Limits: Confessions of a Prodigal Parent', in Gerald R. Winslow and James W. Walters (eds), *Facing Limits: Ethics and Health Care for the Elderly*. Boulder, CO: Westview Press.

Laurance, Jeremy and Cherry Norton (2000). ' "Unresponsive" NHS Ranked 18th in the World', *The Independent*, 21 June.

Lee, Kelley, Kent Buse and Suzanne Fustukian (eds) (2002). *Health Policy in a Globalising World*. Cambridge: Cambridge University Press.

Leeder, Stephen R. (1999). *Healthy Medicine: Challenges Facing Australia's Health Services*. St Leonard's, NSW: Allen & Unwin.

Leichter, Howard M. (1991). *Free to be Foolish: Politics and Health Promotion in the United States and Great Britain*. Princeton, NJ: Princeton University Press.

Leutwyler, Kristin (1995). 'The Price of Prevention', *Scientific American*, April: 124–9.

Lewis, Jane (2001). 'Older People and the Health-Social Care Boundary in the UK: Half a Century of Hidden Policy Conflict', *Social Policy and Administration*, 35 (4): 343–59.

Lieverdink, Harm and Jan H. van der Made (1997). 'The Reform of Health Insurance Systems in the Netherlands and Germany: Dutch Gold and German Silver', in Christa Altenstetter and James Warner Björkam (eds), *Health Policy Reform, National Variations and Globalization*. London: Macmillan.

Light, Donald (1995). 'Countervailing Powers: A Framework for Professions in Transition', in Terry Johnson, Gerry Larkin and Mike Saks (eds), *Health Professions and the State in Europe*. London: Routledge.

—— (1997). 'From Managed Competition to Managed Cooperation: Theory and Lessons from the British Experience', *The Milbank Quarterly*, 75 (3): 297–331.

Lijphart, Arend (1984). *Democracies: Patterns of Majoritarian and Consensus Government in Twenty-One Countries*. New Haven, CT: Yale University Press.

—— (1999). *Patterns of Democracy*. New Haven, CT: Yale University Press.

Lim, Judy (1997). 'Health Care Reform in Singapore: The Medicare Scheme', in T. M. Tan and S. B. Chew (eds), *Affordable Health Care*. Singapore: Prentice Hall.

Locock, Louise (2000). 'The Changing Nature of Rationing in the UK National Health Service', *Public Administration*, 78 (1): 91–109.

Lombarts, M. J. M. H. and N. S. Klazinga (2001). 'A Policy Analysis of the Introduction and Dissemination of External Peer Review (Visitatie) as a Means of Professional Self-regulation amongst Medical Specialists in the Netherlands in the Period 1985–2000', *Health Policy*, 58(3): 191–213.

London School of Hygiene and Tropical Medicine (1999). *Rapid Reviews of Public Health for London. Housing and the Built Environment.* London: London School of Hygiene and Tropical Medicine.

Loo, Mirjam van het, James P. Kahan and Kieke G. H. Okma (1999). 'Developments in Health Care Cost Containment in the Netherlands', in Elias Mossialos and Julian Le Grand (eds), *Health Care and Cost Containment in the European Union.* Aldershot: Ashgate.

Low, J. A., W. C. Ng, K. B. Yap and K. M. Chan (2000). 'End-of-life Issues: Preferences and Choices of a Group of Elderly Chinese Subjects', *Annals of the Academy of Medicine,* 29 (1): 50–6.

Lowi, Theodore J. (1966). 'Distribution, Regulation, Redistribution: The Functions of Government', in Randall B. Ripley (ed.), *Public Policies and their Politics: Techniques of Government Control.* New York: W.W. Norton.

Maarse, J. A. M. (1997). 'Netherlands', in Marshall W. Raffel (ed.), *Health Care and Reform in Industrialized Countries.* University Park, PA: Pennsylvania State University Press.

MacDaid, David (2001). 'European Health Technology Assessment Quo Vadis?', *Eurohealth,* 7 (1): 27–8.

Macer, Darryl (1999). 'Bioethics in and from Asia', *Journal of Medical Ethics,* 25: 293–5.

Mackenzie, Elizabeth R. (1998). *Healing the Social Body: A Holistic Approach to Public Health Policy.* London: Garland.

Maclennan, A.H., D.H. Wilson and A.W. Taylor (1996). 'Prevalence and Cost of Alternative Medicine in Australia', *Lancet,* 347: 569–73.

Malcolm, L., and M. Powell (1996). 'The Development of Individual Practice Associations and Related Groups in New Zealand', *New Zealand Medical Journal,* 109: 184–7.

——, L. Wright and P. Barnett (2000). 'Emerging Clinical Governance: Developments in Independent Practitioner Associations in New Zealand', *New Zealand Medical Journal,* 113: 33–6.

Manning, Anita (2003). 'Experts Tackle Global SARS Policy', *USA Today,* 7 May.

Marinker, Marshall (2002). *Health Targets in Europe: Policy, Progress, and Promise.* London: BMJ Books.

Marmot, Michael and Richard G. Wilkinson (eds), (1999). *Social Determinants of Health.* Oxford: Oxford University Press.

Martin, John and George Salmond (2001). 'Policy Making: The "Messy Reality"', in Peter Davis and Toni Ashton (eds), *Health and Public Policy in New Zealand.* Auckland: Oxford University Press.

Massaro, Thomas A. and Yu-Ning Wong (1996). *Medical Savings Accounts: The Singapore Experience.* Singapore: National Center for Policy Analysis.

Maynard, Alan and Karen Bloor (2001). 'Our Certain Fate: Rationing in Health Care', Office of Health Economics Briefings Page, www.ohe.org/our.htm.

McClellan, Mark and Daniel Kessler (1999). 'A Global Analysis of Technological Change in Health Care: The Case of Heart Attacks', *Health Affairs,* 18 (3): 250–5.

McGinnis, J. Michael and William H. Foege (1993). 'Actual Causes of Death in the United States', *Journal of the American Medical Association*, 270: 2,207.

McKie, John, Jeff Richardson, Peter Singer and Helga Kuhse (1998). *The Allocation of Health Care Resources: An Ethical Evaluation of the 'QALY' Approach*. Aldershot: Dartmouth.

Means, Robin and Randall Smith (1998). *Community Care. Policy and Practice*, 2nd edn. London: Macmillan.

Mechanic, David (1994). *Inescapable Decisions: The Imperatives of Health Care*. New Brunswick, NJ: Transaction.

Medicare and Graduate Medical Education (1995). 'Policy Issues and Questions', www.cbo.gov/showdoc.cfm?index.htm.

Mendelson, Daniel N., Richard G. Abramson and Robert J. Rubin (1995). 'State Involvement in Medical Technology Assessment', *Health Affairs*, 14 (2): 83–98.

Merson, Michael H., Robert E. Black and Anne J. Mills (2001). *International Public Health: Diseases, Programs, Systems, and Policies*. Sudbury, MA: Jones & Bartlett.

Milio, Nancy (2000). *Public Health in the Market: Facing Managed Care, Lean Government, and Health Disparities*. Ann Arbor, MI: University of Michigan Press.

Miller, A. S. and A. Hagihara (1997). 'Organ Transplanting in Japan: The Debate Begins'. *Public Health*, 111: 367–72.

Miller, T. R. and M. A. Cohen (1997). 'Costs of Gunshot and Cut/stab Wounds in the United States', *Accidents Analysis and Prevention*, 29 (3): 329–41.

Mills, Anne, Sara Bennett, Steven Russell and Nimal Attanayake (eds), (2001). *The Challenge of Health Sector Reform: What Governments Must Do?* Basingstoke: Palgrave.

Ministry of Health and Social Affairs (2001). 'Towards Public Health on Equal Terms', Fact Sheet no. 3. Stockholm: Ministry of Health and Social Affairs.

Mitchell, David (2001). 'Q&A: The England–Scotland Divide on Free Personal Care', *The Guardian*, 24 January.

Moran, Michael (1999). *Governing the Health Care State: A Comparative Study of the United Kingdom, the United States and Germany*. Manchester: Manchester University Press.

—— (2000). 'Understanding the Welfare State: The Case of Health Care', *British Journal of Politics and International Relations*, 2 (2): 135–60.

—— and Bruce Wood (1993). *States, Regulation and the Medical Profession*. Cheltenham: Edward Elgar.

Mossialos, Elias and Julian Le Grand (eds), (1999). *Health Care and Cost Containment in the European Union*. Aldershot: Ashgate.

Mueller, Keith J. (1993). *Health Care Policy in the United States*. Lincoln, NE: University of Nebraska Press.

Nadakavukaren, Anne (2000). *Our Global Environment: A Health Perspective*. Prospect Heights, IL: Waveland Press.

Nakahara, Toshitaka (1997). 'The Health System of Japan', in Marshall W. Raffel (ed.), *Health Care and Reform in Industrialized Countries*. University Park, PA: Pennsylvania State University Press.

National Board of Health and Welfare (2000). *Social Services in Sweden in*

1999. Needs – Interventions – Development. Stockholm: National Board of Health and Welfare.

National Center for Health Care Statistics, Centers for Disease Control and Prevention (2002). *Chartbook on Trends in the Health of Americans.* Washington, DC: Government Printing Office.

National Contract for Public Health (2001). *National Contract for Public Health. Declaration of Intent to Cooperate. 2001–2003.* Leiden, 22 February. www.minvws.nl/documents/Health/natcontract.pdf.

National Institutes of Health (1998). 'Economic Costs of Alcohol and Drug Abuse Estimated at $246 Billion in the United States', *News Release,* 13 May.

National Library of Medicine (1998). 'Fighting the Spread of Epidemic Diseases', *Images from the History of the Public Health Service.* Washington, DC: Government Printing Office.

National Organisation for Women (2003). 'Statistics for Battered Women', www.now.org/issues/violence/stats.html.

New Zealand Core Services Committee (1992). *The Core Debate: How We Define the Core.* Wellington: National Advisory Committee on Core Health and Disability Support Services.

New Zealand Ministry of Health (1999). *Health Expenditure Trends in New Zealand, 1980–98.* Wellington: Ministry of Health.

—— (2001). *An Overview of the Health and Disability Sector in New Zealand.* Wellington: Ministry of Health.

—— (2002). *Health of Older People Strategy: Health Sector Action to 2010 to Support Positive Ageing.* Wellington: Ministry of Health.

—— (2003). *Achieving Health for All People: A Framework for Public Health Action.* Wellington: Ministry of Health.

New Zealand Occupational Safety and Health Service (2002). *The Health and Safety in Employment Act.* 20 December.

Newhouse, Joseph P. (1993). 'An Iconoclastic View of Health Cost Containment'. *Health Affairs* 12 (Supplement): 152–71.

Nurse Maude Association (2003). 'Committed to Community Health Care', www.nursemaude.org.nz.

Nuthall, J. (1992). *The Impact of Economic and Social Factors in Health.* Wellington: Public Health Association of New Zealand.

OECD (1987). *Financing and Delivering Health Care: A Comparative Analysis of OECD Countries.* Paris: OECD.

—— (1988). *Ageing Populations: Social Policy Implications.* Paris: OECD.

—— (1990). *Health Care Systems in Transition: The Search for Efficiency.* Paris: OECD.

—— (1992). *The Reform of Health Care Systems: A Comparative Analysis of Seven OECD Countries.* Paris: OECD.

—— (1996). *Caring for Frail Elderly People. Policies in Evolution.* Social Policy Studies no. 19. Paris: OECD.

—— (2001a). *Health at a Glance.* Paris: OECD.

—— (2001b). *OECD Health Data 2001. A Comparative Analysis of 30 Countries.* Paris: OECD.

Ohnuki-Tierney, Emiko (1984). *Illness and Culture in Contemporary Japan: An Anthropological View.* Cambridge: Cambridge University Press.

Okamoto, Kozo (2001). *Public Health of Japan 2001*. Osaka: National Institute of Public Health.

Okma, Kieke G.H. (2001). *Health Care, Health Policies and Health Care Reforms in the Netherlands*. International Publication Series Health, Welfare and Sport no. 7. The Hague: Ministry of Health, Welfare and Sport.

Ovretveit, John (1998). *Comparative and Cross-cultural Health Research*. Abingdon, UK: Radcliffe Medical Press.

Palmer, George R. and Stephanie D. Short (2000). *Health Care and Public Policy: An Australian Analysis*, 3rd edn. Melbourne: Macmillan.

Paton, Calum (1997). 'The Politics and Economics of Health Care Reform: Britain in a Comparative Context', in Christa Altenstetter and James Warner Björkam (eds), *Health Policy Reform, National Variations and Globalization*. London: Macmillan.

Peckham, Stephen and Mark Exworthy (2003). *Primary Care in the UK*. Basingstoke: Palgrave.

Perleth, Matthias, Reinhard Busse and Friedrich Wilhelm Schwartz (1999). 'Regulation of Health-related Technologies in Germany', *Health Policy*, 46(2): 105–26.

Pickard, Linda (2001). 'Carer Break or Carer-blind? Policies for Informal Carers in the UK', *Social Policy and Administration*, 35 (4), 441–58.

Podger, Andrew (1999). 'Perspective – Reforming the Australian Health Care System', *Health Affairs*, 18 (3): 111–13.

Powell, Margaret and Maxzahira Anesaki (1990). *Health Care in Japan*. London: Routledge.

Prager, Linda O. (1998). 'Boards Want Broader Quality Monitory Role', *American Medical News*, 24/31 August: 6–7.

Public Citizen (2003). 'Medical Malpractice: Bush & Congress Should Act to Reduce Medical Errors, Not Reduce Compensation to Injured Patients', www.citizen.org.

Quah, E. and T. L. Boon (2003). 'The Economic Cost of Particulate Air Pollution on Health in Singapore', *Journal of Asian Economics*, 14 (1): 73–90.

Quah, Stella R. (1988). 'Private Choices and Public Health: A Case of Policy Intervention in Singapore', *The Asian Journal of Public Administration*, 10 (2): 207–24.

—— (2003). 'Traditional Healing Systems and the Ethos of Science', *Social Science and Medicine*, 57(10): 1997–2012.

Raffel, Marshall W. (ed.) (1997). *Health Care and Reform in Industrialized Countries*. University Park, PA: University of Pennsylvania Press.

—— and Norma K. Raffel (1994). *US Health System: Origins and Functions*. New York: Delmar.

—— and Norma K. Raffel (1997). 'The Health System of the United States', in Marshall W. Raffel (ed.), *Health Care and Reform in Industrialized Countries*. University Park, PA: Pennsylvania State University Press.

Ramesh, M. and Ian Holliday (2001). 'The Health Care Miracle in East and Southeast Asia: Activist State Provision in Hong Kong, Malaysia and Singapore', *Journal of Social Policy*, 30 (4): 637–51.

Ranade, Wendy (ed.) (1998). *Markets and Health Care: A Comparative Analysis*. London: Longman.

Randall, Teri (1993). 'Demographers Ponder the Ageing of the Aged and Await Unprecedented Looming Elder Boom', *Journal of the American Medical Association*, 269 (18): 2, 330–1.

Rehnberg, Clas (1997). 'Sweden.' in Christopher Ham (ed.), *Health Care Reform: Learning from International Experience*. Buckingham: Open University Press.

Reinhardt, Uwe E. (1990). 'Commentary', in OECD (ed.), *Health Care Systems in Transition: The Search for Efficiency*. Paris: OECD.

Reiss, Cory (2003). 'Malpractice Debate Now A Blame Game'. *Sarasota Herald Tribune* 13 January, p.; 1A.

Reuters (2003). 'Study: Tobacco, Alcohol, Drugs Kill 7 Million a Year', 25 February.

Richmond, Julius B. and Rashi Fein (1995). 'The Health Care Mess: A Bit of History', *Journal of the American Medical Association*, 273 (1): 69–71.

Riska, Elianne and Katarina Wegar (1995). 'The Medical Profession in the Nordic Countries. Medical Uncertainty and Gender-based Work', in Terry Johnson, Gerry Larkin and Mike Saks (eds), *Health Professions and the State in Europe*, London: Routledge.

Robinson, Ray (1998). 'Managed Competition: Health Care Reform in the Netherlands', in Wendy Ranade (ed.), *Markets and Health Care: A Comparative Analysis*. London: Longman.

Romaine-Davis, Ada, Jennifer Boondas and Ayeliffe Lenihan (eds) (1995). *Encyclopedia of Home Care for the Elderly*. Westport, CT: Greenwood Press.

Roos, Noralou, Evelyn Shapiro, and Robert Tate (1989). 'Does a Small Minority of Elderly Account for a Majority of Health Care Expenditures? A Sixteen-Year Study', *The Milbank Quarterly*, 67 (3/4): 347–69.

Ros, Corina C., Peter P. Groenwegen and Dianna M.J. Delnoij (2000). 'All Rights Reserved, or Can We Just Copy? Cost Sharing Arrangements and Characteristics of Health Care Systems', *Health Policy*, 52(1): 1–13.

Ross, Emma (2003). 'WHO Links SARS to Three Small Mammals', AP News Story, 23 May.

Royal District Nursing Service (2003). 'Partnerships and Alliances', www.rdns.asn.au/innovation.htm.

Russell, Louise B. (1994). *Educated Guesses: Making Policy About Screening Tests*. Berkeley, CA: University of California Press.

Saltman, Richard B. (1997). 'The Context of Health Reform in the United Kingdom, Sweden, Germany, and the United States', *Health Policy*, 41 (Supplement): S9–S26.

—— (1998). 'Health Reform in Sweden: The Road Beyond Cost Containment', in Wendy Ranade (ed.), *Markets and Health Care: A Comparative Analysis*. London: Longman.

—— (2002). 'Regulating Incentives: The Past and Present Role of the State in Health Care Systems', *Social Science and Medicine*, 54(11): 1,677–84.

—— and Casten Von Otter (eds) (1995). *Implementing Planned Markets in Health Care: Balancing Social and Economic Responsibilities*. Buckingham: Open University Press.

——, Josef Figueras and Constantino Sakellarides (eds) (1998). *Critical Challenges for Health Care Reform in Europe*. Buckingham: Open University Press.

San Francisco Department of Health (2003). *Healthy People in Healthy Communities*, www.dph.sf.ca.us/PHP/php.htm.

Schepers, Rita M. J. and Anton F. Casparie (1997). 'Continuity or Discontinuity in the Self-regulation of the Belgian and Dutch Medical Professions', *Sociology of Health and Illness*, 19 (5): 580–600.

Schoen, Cathy *et al.* (2000b). *Equity in Health Care Across Five Nations: Summary Findings from an International Health Policy Survey*. New York: The Commonwealth Fund.

—— *et al.* (2000a). *The Elderly's Experiences with Health Care in Five Nations*. New York: The Commonwealth Fund.

Schunk, Michaela (1998). 'The Social Insurance Model of Care for Older People in Germany', in Caroline Glenndinning (ed.), *Rights and Realities. Comparing New Developments in Long-term Care for Older People*. Bristol: Policy Press.

Schwartz, Friedrich F. (1997). *Fixing Health Budgets: Experience from Europe and North America*. New York: John Wiley.

—— and Reinhard Busse (1997). 'Germany', in Christopher Ham (ed.), *Health Care Reform: Learning from International Experience*. Buckingham: Open University Press.

Scott, Claudia D. (1997). 'Reform of the Health System of New Zealand', in Marshall W. Raffel (ed.), *Health Care and Reform in Industrialized Countries*. University Park, PA: Pennsylvania State University Press.

Seedhouse, David (1991). *Liberating Medicine*. Chichester: Wiley.

Shedden, Juliet (2000).'Scotland's NHS Plan – the Main Points', *The Guardian*, 14 December.

Singapore Health Promotion Board (2003). 'Workplace Health Promotion Programme', http://app.hpb.gov.sg.

Singapore Ministry of Health (1993). *Affordable Health Care*. Singapore: Ministry of Health.

—— (1995). 'Traditional Chinese Medicine', *Report of the Committee on Traditional Chinese Medicine*, October.

—— (2000). *White Paper on 'Affordable Health Care'*. Singapore: MOH.

—— (2001). *Health Care Financing in Singapore*. Singapore: MOH.

—— (2002a). 'Health Care Financing in Singapore', www.gov.sg/scripts/moh/newmoh/asp/you.html.

—— (2002b). *Hospital Statistics*. Singapore: Ministry of Health.

Singapore Ministry of Health (2002c). 'Overview of the Singapore Healthcare System', www.gov.sg/moh/mohinfo/mohinfo-a.html.

—— (2003). 'Subsidies for the Elderly', http://app.moh.gov.sg/pro/pro0302.asp.

'Singapore's Health Care Ranked First in an International Comparison' (2001). *Daily Policy Digest, Health Issues*. Singapore: National Center for Policy Analysis.

'Singapore's Health System is Best in Asia' (2000). *The Straits Times*, 21 January.

Society of Occupational Medicine (2003). 'Occupational Medicine in the UK', www.som.org.uk/carinom/car3_omit.html.

Spiers, John (1999). *The Realities of Rationing: 'Priority Setting' in the NHS*. London: Institute of Economic Affairs, Health and Welfare Unit.

Standard Committee of the Hospitals of the European Union (2003). 'Hospitals and Occupational Health in Germany', www.hope.be/07publi/leaflet/occup/de.htm.

Stanton, Glenn T. (2003). 'How Marriage Improves Health', www.divorcereform.org/mel/abetterhealth.html.

Starfield, Barbara (2000). 'Is US Health Really the Best in the World?' *Journal of the American Medical Association* 284(4): 483–5.

State Coverage Initiatives (2002). 'Who are the Uninsured in the United States?', www.statecoverage.net/who.html.

Stone, Diane (1999). 'Learning Lessons and Transferring Policy across Time, Space and Disciplines', *Politics*, 19 (1): 51–9.

Sultz, Harry A. and Kristina M. Young (1999). *Health Care USA: Understanding its Organisation and Delivery*, 2nd edn. New York: Aspen.

Tatara, Kozo (ed.) (2001). *Public Health of Japan 2001*. Japan Public Health Association, www.jpha.or.jp/jpha/english/alpha/top.html.

Teo, Peggy, Angelique Chan and Pauline Straughan (2003). 'Providing Health Care for Older Persons in Singapore', *Health Policy*, 64(3): 399–413.

Terris, Milton (1999). 'National Health Insurance in the United States: A Drama in Too Many Acts', *Journal of Public Health Policy*, 20 (1): 13–26.

Tester, Susan (1996). *Community Care for Older People. A Comparative Perspective*. London: Macmillan.

—— (1999). 'Comparative Approaches to Long-term Care for Adults', in Jochen Clasen (ed.), *Comparative Social Policy: Concepts, Theories and Methods*. Oxford: Basil Blackwell.

Theobald, Hildegard (2003). 'Welfare System, Professionalisation and the Question of Inequality', *International Journal of Sociology and Social Policy*, 23 (4/5): 159–85.

Thorpe, Kenneth E. (1992). 'Health Care Cost Containment: Results and Lessons from the Past 20 Years', in Stephen M. Shortell and Uwe E. Reinhardt (eds), *Improving Health Policy and Management*. Ann Arbor, MI: Health Administration Press.

Timmermans, Arco (2001). 'Policy Making in Comparative Perspective: How Policy Arenas Affect Opportunities for Entrepreneurs and Veto Players', unpublished paper.

Tong, Mee Mien (2003). Singapore Health Care Services, www.tradeport.org/ts/countries/singapore/isa/isar0018.html.

Trappenburg, Margo, and Mariska De Groot (2001). 'Controlling Medical Specialists in the Netherlands: Delegating the Dirty Work', in Mark Bovens, Paul t'Hart and B. Guy Peters (eds), *Success and Failure in Public Governance. A Comparative Analysis*. Cheltenham: Edward Elgar.

Trydegård, Gun-Britt, and Mats Thorslund (2001). 'Inequality in the Welfare State? Local Variation in Care of the Elderly – the Case of Sweden', *International Journal of Social Welfare*, 10(3): 174–84.

Turner J. B. (1995). 'Economic Context and the Health Effects of Unemployment', *Journal of Health and Social Behavior*, 36: 213–29.

Turnock, Bernard J. (2001). *Public Health: What It Is and How It Works*. New York: Aspen.

Twaddle, Andrew C. (1999). *Health Care Reform in Sweden, 1980–1994*. London: Auburn House.

Twigg, Julia (1989). 'Models of Carers: How Do Social Care Agencies Conceptualise Their Relationship with Informal Carers?', *Journal of Social Policy*, 18 (1): 53–66.

—— (1996). 'Issues in Informal Care', in OECD (ed.), *Caring for Frail Elderly People. Policies in Evolution*. Social Policy Studies no. 19. Paris: OECD.

Ubel, Peter A. (2001). *Pricing Life: Why it's Time for Health Care Rationing*. Cambridge, MA: MIT Press.

United Nations High Commission for Refugees (2001) 'Asylum Applications in Industrialized Countries: 1980–1999', http://www.unhcr.ch/pubs/statistics/nov2001/toc2.htm.

United States Department of Health and Human Services (2000). *Healthy People 2010*. Washington, DC: US Government Printing Office.

United States Environmental Protection Agency (2002). 'Global Warming – Impacts: Health', http://yosemite.epa.gov/oar/globalwarming.nsf/content/impactsHealth.html.

United States Public Health Service (1995). *For a Healthy Nation: Returns on Investment in Public Health*. Washington, DC: US Government Printing Office.

—— (2002). *Healthy People 2010: A Systematic Approach to Health Improvement*. Washington, DC: US Government Printing Office.

Vasoo, S. (2001). 'Health Care in Singapore: Policy Issues and Challenges', www.hku.kk/socwork/dept/hepl/hepl.html.

Ven, Wynand van de (1997). 'The Netherlands', in Christopher Ham (ed.), *Health Care Reform: Learning from International Experience*. Buckingham: Open University Press.

Victorian Department of Human Services (1996). *Towards a Safer Choice: The Practice of Traditional Chinese Medicine*. Melbourne: Department of Human Services.

Victorian Ministerial Advisory Committee on Traditional Chinese Medicine (1998). *Traditional Chinese Medicine: Report on Options for Regulation of Practitioners*. Melbourne: Department of Human Services.

Wagenaar, A.C. and M. Wolfson (1995). 'Deterring Sales and Provision of Alcohol to Minors: A Study of Enforcement in 295 Counties in Four States. *Public Health Reports* 995 (110): 419–27.

Wall, Ann (ed.) (1996). *Health Systems in Liberal Democracies*. London: Routledge.

Ward, Lucie (2002). 'Health Service Failing Homeless', *The Guardian*, 17 December.

Wasem, Jürgen (1997). 'A Study of Decentralizing from Acute Care to Home Care Settings in Germany', *Health Policy*, 41 (Supplement): S109–29.

Watson, Elizabeth A. and Jane Mears (1999). *Women, Work and Care of the Elderly*. Aldershot: Ashgate.

Wenger, Eldon L. (2001) 'Restructuring Care for the Elderly in Germany', *Current Sociology*, 49 (3): 175–88.

Wennberg, John E. (1998). *Dartmouth Atlas of Health Care*. Chicago, IL: American Hospital.

Werkö, Lars, Julia Chamova and Jan Adolfson (2001). 'Health Technology Assessment. The Swedish Experience', *Eurohealth*, 7 (1): 29–31.

Whitehead, Margaret (1998). 'Diffusion of Ideas on Social Inequalities in Health: A European Perspective', *The Milbank Quarterly*, 76 (3): 469–92.

WHO (1996). 'Traditional Medicine', Fact Sheet no. 134, September. Geneva: WHO.

—— (2001). *Global Status Report on Alcohol*. Geneva: WHO, June.

—— (2002). *Alcohol Control Policies*. Geneva: WHO. www.WHO.int/substance_abuse/PDFfiles/global_alcohol_status_report/8Alcoholcontrolpolicies.pdf.

WHO (2003). *Moving towards a Tobacco-free Europe: The European Report on Tobacco Control Policy, 1997–2002*. European Ministerial Conference for a Tobacco-free Europe Copenhagen: WHO.

WHO, Regional Office for Europe (2003a) *European Environment and Health Committee*, www.euro.who.int/eprise/main/who/progs/eehc/home.

—— (2003b) 'Global Change and Health', www.euro.who.int/eprise/main/who/progs/gch/home.

—— (2003c) 'National Environmental Action Plans', www.euro.who.int/envhealthpolicy/Plans/20020807_1.

Wiener, Joshua M. (1992). 'Rationing in America: Overt and Covert', in Martin A. Strosberg, Joshua M. Wiener and Robert Baker (eds), *Rationing America's Medical Care: The Oregon Plan and Beyond*. Washington, DC: The Brookings Institution.

Wilkinson, R. G. (1992). 'National Mortality Rates: The Impact of Inequality?', *American Journal of Public Health*, 82: 1,082–4.

Wilkinson, Richard G. (1997). *Unhealthy Societies: The Afflictions of Inequality*. London: Routledge.

Wilsford, David (1994). 'Path Dependency, or Why History Makes it Difficult, but not Impossible to Reform Health Systems in a Big Way', *Journal of Public Policy* 14(3): 251–83.

Winkleby, M. A., D. E. Jatulis, E. Frank and S. P. Fortmann (1992). 'Socioeconomic Status and Health: How Education, Income, and Occupation Contribute to Risk Factors for Cardiovascular Disease', *American Journal of Public Health*, 82 (6): 816–21.

Winslow, Ron (2001). '1 Patient, 34 Days, $5 Million', *The Wall Street Journal*, 3 August, p. 1A.

Witherick, Michael E. (2002). *States of Health and Welfare*. Cheltenham: Nelson Thornes.

Wong, Margaret (2003). 'WHO Removes Hong Kong from SARS List', Associated Press, 23 June.

Woodman, Richard (2001). 'UK Hospitals Face 3.9 Billion Negligence Bill', Reuters News, 4 May, http://dailynews.yahoo.com/h/nm/20010504/hl/hospitals_1.htm.

Wooldridge, Michael (2001). 'More Doctors for Rural Australia', Department of Health and Aged Care, Media Release (6 June).

World Drink Trends (2002). Henley on Thames: World Advertising Research Center Ltd.

World Factbook (2003). http://education.yahoo.com/reference/factbook.

World Health Organization (1946). 'Preamble to the Constitution of the World Health Organization as adopted by the International Health Conference,' New York, 19–22 June, 1946; signed on 22 July 1946 by the representatives of 61 States, and entered into force on 7 April 1948.

Yamauchi, Toyoaki (1999). 'Healthcare System in Japan', *Nursing and Health Sciences*, 1 (1): 45–8.

Yoshikawa, Aki, Jayanta Bhattacharya and William B. Vogt (eds) (1996). *Health Economics of Japan: Patients, Doctors, and Hospitals under a Universal Health Insurance System*. Tokyo: University of Tokyo Press.

Zwillich, Todd (2001). 'Medical Technologies May Drive Up Health Costs', Reuters News Service, 6 March.

—— (2003). 'US Spent Record $1.4 Trillion on Health in 2001', Reuters News Service, 8 January.

Index